The Bureaucracy of Truth

By the same author

Eagles in Cobwebs: Nationalism and Communism in the Balkans
Anti-Semitism in Eastern Europe

THE
BUREAUCRACY
OF TRUTH

HOW COMMUNIST GOVERNMENTS
MANAGE THE NEWS

Paul Lendvai

 BURNETT BOOKS – LONDON
WESTVIEW PRESS – BOULDER, COLORADO

First published 1981 by Burnett Books Limited
in association with André Deutsch Limited
105 Great Russell Street London WC1

Typeset in Great Britain by
King's English Typesetters Limited, Cambridge
and printed by
Lowe & Brydone Printers Limited
Thetford, Norfolk

ISBN 0233 97290 0 (hardback)

Published in the United States of America in 1981 by
Westview Press
5500 Central Avenue
Boulder, Colorado 80301
Frederick A. Praeger, Publisher

ISBN 0-86531 -142-0
Library of Congress Catalog Card Number 80-5925

For Margaret

The censored press has a demoralising effect . . . The government only hears its own voice, knows that it only hears its own voice, yet acts under the illusion that it hears the voice of the people, and demands from the people that they should accept this illusion too. So the people for their part sink partly into political superstition, partly into political disbelief or withdraw completely from civic life and become a rabble . . . Since the people must regard free writings as illegal, they become accustomed to regarding what is illegal as free, freedom as illegal, and what is legal as unfree. Thus the censorship kills civic spirit.

KARL MARX

In a free society everything can be published – and is forgotten because it is all seen at a glance. Under absolutism everything is hidden, but may be divined; that is what makes it interesting.

MARQUIS DE CUSTINE, 1839

Contents

Introduction

ACCORDING TO THE Universal Declaration of Human Rights it is a basic right of all peoples, 'to seek, receive and impart information and ideas through any media regardless of frontiers'. This apparently simple principle has become the subject of bitter political and ideological confrontation. Gradually, and to the wider public, imperceptibly, two major developments have combined to project into the centre of the international stage the twin issues of the freedom of the press, and the 'free' versus the 'balanced' flow of information between nations.

The dispute over the first issue derives from the so-called Final Act, a complex, 40,000 word-long document adopted at the Conference on Security and Co-operation in Europe (CSCE) and signed in Helsinki on 1 August 1975 by the leaders of thirty-three European countries, the US and Canada. The provisions of what *Le Monde* called a 'diplomatic master-piece' were intended to improve political relations, to ease military tensions, to stimulate trade and the flow of people and ideas between East and West. The actual implementation of the provisions was subsequently reviewed by the signatories in Belgrade during five months of acrimonious public and closed debate from October 1977 to March 1978. Despite reaching a deadlock over the assessment of their respective records of implementation and over future steps, the diplomats finally agreed to hold the next follow-up meeting in Madrid in the autumn of 1980. Of the sixty-two pages of the Final Act only some three and a half deal with information, but conflicting interpretations of these provisions inject an element of permanent polemic into East-West relations.

The second factor keeping the issue of the mass media on

the international agenda is the campaign of the Third World countries against what they perceive as a monopoly of information media by a handful of transnational news agencies, operating from a few industrialised Western countries. The Paris-based UN Educational, Scientific and Cultural Organisation (Unesco) seeks to establish ground rules for a 'New Order For Information' to put an end to the alleged world-wide domination of the mass media by the so-called Western model. As part of the Unesco campaign, a small commission, under Sean MacBride, the former Irish Foreign Minister, and a winner of the Nobel and Lenin Peace Prizes, has completed a highly controversial report on communications, the outcome of two years of debate. Despite the fact that the commission made several compromises, the MacBride report is still seen by most Western observers as a potential threat to free and accurate reporting.[1]

Though the first dispute is primarily concerned with East-West relations in Europe, and the second focuses on Unesco's communication policies and the aspirations of the developing countries concerning control over the use of media, the controversies about the freedom of news reporting and access to information constitute an intimate, albeit often ignored, link between the two seemingly disparate exercises in international diplomacy. The literature, supplemented by a steadily growing mass of statistics and official papers, both on communications and the CSCE process, has become enormous, indeed almost unmanageable. Yet for all the publicity it is startling how few people are aware of the character, structure and role of mass media in the 'socialist' countries east of the Elbe. Neither the implications of the negotiating process over East-West détente, nor the potential consequences of the various proposals for a new information order can be properly grasped if one ignores the Soviet bloc's record in what Unesco calls 'responsible, comprehensive and objective reporting'.

Who decides what is communicated in countries where the print and broadcast media are state-owned and treated as 'the sharpest weapon' of the ruling Communist parties in the battle for the minds of the people? What are the accepted criteria, norms or standards for judging what is 'newsworthy'? How is the treatment of the outgoing and incoming information controlled and what are the values of the 'gate-keepers', the people who govern news priorities? What is the response of ideologically-structured régimes to the challenge of the communications revolution? Why has the information issue (alongside the much more publicised problems of human rights and human contacts) become one of the dominant elements in the great debate over the Helsinki accords? What does the post-Helsinki and post-Belgrade balance sheet look like on implementation of the provisions for the free dissemination and exchange of information, and those dealing with working conditions for foreign journalists and the access to foreign publications in the participating countries?

These questions are examined in this book, mostly on the basis of primary sources; a considerable part of the information was collected by the author during his time as a journalist in Hungary (1948–1956) and on frequent trips during the past fifteen years or so to the countries of Eastern Europe. I have studied the theory and practice of Communism since 1946, and, since the early sixties, regularly visited all the Soviet bloc countries, and have also spent considerable time in Yugoslavia. During the same period I had ample opportunity to discuss most of the problems described here with well-informed and often highly-placed media representatives, ranging from Central Committee members and chief editors to reporters and sub-editors. On-the-spot coverage of the two months of preparatory discussions and five months of substantive talks at the Belgrade Follow-Up Meeting on the implementation of the CSCE Final Act also contributed to my understanding of the tactical manoeuvring sketched out in the third part of this study. To my journalistic colleagues, for giving me background information, and to the diplomats, for allowing a study of the documents, I am most grateful; they all, of course, have to remain nameless.

The personal element should be mentioned, for it does provide, not only the necessary background and special interest, but also, I believe, a certain feel and understanding which is difficult to acquire from the study of newspapers and archives alone. To understand, for example, some of the reasons for the strikingly different attitudes towards the external and internal flow of information, the media treatment of air crashes and natural disasters and last, but not least, the implementation of the Helsinki accords, in short to gain a glimpse into the back-stage workings of a state-controlled press, the observer has to consult human sources at first hand, checking and counter-checking their statements. Though it has become commonplace to warn against sweeping generalisations about a unique Soviet model imposed throughout Eastern Europe by an all-powerful Kremlin, there is still a persistent tendency to lump together the Soviet Union and the smaller Central and East European states: Bulgaria, Czechoslovakia, the German Democratic Republic, Hungary, Poland and Romania. It is not just sheer size and military-economic potential that explain the enormous difference between the Soviet Union and its smaller Warsaw Pact partners. The differences in the political climate between the Soviet Union and its allies on the one hand, and between the small east bloc countries themselves on the other, are due to historical differences in the motivation and behaviour patterns of the ruling élites, in attitudes and policies towards the outside world, in press traditions and lifestyles, geographical proximity to the political and cultural centres of the West and widely varying historical and political experiences.

Despite decades of professed adherence to the tenets of Marxism-Leninism and membership of the Soviet-run military and economic bloc, the emphasis is on diversity rather than on uniformity in internal policies. The quest for national identity has proved – not only in the case of Romania – stronger than ideological bonds. Yet, at the same time, the extraordinary difference between the mass media in, say, 'occupied' Hungary and independent-minded Romania is in no small degree due to such 'unideological' factors as the different personalities, public relations style and tactical dexterity of the respective leaders.

But awareness of the manifold variations and differences in communication policies within the bloc as a whole should not make us forget the limits of the experimentation nor overstate its real significance and durability. To equate certain innovations in style and content, increasing professionalisation and sophistication in the mass media of certain countries, with basic changes in the Communist approach to the control and function of the press would be to lose all sense of proportion.

A few words of explanation about the terms used in this study may also be appropriate. For the sake of convenience and brevity, 'East' or 'Soviet (Communist) bloc' will, for the present purpose, always mean the Soviet Union and the six other Warsaw Pact (and Comecon) member states. When dealing with variations in censorship practices, the implementation of the Helsinki accords or the coverage of major events such as, for example, the Pope's visit to Poland, the countries concerned will be dealt with separately. No attempt will be made to analyse the information policies of China and North Korea or of the non-European allies of the Soviet Union: Cuba, Mongolia and Vietnam.

Non-aligned Yugoslavia, though also a one-party system, is of course a very special case. The decades of economic self-management and administrative decentralisation coupled with the opening of frontiers and freedom of movement have produced a press that is in many ways qualitatively different. Thus my general observations on practice – and on the Helsinki accords – will be confined to the Soviet bloc countries. Nevertheless, Yugoslavia's experiences of reporting by Soviet news media as well as the reflection of political and national upheavals in the handling of press control by the party will briefly be examined.

'West' is used to describe the industrialised Western democracies, by no means restricted to the NATO countries, but including such distinctly neutral states as Austria or Switzerland. When dealing with the Belgrade review conference, certain national positions will be singled out. Finally, the Third World will be referred to only in connection with news reporting in bloc media and as a subject for the proselytising efforts of the Prague-based International Organisation of Journalists and the journalist training centres in East Berlin and Budapest.

'The man who ventures to write contemporary history,' Voltaire wrote to Bertin de Rocheret, 'must expect to be attacked both for everything he has said and everything he has not said.' The present book, with all its limitations and imperfections, is to the best of my knowledge the first attempt to combine an analysis of continuity and change in the Communist mass media in theory and practice with the study of the impact of both international broadcasting and the

Helsinki accords, including the implementation debates at and since the Belgrade review conference.

I believe that the matters discussed on the following pages not only affect the daily life of almost 370 million people living in the countries concerned, but also, in one way or another, influence East-West relations and the great international debate on the future of communications. It would be both dishonest and foolish to pretend that there are no restraints on the freedom of the press in Western societies, or to underestimate the increasingly serious threats to independent reporting and the diversity of Western media. But the fact remains that the real or perceived failings of Western news reporting and the international action programme to produce a 'balanced flow of information' are discussed constantly in countless monographs, books and conference papers, while there is a dearth of factual material about Communist information policies in action. Avoiding both Cold War clichés and the temptation to take Communist propaganda messages at face value, this book is meant to be a modest contribution to the study of communication policies; policies which are complex and ambiguous, reflecting both actual conditions in each East European country and changes in the broader context of East-West relations.

The first part of this volume deals with the Communist mass media, their structure, function and control, combining common features and variations in each country. Part Two covers the problems connected with international broadcasting to Eastern Europe, including a description of major broadcasters, audience impact and the countermoves, including jamming, by the Soviet bloc. In Part Three the significance and consequences of the Helsinki accords and the Eastern record of implementation in 1975–80 are described and analysed.

My position on the subjects discussed emerges from the following pages. My main intention is to avoid sweeping generalisations and to provide a truthful and dispassionate account, even of policies and actions which I deplore.

Vienna, 1980

PART I
Communist Mass Media

We need complete, truthful information. And
the truth should not depend on whom it is to
serve.

V. I. LENIN

1   *The Party's Sharpest Weapon*

SOME WESTERN OBSERVERS tend to regard the Soviet Union
as a country 'like any other'. Many people are convinced that
industrialisation and modernisation, trade with the West and
growing indebtedness are bound to lead to greater political
freedom. Optimistic commentators and businessmen still
predict an inevitable convergence of the Communist and
Western systems. More cautious observers forsee, at the very
least, a gradual opening vis-à-vis the West.

There have been such major changes since Stalin's death
that certain Western scholars reject the use of the term
'totalitarian' when applied to the Soviet system as 'a relic of
the Cold War' or at best an outdated adjective. The meanings
of the term are as numerous and varied as the authors who
have attempted to define it. Most serious students of Communist affairs tend to agree today that it is neither terror nor
one-man rule by a dictator over a single-party system which
can be seen as the most important feature of totalitarian
régimes. What distinguishes the Soviet-type Communist systems from ancient despotisms and modern dictatorships is,
above all, the ideology; or put in another way, the assumption of a sole and exclusive truth in politics, which can be
defined in any situation and at any given moment only by the
true prophets of the Marxist-Leninist faith.

For all the great and visible differences in atmosphere,
lifestyle and standard of living between Moscow, East Berlin
or Budapest, none of the Communist ruling groups has
abandoned unconditional loyalty to the doctrine in the name
of which Lenin seized power sixty years ago and which
justifies its monopoly of power. J. L. Talmon calls it 'political
Messianism in the sense that it postulated a preordained,

harmonious and perfect scheme of things, to which men are irresistibly driven, and at which they are bound to arrive'.[2] Faced with the critical problem of credibility, the ideology of Marxism-Leninism constitutes both a principle of legitimacy and an instrument to bridge the gap between reality and vision for 'future-oriented' systems claiming the capacity to work miracles and commit only 'temporary errors'.

It is irrelevant whether individuals believe in the dogma as long as the unity of power and ideology is preserved and the effective power of enforcement by the leadership, acting as the only authentic representatives (vanguard) of the working class, is maintained. The essence of these Soviet-type régimes in Eastern Europe which the Communists call 'socialist' still lies in the fact that statements on any issue of political significance which the leaders declare to be the doctrinal truth at any given moment must be accepted by their subjects. Any questioning of ideology would undermine the monopoly of power.

Full control of all relevant means of mass communications and political indoctrination is the natural and inevitable by-product of such ideologically structured systems. It is beyond the scope of this study to pursue the enquiry as to whether the word 'totalitarianism' is an 'insult' or a correct definition when talking about present-day Eastern Europe.[3] But if it is true that all the changes since Stalin's day have not basically affected the total control of the media from above and their close integration with the other instruments of power, then one is inclined to accept the view that the question is not really whether Czechoslovakia, Hungary, Romania, etc, are totalitarian systems. but only to what extent in each case.[4]

Even if using a different vocabulary, Western scholars and authoritative ideological spokesmen in the East profess surprisingly similar views about the essentially unchanged structure and function of Communist mass media. Thus Richard Lowenthal describes the mechanism in these words:

The monopolistic control of all channels of public communications, from the press and other mass media to all forms of education, of literature and arts, with the aim not merely of preventing the *expression* of hostile or undesirable opinions by a kind of censorship, but of controlling the *formation* of opinion at the source by the planned selection of all the elements of information (emphases in original).[5]

Both the 1936 and the 1977 Soviet Constitutions declare that the citizens of the USSR 'are guaranteed freedom of speech, of the press, and of assembly, meetings, street processions and demonstrations'. The Brezhnev version is certainly 'more honest' because it limits these rights more clearly, making them all contingent upon acting 'in accordance with the interest of the people and in order to strengthen and develop the socialist system . . . in accordance with the aims of building communism'.[6]

What does this mean in practice? To start with, under the conditions of state ownership, a centrally planned economy and a single-party system, media supervision cannot be narrowed down to the classical instruments of censorship. From the printing plant, working capital and newsprint, to the typewriters, stationery and waste paper baskets, literally everything has to be provided by government departments, closely following the decisions taken by the Politbureau or Secretariat of the ruling party and the detailed instructions of the Press Sections of the all-powerful Agit-Prop (Agitation-Propaganda) Departments.

It is not for the sake of appearances, but in accord with the time-honoured practice of the division of labour, that the party and its apparatus play the role of the vanguard and guiding force, leaving the day-to-day executive functions to the government bureaucracy. In any case, the staffing, even of formally 'non-party' (i.e. government, union, youth or popular) papers, with reliable journalists is controlled by the Agit-Prop and Personnel Departments of the Central Committees. This control is exercised with special care when it comes to jobs with decision-making powers ('quantitative and qualitative gatekeeping') over the selection and editing of news and commentaries.

As *Pravda* put it:

A journalist is an active fighter for the cause of the party. It is not enough for him to have good intentions, he must also have clear views, a knowledge of life and the ability to present his thoughts convincingly and brilliantly from Leninist positions. The journalist and the public activist writing in the press must constantly perfect his knowledge and skill in order to see life in all its diversity, to know how to single out at the right moment what is practically important and to focus attention on the unsolved tasks of the day.[7]

It is often forgotten by Western observers, including academic communications experts, that the structure, function and circulation of Communist mass media bears hardly any relation to the place, values and changing fortunes of the press in Western societies. The introductory part of the latest Soviet party resolution not only explains the reasons why such high standards of moral and professional behaviour are expected of the almost 70,000 'workers of the pen, TV screen and radio microphone'. Its exhortations (and perhaps even more its harsh criticism of the entire indoctrination apparatus) provide striking proof that the observations of Lowenthal and other Western scholars are as valid as ever on the threshold of the 1980s:

A powerful information and propaganda apparatus provided with modern equipment – an extensively developed press, TV and radio – has been created in the country. Its main task is to arm the Soviet people and each new generation with the invincible weapon of historical truth and a profound understanding of the laws and prospects of social development, relying on the unshakeable foundations of the Marxist-Leninist teaching.[8]

Can anyone imagine Austria's Socialist government, the British Conservatives or even the military junta in Argentina or Chile issuing such a resolution? The 'abridged version' of it filled an entire page, of *Pravda*. It scolded the media, for example, for 'hushing up shortcomings and difficulties', failing to fight resolutely against such 'ugly vestiges of the past' as greed, bribery, waste, negligence, drunkenness, bureaucracy, callousness and indifference, and urged government ministers and leading state officials to write regularly in the press and to 'answer questions put forward by the people'.

The successors of the Bolsheviks are not only in the possession of 'truth', but also of an enormous communications system which is used to reproduce and to convey the political messages of the party and, if necessary, to substitute for reality what Alain Besançon calls 'surreality', a new dimension resulting from the Communists' idea of a future conforming to ideology. The media have the key function of producing a popular consciousness that is blind to the yawning gap between what these societies are and what their leaders pretend they are. Total control of the news filtering process, reflecting every change in foreign and domestic policy priorities. and the permanent, intensive and consistent repetition of simplified political messages are the outstanding features of the Communist propaganda technique.

The character of the Communist press reflects an amazing continuity since 1902 (!) when Lenin in his pamphlet (*'What is to be done'*) spelled out that:

> A newspaper is not only a collective propagandist and collective agitator, but also a collective organiser. In this respect it can be compared to the scaffolding erected around a building under construction; it marks the contours of the structure and facilitates communication between the builders, permitting them to distribute the work and to view the common results achieved by their organised labour.

In this sense the journalist is a party functionary. Three years later, Lenin in an oft-quoted article on *Party organisation and party literature* (November 1905) also argued that articles contributed to the party press must conform absolutely to the party doctrine. Party-mindedness (*partiinost*), the most frequently mentioned personal characteristic demanded of a Soviet and East European newspaperman, means that a Communist must judge every issue from the point of view of his proletarian party, thus implying an absolute devotion to the party and obedience to its instructions.

The point is, however, that these statements were meant as a guideline for a small and intransigent sect fighting for superiority within the Russian social democratic movement seven decades ago. In the meantime, in the words of Raymond Aron, 'Lenin's fanaticism has become the orthodoxy of an empire' and Marxism-Leninism 'the camouflage for a satisfied bureaucracy'.[9] The threefold function of the media, though formally upheld, has in fact been turned into its opposite. Mobilisation of the masses is not intended to change, but to strengthen, the established political order, to stifle deviant values, to counter the danger of apathy or opposition among the population, in short to stabilise, rather than to transform social-political relations.

How is it ensured that, in a world where actual conditions both abroad and at home are changing, at times with extraordinary speed, the press does not get out of control, but still operates as an obedient conveyor belt for the word of the leadership? The function of the media, now of course including television and broadcasting, is not to take a critical view of major decisions and to suggest alternative solutions (for example, a shift in investment priorities or farm policy), but to engage in political persuasion and a public relations exercise on behalf of the decisions already taken, usually behind closed doors, and to provide for their acceptance and active support by the population.

The primary task of the media is therefore not to chronicle daily events and to compete through credibility for the public's confidence, but to serve the party. The editors do not have to worry about circulation figures since there is no competition. Newsprint, as indeed news itself, is regulated and rationed according to political priorities and propaganda. The reactions of the readers are of no consequence whatsoever for the circulation nor for the standing of the individual publications, their editors and columnists.

It is true that, in addition to the much publicised institution of so-called volunteer worker and farmer correspondents, every larger newspaper from East Berlin, Prague and Moscow to Leipzig, Debrecen and Irkutsk has special editors for dealing with the influx of readers' letters, ranging from a dozen to a hundred each day, or even to over a thousand in the case of *Pravda* where a staff of forty-five researchers carefully screen the incoming complaints and refer them to the relevant party and government agencies.[10] What is often hailed as a great feat of socialist democracy, a contrast to the bourgeois world where a few wealthy people or large corporations control the access to the media, is merely a safety valve and a substitute for the lack of civil rights associated with constitutional government and political freedom. People write to the newspapers or radio simply because there are no other places where they can publicly complain about discrimination in the allotment of communal flats, poor service, bribery, waste and illegal profiteering. Their letters are also used by the party leadership for gauging certain trends in public opinion. But only a few, carefully selected letters get printed and these either refer to shortcomings and problems at enterprise and local level, or praise the 'timeliness' of a given government decree or party resolution. Those who disagree with basic policies or major measures taken by the régimes have no access to public channels of communication.

Though newsprint is generally in short supply, prices of newspapers are kept artificially low throughout the Communist world and, except in Hungary, most authoritative central newspapers, the ones with the largest staffs, have no, or very little, income from advertising. Given the nature of the communications system, it is not surprising that *Pravda* has a circulation of almost eleven million copies for a population of over 250 million. The East European fraternal party papers far surpass even this per head ratio. Thus the Bucharest *Scînteia* boasts of a circulation of 1.3 million for twenty-two million people, *Neues Deutschland* in East Berlin prints about one million (population: 16.8 million), *Trybuna Ludu* in Warsaw also around one million (thirty-five million population) and *Rabotnichesko Delo* in Sofia some 830,000 for a population of 8.8 million. The circulation of the Hungarian central party organ, *Népszabadság*, reaches an average 750,000 people on weekdays and that of *Rudé právo* in Prague over 900,000 with populations of 10.5 million and some fifteen million respectively. More important is the fact that the circulation of the party papers, which are everywhere considered to be boring by readers and colleagues alike, is at least three times higher than the sales of other morning and afternoon dailies with a more varied and interesting content. The relationship between sales of *Pravda* and those of the other Soviet dailies is more balanced, but in Russia, too, the dullest newspaper has by far the highest circulation.

How, then, does one explain that the circulations of journals in great demand are kept well below optimal levels and people are forced to subscribe, and often to queue up at the news stands, for publications such as *Pravda*, *Rabotnichesko Delo* or *Scînteia*, none of which could be called a newspaper in any accepted sense of the word? It is not just the scarcity of newsprint and the shortage of foreign exchange, but primarily the unique mixture of centralised resource allocations and political priorities which constitute the background to the bizarre world of Communist news media.

The example of Yugoslavia shows how quickly and drastically readership preferences can change even under the conditions of a single-party system. When Yugoslavia abandoned state subsidies to the media and allowed market demand to operate and began to change newspapers from government institutions into autonomous enterprises run by workers' councils and management boards, circulation of the Belgrade *Borba*, the former party organ, dropped by two-thirds from 650,000 copies in 1949 to 234,000 by 1958. Later, growing freedom and improved quality further sharpened the competition for the public in the decentralised market with the result that *Borba*, though certainly livelier and better than any 'serious' paper in the orthodox Soviet bloc countries, could only sell about 30,000 copies by the mid-1970s. During the same period, Belgrade's leading daily, *Politika* doubled its circulation to 265,000.[11] One should also recall that during the high point of liberalisation after the 'Polish October', the circulation of *Trybuna Ludu*, the Warsaw party paper, was halved.

It may be of some relevance to these sales figures to quote Jerzy Turowicz, the editor of the Polish Catholic weekly, *Tygodnik Powszechne*, who in 1978 complained that the censor had not allowed him to publish a comment in his own paper on an article about the Church-State dialogue originally printed in *Polityka*, the Warsaw weekly. Turowicz stressed the discrimination against Catholics in predominantly Catholic Poland and added as yet another revealing example that the Marxist weekly to which he had wanted to reply prints 300,000 copies, while *Tygodnik Powszechne* is only permitted a printing of 40,000 copies, although the Catholics have no access at all to other media.[12]

All these examples confirm the general rule that the thing media people in the Communist countries really worry about is not the reaction of their readers, viewers and listeners, but the reaction of their bosses. These are not the ministers nor the top officials of the institutions which formally publish the so-called central non-party papers such as the government dailies, and the organs of the youth organisations, the trade unions, the agricultural sector, the capital city and (outside the Soviet Union) the organs of the People's or National Fronts (which comprise all mass organisations) or of nominally existing, but totally irrelevant, non-Communist parties in Poland, Czechoslovakia and East Germany. The personal fate, career, promotion, and last but not least the selection for the much sought-after trips to the West are ultimately decided by the overseers, more often than not professional functionaries, in the press section of the ruling party who have rarely if ever worked on a news desk or held a microphone in their hands.

If one seeks to understand just how the press is supervised, the first and most fundamental point to remember is that it is everywhere the Communist Party leadership which acts as the supreme board of directors of gigantic multi-media companies in the individual countries. By far the largest communications corporation in the world is of course the USSR Inc.; it not only controls 7,923 newspapers, 4,670 periodicals, and studios and transmitters providing programmes for almost sixty million television and over 122 million radio sets (half of them wired receivers) but also possesses the most powerful external broadcasting organisation in the world, transmitting 2,019 hours a week in eighty-four languages. Furthermore, *Novosti* (or APN), the public relations and features agency, launched in 1961 'to counter hostile bourgeois propaganda abroad about Soviet life . . . and to unmask the enemies of peace and social progress', is today active in over one hundred countries. It supplies 100,000 articles and 1.7 million photos annually for some 7,000 foreign papers: publishes fifty periodicals and ten newspapers in fifty-six languages with total circulations of 2.5 million;

and in addition publishes 300 books and pamphlets in several different languages, twenty million copies of which are distributed per annum by the APN publishing house in Moscow and abroad.[13]

Foreign observers tend to realise just how much attention is paid to propaganda operations by the Soviet leadership when spectacular personnel shifts take place, as happened, for example, in 1978 when Leonid Zamyatin, former director general of TASS, the central news agency, was put in charge of a new high-powered international information department of the Central Committee with the former Bonn Ambassador Valentin Falin as his deputy. In every Communist system the domain of agitation and propaganda encompasses oral agitation, propaganda, publishing, literature, arts, film, radio-television, central and provincial press, contacts with foreign media, and even sport and, in some countries, science and education. Propaganda and agitation are used as different terms, going back again to Lenin, who in 1902 approvingly quoted his erstwhile teacher and, subsequently, bitter enemy, G. V. Plekhanov: 'a propagandist presents many ideas to one or a few people, an agitator presents only one, or few ideas, but he presents them to a mass of people'. Under the impact of the modern means of communications the division has become blurred, with the 'propagandist' having a more 'intellectual' connotation, while the 'agitator' is seen more as an activist spreading the party's more simple slogans in a down-to-earth fashion through personal contacts.

The Politbureau and Secretariat of a ruling Communist Party decide not only the broad priorities and very often the details of foreign and economic strategy, but also external propaganda and internal indoctrination strategy. The enormous apparatus has to carry out the general party line, elaborated in detail by the Central Committee Secretariat and transmitted in the form of instructions by the senior officials who are themselves often secretaries of the Central Committee. Currently, in most ruling parties, at least two CC secretaries, sometimes even more, often also full or candidate Politbureau members, are in charge of propaganda and ideology in the broad sense. One of them is always the supreme overseer of the printed and broadcast media which in turn are controlled on a day-to-day basis by numerous sections and sub-sections.

The selection, control and, if necessary, the sacking of journalists provides only the most elementary conditions for the smooth operations of the media. Turning to ideological, political and operational guidance, we must differentiate between the central news agency, the central party paper and the rest of the media. The central news agency fulfills two basic functions in every single Communist-ruled state. First, it serves as the main day-to-day channel for the transmission of information which is politically fit or doctored enough to print in the press and to broadcast. Its second and perhaps even more vital task, the dimensions of which are not generally known to outsiders, is the compilation, processing and distribution of so-called 'special' or 'confidential' news bulletins. Information as a privilege, and as one of the rewards of the élite, will be dealt with later on.

Even in their publicly known activities, TASS, PAP, MTI and the other official news agencies cannot remotely be compared to normal Western news agencies, be it on a transnational or on a more modest national scale. The point is that they serve as the main and quickest instrument for the regulating, rationing and filtering of any kind of news. For example, the ticker of the agency carries press releases from the party and the government apparatus with the headline and length already indicating their relative importance. Speeches, communiques and what the French call 'protocol news', dealing with the arrival and departure of delegations and the progress of their talks, have to be carried in the same way, with same order of names and at same length as the originals transmitted through the agency.

Any Western reporter who has tried to visit any kind of factory or enterprise in Eastern Europe has experienced the obsession with secrecy. Even in the currently most relaxed Soviet bloc country, namely Hungary, journalists always need a permit to go to a factory. No one can be interviewed or make a statement to a news reporter without permission from the ministry concerned. Thus it is no wonder that any substantive information about foreign, domestic, economic or cultural policy must come either from the centrally controlled, edited and if necessary adapted, agency tape, or must be cleared with the relevant government or party department.

As the press is an integral part of the state and party apparatus, the agency – without, of course, having the right to issue any directives of its own – serves as a useful tool for both the sender and receiver groups within the vast apparatus. At the same time, the leadership avails itself of the news agency to transmit politically significant signals for foreign and domestic consumption. A few examples will illustrate that the continuity or the changing of the party line is signalled as much by what is suppressed as by what is published.

When, in the early 1960s, Romania embarked on its successful go-it-alone foreign policy, its leadership skilfully used a mixture of omissions and deliberate leaks to alert the world at large and the public at home. This 'news management' became particularly evident in the spring of 1964 when the entire Romanian press simply ignored the open eruption of the Sino-Soviet conflict. The Bucharest papers, monotonous as ever and relying on the *Agerpress* agency, presented their readers with foreign news pages unparalleled in either the West, or the East. On 10 April, for example, *Scînteia*, the party paper, reported President Johnson's press conference, in thirty-two lines. The famous speech by Nikita Khrushchev about 'goulash Communism' in Hungary rated only fifteen lines.

This curious way of 'news' reporting has by now become a well-known ploy to underscore Romanian irritation or opposition towards her powerful Russian neighbour. Thus ten years later, at the end of 1974, *Agerpress* carried only seven lines about the Ford-Brezhnev summit meeting in Vladivostok, but a much longer report about the independence of the African islands, Sao Tome and Principe. One day later there was a somewhat more extensive item about the US-Soviet communique. However, an even lengthier report on the presentation of the credentials of the Romanian Ambassador in the Central African Republic was carried more prominently.

The same type of politically-motivated slanting can be observed in the work of other Communist-controlled news agencies. The Hungarian MTI, for example, simply ignored the news that President Brezhnev handed the Lenin Order to the Romanian Party chief and head of state, Nicolae Ceauşescu, when the latter paid him a visit in the Crimea in the summer of 1979. The entire Hungarian press kept silent because no desk editor would dream of touching such a dangerous subject on his own. This demonstrative insult to the leader of a neighbouring country and fellow Warsaw Pact partner was a piece of tit-for-tat in the tense period after the Romanians closed their frontiers to motorists who could not pay in convertible currency (or equivalent vouchers) for petrol, a surprise move which had primarily hit Hungarians seeking to visit their two million kinsmen in Transylvania.

One could ask whether the Soviets did not resent what could have been taken as a calculated insult to Brezhnev, who only a couple of months earlier had been celebrated in Budapest as the 'great, respected and trusted friend'? Surprisingly, not at all; they had been informed in advance that, at a time when the leadership had to face an eruption of feeling over the Romanian border measures, reporting the award to Ceauşescu would, if anything, have been, 'objectively', an anti-Soviet provocation. They understood the Hungarian motives, not least because they themselves had often resorted to the same tricks in their occasionally turbulent relations with their Romanian comrades.

When, for example, after the Warsaw Pact summit meeting in Moscow in November 1978, President Ceauşescu defied the Kremlin by speaking out openly against increased military spending and mobilised the usual 'wave of enthusiastic support' from the party and population, TASS did not publish a single word on the subject. Nor did any other East European news agency, except Yugoslavia. The kind of bloc-wide regimentation and uniformity (*Gleichschaltung*) which Stalin imposed is long gone.

In the early 1950s Soviet material provided the basis for the general news service in the bloc. In those days, for example, the editor-in-chief of the Hungarian news agency, a veteran emigrée who had lived for decades in Moscow, fired a desk editor because he dared to cut a TASS dispatch, leaving out some insignificant sentences. When there was no Soviet source, she simply phoned Moscow and held up the domestic wire service until she had proper documentation, even if the event had already been reported in the world press. For example, when the Italian Communist leader, Palmiro Togliatti, made an important statement about polycentrism in the Communist movement, the chief of the MTI managed to prevent publication of the text in all Hungarian papers for an entire week, after which the party paper printed doctored fragments.

Shift editors are no longer sacked, let alone jailed, for omitting a phrase or letting through a misleading translation. In fact, their decision-making power today in handling daily news requirements is much greater than is ordinarily assumed. It may be noted that the tested instrument of self-censorship, based on training, experience and political instinct, has on the whole been as successful in Hungary, where there has never been a formal censorship apparatus installed, as in the other bloc countries with a cruder type of 'thought control'.

Yet for all the salutary changes – affecting even the staid TASS, which now discloses population and output statistics which would have been regarded as treason in Stalin's day – Communist news agencies continue to be used primarily to convey the word of the party and are regarded by the national and bloc media as the only source of official, that is reliable, information. There is tacit agreement, for example, that the news agency of one Soviet bloc country reports events in another bloc country only on the basis of releases by the agency in the country concerned. Thus it would be inconceivable that, under normal circumstances, news items about, say, a trial of Czech human rights activists would go on the general service wire in Hungary, or that a report on the 1976 strikes in Poland would be carried by the Bulgarian BTA without an appropriate release from the Czech or Polish agencies.

It is important to note, that, despite the diversity in politics and communications methods, TASS operates even today as a kind of bloc gate-keeper, a communications centre transmitting, withholding or slanting information when there is a sudden, unexpected switch in Soviet policy or in world affairs. Thus when the agency remained mute about the sensational release of Alexander Ginzburg and four other prominent Soviet dissidents in exchange for two convicted Soviet spies, arranged at the highest level before the Carter-Brezhnev summit in Vienna in June 1979, the same silence descended upon the news media all over Eastern Europe. The Soviet lead was also followed by the bloc media in the treatment of such sensitive items as the high points in the Moscow-Peking conflict, the expulsion of Soviet military advisers by Egypt, massive grain imports from the West, the Soviet intervention in Afghanistan, or, for that matter, the death of Nikita Khrushchev in September 1971. The entire press in Eastern Europe was waiting for TASS. It took thirty-six hours until a six-line announcement was released in Moscow about the death of 'pensioner Khrushchev'. Then at last the news (already broadcast by the Western radio stations and covered by the world press in obituaries which, in the *New York Times* for example, ran to 10,000 words) could also be carried by the fraternal papers in Eastern Europe. Then, as Khrushchev's name disappeared down the Orwellian 'memory hole' in Moscow, he also had to be made into an 'unperson' in the Soviet-controlled part of the Communist world. No wonder that an opinion survey among young Hungarians in 1976–77 revealed that fifty-nine percent had no idea at all who Khrushchev was. A young white-collar employee thought that 'Khrushchev was the first man in space', while a skilled worked wondered whether he had not been 'a US President in the sixties' and finally another highly qualified labourer recalled that the man 'had worked as a successful *kolkhoz* chairman' . . .[14]

The point is that the man who between 1953 and 1964 dominated not just Soviet affairs but international Communism and East European politics, has had to disappear completely from the East European media. Many years after Khrushchev's fall and death, the Bulgarian radio and newspaper commentator, Vladimir Kostov, reported in a broadcast from Moscow that the Muscovites with whom he had spoken 'had expressed their satisfaction with Leonid Brezhnev and considered him to be a better leader than N. S. Khrushchev.' Back home in Sofia, Kostov was severely reprimanded for having mentioned the name of Khrushchev at all. He had committed an 'unforgiveable sin'. Relating this characteristic episode after his defection in Paris in a series broadcast by RFE in October 1977, Kostov added ironically: 'since Khrushchev no longer held the leading post which was tantamount to his never having held it, such a person had simply never existed.'

The experiences of Yugoslav correspondents in Moscow are, in a different way, instructive. In January 1970 the correspondent of the Belgrade *Politika* reported the case of two Italians who had distributed leaflets in a department store in Moscow demanding the release of some Soviet dissidents and appealing to Prime Minister Kosygin to grant freedom of speech. Two weeks later the mass circulation weekly, *Literaturnaya Gazeta*, publicly castigated the 'disgraceful' behaviour of the Yugoslav correspondent who had informed his readers 'about the content of that filthy anti-Soviet sheet' instead of simply condemning the 'provocation' of the two Italians.

Even reporting what the Soviet papers actually write can be a risky enterprise in a world where information is treated as a state monopoly. Miodrag Marović, the international Communist affairs commentator of *NIN*, the Belgrade weekly, recalled in December 1977, a time of sharp polemics between Yugoslavia and some pro-Soviet ruling parties over the assessment of Euro-Communism, his experience in the country (he meant, but did not name, the Soviet Union) where he was earlier working as a permanent correspondent. One day he was called to a high official, who, looking very serious, admonished him: 'You write about things you should not'. Marović replied: 'I only report what your press has written and not gossip picked up on the street'. To Marović's great amazement the official declared 'Our press writes for our readers and not for yours . . .'[15] In the opinion of the Soviet official, the Communist correspondent from Yugoslavia had evidently violated the 'code of good behaviour' agreed upon by Tito and Brezhnev during the latter's visit to Belgrade in 1971. The famous and (within Yugoslavia itself) highly controversial paragraph stressed that 'the mass media should work for the sake of strengthening mutual respect and friendship between the people of the Soviet Union and Yugoslavia;' they should also explain 'objectively and with goodwill' and contribute to the construction of socialism. We will not dwell on Yugoslav-Soviet polemics, except perhaps to note that Veljko Mičunović, twice Yugoslav ambassador to Moscow, repeatedly refers in his revealing memoirs to 'half-truths' and complete 'distortions' of Yugoslav statements by TASS and *Pravda*.[16]

The above is, inevitably, much too simple a picture of the operations of TASS, which is after all primarily supplying its subscribers at home and abroad with a steady stream of straightforward items about the manifold successes of the Soviet Union and its constitutent republics in industry, agriculture and the cultural and educational fields, coupled with gloomy news about troubles in the capitalist world. Yet advocates of the 'new international information order' often overlook the fact that TASS and its sister organisation, *Novosti* (APN), together constitute what could arguably be called the largest transnational news agency in the world.

On the eve of the Soviet-sponsored International Journalists' Seminar on Communications in Tashkent in September 1979, Yuri Kashlev, the executive secretary of the Soviet Unesco Commission, stressed in a *Pravda* article that Soviet aid for the media of the developing countries has 'no political strings' attached, and that the Soviet Union does not seek – as he claimed the capitalist countries do – to establish its 'financial and ideological control over information services being set up in the developing world'.[17] There is no reason to doubt the sincerity of his words. But it is useful to recall at least some of the experiences of the Yugoslav media with the least known, but best organised, transnational news agency complex. Political priorities can and do alter and the form and instruments of bloc-wide propaganda co-operation are also subject to many changes. Yet, as we have briefly seen, the Soviet political, ideological and information centre is still well-placed to set the bloc-wide propaganda priorities and to enforce, if no longer in detail then in essence, the loyal and disciplined co-operation of the vast Agit-Prop apparatus east of the Elbe – with the significant exception of Romania. There, however, qualitative differences are restricted only to the area of foreign policy and self-assertive nationalism, with no deviation whatsoever from the Soviet tradition as far as the internal information flow is concerned.

If TASS is the operative instrument of internal and, in truly important matters, external *Gleichschaltung* in news selection, so *Pravda* remains the ideological and political guide for the press and the media as a whole. The central party papers from East Berlin to Bucharest were founded after World War II as faithful copies of the great example in Moscow. Everything was of course on a smaller scale. But, from the institution of the so-called small collegium of editors to the daily, weekly and monthly plans, stating exactly how much 'anti-imperialist', 'Soviet' and 'people's democratic' material the papers intended to use in any given period, from the mechanism of the special channels of communication to the party leaders down to the special privileges enjoyed by the editorial staff, all was closely patterned on *Pravda*.

The total uniformity of those days is irrevocably gone. The difference between *Pravda* and its sister papers in lay-out, style and presentation of news has become very visible, even to the casual reader. The progress towards a greater degree of internal diversity in each Communist country has also allowed the local press to develop along more individualistic lines. Traditions, the level of economic and cultural development, the availability of trained journalists and printers and readership habits may have contributed much more to the difference between the leading papers in Hungary and those in Bulgaria, for example, than changes in political tactics.

What matters more, however, is what has *not* altered. While appearances may have changed, the principle of absolute domination of the national press by the central paper has remained. All the central papers resemble ministries or government offices rather than real newspapers. Their editors are at least Central Committee, often even Politbureau, members and are invariably close enough to the top to exercise their own discretion as to how to apply the general line. The

Party's line takes care not only of everything which has happened, is happening and might happen, but allows the experienced editor to present even the unexpected as a stunning confirmation of the leadership's wisdom.[18]

The editorials of *Pravda*, *Népszabadság* in Budapest, *Rabotnichesko Delo* in Sofia, etc are taken in the countries concerned as significant pointers. If the title or main topic is the 'unshakeable unity of the party', or the exhortation to 'respect the collective leadership', the alert reader knows even before a formal announcement that the top leadership has just been shaken by a power battle which further strengthened the position of the Number One or that the preparations for a reshuffle are in full swing with the Number Two or the potentially most dangerous rival in the wings just about to be eliminated.

The preeminence of *Pravda* as the only source of really authentic information was such that it took a special party resolution in 1960 to authorise TASS to transmit topical news directly to the broadcast media, by-passing *Pravda*. Previously even Moscow Radio could not broadcast an account of an event before it had been duly carried in *Pravda*. Even today, however, there is no Communist country where a paper could break an important story before the party mouthpiece.

The central paper is directly linked to the central apparatus at several levels; the editor can pick up the telephone and consult even top leaders over a sudden change of domestic or foreign policy, and the chiefs of every department have connections to the departmental heads at the Central Committee or, occasionally, even to members of the Politbureau. Such close ties are of course fraught with dangers if and when there is a significant change in the Politbureau or Secretariat.

It goes without saying that the journalists on the party central paper in most bloc countries, certainly in the Soviet Union, Romania, East Germany and Bulgaria, use the exclusive hospital and resort facilities reserved for the higher echelons of the party and enjoy unquestioned priority in obtaining new flats and new cars.

It might be asked why other papers were and are necessary at all? From the first, the Bolshevik founding fathers sought to create the impression of a manifold, lively press. More important still, the various papers were given definite tasks – among youth, the workers, the farmers, the government bureaucrats and so on. This pattern was imposed, with some local variations, on all client states. However, more than six decades after the October Revolution, the Soviet party has had to warn once again that 'newspapers must have their distinctive style'.

When it comes to the co-ordination of bloc-wide propaganda on issues like the campaign against China, the American plans to develop the neutron bomb, NATO's decision to deploy medium range missiles in Europe, the challenge represented by the Euro-Communists, and – at a different time and in a different fashion – the confrontation with Yugoslavia, the Kremlin does not have to issue detailed blueprints. Even in Stalin's day competent manipulation of news and comment was assured, mainly through functionaries, editors and commentators who approached all new problems from a 'class' and 'party-minded' standpoint. There were even special instances when, for example, the Hungarian, or Bulgarian or other East European papers were allowed to precede *Pravda* in commenting on certain events.

Thus in the period between 1949–53 the satellite press supplied the Soviet papers with distorted information about internal conditions in Yugoslavia. Anti-Tito propaganda was not confined to the exile Yugoslav papers, run by the functionaries of Cominform, the international Communist organisation (set up by Stalin in 1947 and dissolved in 1956) in Budapest, Prague, Bucharest and Moscow; the local party newspapers throughout the bloc had to 'plan' ahead when and how anti-Tito material would appear. Often the same article, based on full-blown lies about, say, bridges blown up by 'genuine Communist resistance fighters in Tito-Yugoslavia', would appear several times in a slightly altered form (tunnel instead of bridge for example) in the party papers all over Eastern Europe.

This Soviet practice of using intermediaries was not abandoned with the Stalinist past, but is still very much alive in the bloc media. In 1958 the Soviet Marshal Koniev wrote an article in the Prague *Rudé právo* on the fortieth anniversary of the Red Army. Significantly, he 'forgot' to mention Yugoslavia (the country with the largest partisan movement in Eastern Europe which relied essentially on its own strength to defeat the Axis occupation armies) among the countries which contributed to the victory over the Third Reich. After furious protests by the Belgrade government, the Czechoslovak Ambassador apologised to his Yugoslav colleague in Moscow, saying that the omission was a 'printing mistake' committed by *Rudé právo*.[19]

Ironically, seventeen years later in 1975, another Soviet Marshal, the then supreme commander of the Warsaw Pact forces, Marshal Ivan Jakubovsky published a similar article in the same Prague paper, depicting the Red Army as Yugoslavia's real liberator. The outcry in Yugoslavia was such that even President Tito sharply attacked 'all those' who tried to defame the heroic struggle of his partisans. This time there was no talk about a 'printing mistake'. The Yugoslav Minister of Defence, Nikola Ljubičić, was allowed to set the record straight two weeks later in a *Pravda* article; at the same time a senior Yugoslav party leader, Stane Dolanc was allowed to spell out the Yugoslav view in *Rudé právo* itself.

The same type of centrally-orchestrated 'cross-reporting' was repeatedly evident in the treatment of China. When, for example, the Romanian President Ceauşescu visited China and the former arch-enemies, Tito and Mao Tse-tung, gave the green light to a high-level dialogue, a Budapest paper, seemingly out of the blue, warned against 'a Belgrade-Bucharest-Tirana axis' supported by Peking. The article was published at the time of wild rumours about Soviet troop movements in Hungary. The Soviet, East German and Czechoslovak press immediately reprinted the ominous phrase. Yugoslav and Western observers saw in the coincidence of these events a psychological attack on the independently-minded Balkan states and a proof of Soviet concern about the appeal of their independent foreign policy to other Warsaw Pact countries.[20]

The central party organs are also used to rebuke the editorial staff on other journals if they happen to fall prey to what is called 'objectivism' (in very bad cases even 'bourgeois objectivism'), meaning, in party jargon, the presentation of events without an appropriate 'partisan' and 'class' evaluation. Here again, substantial progress since the mid-1950s cannot be denied. A handful of desk editors and reporters may have been demoted or even sacked, but not one of them appears to have been arrested, let alone shot, after criticism in *Pravda*, *Népszabadság* or *Rabotnichesko Delo* of any political daily, cultural weekly or scholarly monthly. We are talking here of course about loyal and reliable newsmen in good standing, and not about intellectuals in opposition to the régime or editors and contributors to underground publications.

Of course, political error and lack of vigilance cannot be allowed to pass. To take an apparently minor example, the coverage of Princess Alexandra's visit to Vienna in the late sixties by the correspondent of a Budapest popular daily was apparently found not worthy of the accepted reporting standards in a 'socialist' country. *Népszabadság* took him to task for his use of glowing adjectives and the entire tone of his truly innocuous dispatch. The defection of the journalist some time later was by all accounts a pure coincidence. At any rate the message was grasped by the other newsmen: it is safer to print an interview with groups of 'merited collective farms' chairmen' or 'outstanding workers' returning from Soviet Latvia or Moldavia under headlines – 'Two wonderful weeks', 'Meeting with Soviet people' or 'Dreams coming true' – than to show too much enthusiasm about the human touch displayed by a member of the British Royal Family.

The case of the Sofia weekly *Anteni*, with a circulation of 260,000, was more serious – also more mysterious. In December 1977 the political-cultural journal published an article arguing against the hasty decentralisation of higher education and the removal of some university faculties from Sofia to the provinces. Almost three months later five full-length columns in *Rabotnichesko Delo*, the party organ, were devoted to a vicious attack on the 'harmful', 'totally wrong', 'superficial' allegations of an article which most people had already forgotten. Veselin Yosifov, the editor, lost no time in apologising, reprinting the full text of the attack in the very next issue of his weekly. In the small world of Bulgarian media, the event had the effect of a minor earthquake. Why this sharp attack, why so late and why so sudden? Yosifov was after all not just any editor, but also Chairman of the 4,000-strong Journalist Federation and even a member of the Central Committee of the party. His meek submission baffled domestic observers.

When I met the lively, quick-witted Yosifov six months after his self-critical statement in Sofia, my persistent questioning failed to shed light on the mysterious affair. 'As you see I am still around. The criticism of our piece was fully justified. I said it then and repeat it now, we journalists cannot be specialists on everything. It would have been better not to raise the subject', he said smilingly, and elegantly avoided my question as to just why the party paper took such a long time to attack him and then so sharply. When I disrespectfully raised the delicate question of why *Rabotnichesko Delo* devoted so much space to an issue which by no stretch of the imagination could be of crucial importance to Bulgaria's destiny, yet maintained total silence on the reasons for the overnight disappearance from the political scene of Boris Velchev, the country's Number Two political figure for two decades, Yosifov shot back angrily: 'Yes, we don't write about internal party matters, but we have no terrorism, no bombing outrages, no mass unemployment as in your countries. We write rather about China and the danger of war against Vietnam.'

This affair, seemingly so minor, is a pointer to the very special place of a central party organ as the privileged voice of the top leadership. Ironical remarks by outsiders about the editor's submission to humiliating ritual would be out of place. According to the sacred principle of democratic centralism (coined by Lenin during his fight for supremacy in 1905 and incorporated into the Bolshevik party statutes in 1917) all decisions of the higher party bodies are unconditionally binding on the lower ones; discussions are possible only before a decision has been taken; and the minority or the individual party members must observe 'strict party discipline'. If one knows that Yosifov himself had gone through hell in the early fifties during the so-called 'cult of personality' period, having no respectable job for seven years and losing some of his teeth during interrogation sessions with the secret police, his behaviour is less surprising.

It is, however, not a question of personalities, or even issues. The record shows what the accusation of deliberately malicious reporting, even on a side issue, can do to news perspectives and professionalism. No party-minded journalist on another paper could even dream of ignoring, let alone rejecting, the views of a central party organ, the authoritative voice of what Robert Havemann, the East German Marxist scholar once called 'the Main Administration of Eternal Truths'. Only in exceptional and transitory periods of major political crisis such as the Hungarian uprising of October-November 1956, the Polish upheaval in 1956–57 and the peak phase of the 'Prague Spring' in 1968 could any paper dare to answer back to a central party organ – without immediate retribution. But simple malleability, the grasp of what is required by authority, can advance a career just as effectively as ideological purity.

The recent media history of Hungary, Poland, Czechoslovakia and even East Germany confirms that under certain circumstances nominally non-party journalists and, among the older generation, even former right-wing and erstwhile Fascist journalists, can prove to be more reliable than some party members who still cling to their ideals rather than let themselves be guided by the instinct for survival. This was shown by some breathtaking careers in Hungary after 1956 and also during the large-scale 'anti-Zionist', i.e. anti-Semitic and anti-intellectual, campaign in 1968 in Poland. But to my knowledge nothing can equal the unique phenomenon of East Germany, where the chief of the government's press office and the deputy editor-in-chief of *Neues Deutschland* along with thirty-seven other influential journalists were registered Nazi party members, according to a survey compiled by Simon Wiesenthal – and never refuted by the office-holders listed.[21]

But mishaps can happen in the absence of malicious intent. Consider the curious history of a speech delivered by Prime Minister Jenö Fock at the eleventh Hungarian party congress in 1975. This able but impulsive politician, probably embittered and frustrated by the long factional infighting about the pace and scope of the economic reforms, surprised, some say even shocked, his colleagues with some very blunt speaking about the weaknesses in government policy. The Prime Minister did not mince words about his own responsibility either.

Such behaviour was most unusual at a party congress and according to Communist protocol would have been more appropriate to a closed session of the Central Committee or the Politbureau. As Leonid Brezhnev also spoke on the same day and as Fock had obviously added his self-critical and critical remarks to his prepared speech at the last minute (the text had as usual been circulated among his Politbureau colleagues), the full text was routinely released. By the time those in charge of information went into action to delete the two sensitive paragraphs, it was too late. Hundreds of thousands of subscribers could read the full text in the early editions of the party organ and the provincial papers. But the party members and the public at large who got later editions in Budapest and its environs were kept in the dark about the complaints of Fock, who resigned two months later.

Even more mysterious was the fate of a speech delivered by the Romanian Prime Minister Ion Gheorghe Maurer in 1973 at a party conference in the city of Cluj. In a seemingly routine way he referred to Lenin's oft-quoted last article *Better less, but better*, warning against reckless haste in the organisation of the economy. Maurer's public statement was of great political significance because it indirectly, but clearly, deviated from President Ceauşescu's all-out industrialisation policy with the highest investment ratio, through enforced savings, in the Communist world. But Maurer's words reached, apart from his audience, only the readers of the local party paper. Not one word of the speech made by the second-ranking figure in the hierarchy was printed in the central press! He was made to resign only a few months later – but he was politically dead the moment his contact with the public was severed by that one quick stroke.

Professor Mihailo Marković, the Yugoslav Marxist philosopher, has remarked that the 'history of the countries which call themselves socialist, is to a high degree shaped by power battles within their ruling élites.'[22] Access to, and control of, the press is a vital factor in such battles.

The third segment of the mass media – after the news agencies and central party organs – consists of the other, formally non-party, national papers and the provincial party papers together with radio and television. It goes without saying that in these domains, too, the key positions are occupied by trusted party members.

The other papers, daily or weekly, published in the capital have a kind of double or even triple supervision. Selection of staff and direction of policy is handled by the institutions which nominally publish the papers, that is the trade unions, the youth organisations, the People's Front, the party organisation or municipal council of the capital city, and in some countries, the army, or rather its political directorate. Radio and television are run by a special committee and there is also a government press office. In countries with a formal institution of censorship all these outlets are more tightly controlled and their output more thoroughly scrutinised than the select party papers with their own long established supervisory system. Yet at the same time, ultimately, all the media (and of course the censors too) are controlled and run by the Agit-Prop Departments of the Central Committees. The party journals in the provinces or in the Soviet Republics are of course subject to supervision by the local party bodies. The careers of the local media executives depend to no small degree on whether their bosses are transferred to the political centre and co-opted into the top leadership.

Even before the advent of the television age, and although never faced with the daunting prospect of free elections, Communist leaders were traditionally closely involved in controlling, directly or indirectly, the content and mix of the internal and external political news flow. The tradition goes back originally to Marx, Rosa Luxemburg, Trotsky and Lenin – the last left an indelible imprint on the life and working conditions of successive generations of journalists working in the Communist-controlled media. But there was of course a world of difference in the way in which the founding fathers regarded the press and the information policies of some of their successors at the helm of certain ruling parties. Common to all party secretaries is the attention they pay to the media, both that which is published and their more confidential sources of news.

Nevertheless the Hungarian party chief who engineered the Communist seizure of power (1945–47) and ran the country as 'Stalin's best Hungarian pupil' until the summer of 1956, Mátyás Rákosi, probably remains unique: towards the end of his rule he personally supervised the publication of his speeches in *Szabad Nép*, the then central paper. The fuse that ultimately ignited the powder keg of pent-up resentment in 1956 was Rákosi's role in the show trial of László Rajk, the former Minister of Interior who, together with seven other high-ranking functionaries was tried and hanged in 1949 as 'an agent of the Tito-gang, the American imperialists and the French secret service'. With Khrushchev's destalinisation campaign in full swing, pressures from below and from the Yugoslavs were rapidly pushing Rákosi on to the defensive. Then in the spring of 1956 speaking at a meeting in a small town, the man who had publicly boasted of having spent 'sleepless nights' in unmasking the Rajk conspiracy and sending the 'spy' to the gallows, now unexpectedly called his victim a 'comrade' and announced his 'innocence'.

The text of his speech was set up in print for page two. Alerted by one of his many informers, the party chief rushed personally to the party paper's office, appeared dramatically in the printing plant, and personally supervised the correction of the error. Two months later fighting for his political life, Rákosi engaged in a sickening example of 'self-criticism' at a mass meeting. That very night he was once again in direct touch with the editors and printers on how to handle the story. But then, as Trotsky prophetically noted about Stalin: 'The vengeance of history is more terrible than the vengeance of the most powerful secretary general . . .'

At present, the Communist leader in Europe most intimately involved in personal supervision of the media may well be Romania's Nicolae Ceauşescu (if we exclude the special case of Enver Hoxha in isolated Albania, who himself writes most of the editorials on ideology and foreign policy in the party organ in Tirana). For the past few years, no editor of a newspaper, even of a minor cultural weekly, has been allowed to leave the country without President Ceauşescu personally counter-signing the exit permit. The same procedure is applied to all academics invited to international conferences with the result that advance notification of 'at least' forty days is needed to get a smooth passage for an application through the bureaucracy.

When a foreign correspondent of *Agerpress*, the news agency, defected in Paris in 1976, the President was so outraged that he ordered the immediate recall to Bucharest of all agency and newspaper correspondents. Ever since then Romania has been the only East European country with no permanent foreign correspondents abroad. A man of puritanical convictions and a penchant for quick decisions, Ceauşescu has applied Lenin's teaching – 'we must systematically set to work to create a press that will not entertain and fool the masses with political sensations and trivialities.' In the course of an ideological spring-cleaning, he ordered an immediate stop to the TV transmissions of some popular American thriller and Western series. In a further move, to save sparse hard currency and to leave more time for the reporting on the President's manifold activities at home and abroad, Romanian television was prevented from showing any matches, even the finals, during the World Cup in Argentina in 1978, thereby provoking widespread, but futile, resentment among millions of soccer fans.

Why do such seemingly minor matters as the personal taste of a President have political relevance and a definite impact on the life of an entire population? The central determination of news criteria is only part of the picture. It should also be remembered that under a Soviet-type system, the fact that the authority of a man 'at the head of the party' is accepted inevitably entails glorifying him. The image of the party 'closely knit around its Leninist leadership', makes it mandatory to extol the wisdom of its decisions and therefore that of the chief.[23] The picture is only different if the leader expressly forbids any tribute to himself, as is done by the Hungarian party chief, János Kádár, or if, instead of one leader, there are several men temporarily sharing power, jealously watching over one another as in Bulgaria between 1956–1961, or, for several years after the triumph of the collective principle in October 1964, in the Soviet Union.

Regardless of the given degree of cult, the world view of the man at the helm of a Communist party and the ideological blinkers through which he sees political, social and cultural developments have a permanent (and in the case of an exalted, adulated dictator even all-pervading) impact on the entire range of media output. The following story, related by Jiři Pelikán, the former director general of Czechoslovak Television in his autobiography,[24] is an instructive example of how Communist office-holders see themselves and the function of the mass media in the world.

During the 'Prague Spring', the 1968 reform movement under the leadership of Alexander Dubček, both the printed press and broadcast media played an enormously important role in forcing the pace of liberalisation and mobilising public opinion. The impact of unaccustomed investigation and the persistent questioning of high-ranking officials before the TV camera was such that a government commission, headed by the then deputy Premier Dr Gustav Husák took Pelikán to task for the cheeky behaviour of the TV reporters: 'Could you imagine that the BBC or the French TV would publicly criticise cabinet ministers or allow Communists to speak before the cameras?'. 'It is very easy for me to imagine it,' Pelikán retorted, 'I saw such things happening with my own eyes'. Husák seemed somewhat perturbed and momentarily dropped the matter. During a pause, however, he drew Pelikán aside and asked him in a low voice: 'What were you saying? Can Communists really speak on capitalist television?'. Pelikán replied calmly: 'That is the truth. On French or Italian Television it is quite normal for the leaders of the Communist parties to be invited to state their views about this or that subject.' And, as the deputy Premier still appeared disbelieving, Pelikán added: 'One can also criticise the government. I myself saw a report on the BBC which not only criticised the government but even made insulting remarks about its policies.'

Pelikán did not know whether he had succeeded in convincing Husák, who like Gomulka in Poland between 1956–1970, did not know the West and was one of those Communist leaders who remained 'prisoners of their own propaganda'. In the meantime, Husák became both the first secretary of the party and head of state. The politically disastrous fashion in which his régime has handled the 'Charter 77' human rights movements and staged the trials of dissident journalists, writers and academics indicates that Pelikán's scepticism was more than justified.

When we talk in a broad sense about the guidance of the media from above, we must differentiate between the formal, large-scale propaganda conferences, events which are on the public record, and the regular but confidential supervision and manipulation of news reporting. Observers, unfamiliar with the actual operations and the inner structure of such systems tend to ignore such 'informal channels' of guidance and communication within the apparatus itself. Yet the speeches or resolutions at national ideological conferences, the overall propaganda directives concerning the Five-Year Plan or a forthcoming party congress, as spelled out in specialised publications, and even the very occasional encounters like those the Polish party chief Edward Gierek* had with large groups of editors and commentators on an 'informal basis', do not match the impact of the constant, day-to-day or week-to-week, guidance of the apparatus, even on matters quite trivial by Western standards. The following brief and necessarily oversimplified sketch is applicable to the entire Soviet bloc (and also to Yugoslavia until the early fifties when Milovan Djilas was in charge of the Agit-Prop sector). The rank of the functionaries and the frequency of conferences may vary from party to party, but the manner of supervision and direction, borrowed from the 'fatherland of the proletariat' – first completely and slavishly, later 'adapted to local conditions' – is similar everywhere.

In societies where so much is protected by a veil of secrecy, and where access to information in the form of confidential bulletins depends on a person's rank in the hierarchy, access to confidential 'briefing' is in turn regulated by an official's position within the special bureaucracy of communicators. Thus by far the most important meeting, generally held twice monthly, involves only the editors-in-chief of the news agency, the central papers, radio, television news and political departments and the head of the government's press office.

* This book went to press before events in Poland in the summer of 1980 could be fully taken into account.

Such meetings are usually chaired by the chief of the Agit-Prop Department, who is often also secretary of the Central Committee. In some countries the editors of the formally non-Communist newspapers also attend; but in Czechoslovakia, for example, they used to be informed through the government press office. Due to the existence of their own special channels, the central party papers are generally represented only by their first deputy editor.

The propaganda chief gives a short account of new developments in foreign, economic and cultural policies, issues broad directives, answers some queries and occasionally criticises the past performance of certain papers or sectors of the mass media. Whenever the leadership is concerned about the danger of a political crisis, or there is popular disaffection in the wake, for example, of a price increase, special conferences of the top media executives are convened.

At this level, overall priorities are stressed rather than technical details. But even so decisions may be taken which would appear rather strange to a Western reader; for example the directives in Prague and Budapest as to which papers or media should comment at all on the Pope's visit to Poland in the summer of 1979 (the detailed instructions and their results will be described later). But if one believes, and there is no reason to doubt the authenticity of the story, that in the fifties the supreme leadership in Prague had to decide whether the news of some totally insignificant price reductions in neighbouring East Germany should be published, then nothing can be excluded. As a matter of fact, the then President of the Republic and the Prime Minister were attending a theatre performance with a distinguished foreign delegation when an anxious CTK editor and party officials consulted them. They had to leave the presidential box to discuss the vital issue and to decide finally that it would not be 'in the interest of the Czechoslovak people' if they were told about the East German price reductions for shoe cream and marmalade.[25]

Decisions about the handling of a crisis situation in another bloc country, for example Czechoslovakia in 1968, the Polish riots at the end of 1970 and the strikes in 1976, or dramatic events such as the assassination of President Kennedy or Khrushchev's fall, are naturally taken at the highest level.

Even less important matters can not always wait to be settled at the regular meetings. But if possible, the top leadership prefers to prepare public opinion 'in the usual way', that is after a background information session with those in charge of running the print and broadcast media. Of course, the details of the execution are not, save in super-sensitive matters (like the placement of the news about the ousting of Khrushchev), the direct concern of the top leaders.

The names of the functionaries currently handling the regular information sessions in the various countries are of no great importance. More interesting may be the fact that at critical junctures even such senior Politbureau members as Mikhail Suslov or his veteran right-hand assistant Boris Ponomarev, meet with the editors of the Soviet central media to give them broad directives and information concerning such events as the proper coverage of the 1976 international Communist conference in East Berlin, the Sino-Soviet dispute or the SALT negotiations with Washington. The potential dangers of the China-Vietnam War in 1978, for example, only became fully evident to the best informed Hungarian journalists when they heard that party chief János Kádár had himself chaired the regular meeting with the leading editors, and given them the background.

The editors of the weekly papers have the privilege of receiving instructions only from the chief of the press sector of the Agit-Prop Department or his deputy. For the foreign editors, the regular information sessions are handled by the chief of the Foreign Ministry's press department or a high official of the Central Committee's international department. Occasionally, ambassadors on home leave or from a country with which it is thought desirable to improve relations talk to the international specialists.

Similar channels of communication are used between the heads of relevant departments and the agricultural, industrial and cultural editors. It has to be remembered that central newspapers are almost everywhere heavily over-staffed by normal Western standards. *Pravda* and *Izvestia* have, on their own admission, a permanent writing staff 250 to 300 strong (including full-time correspondents) to fill six pages; with about sixty percent of the turgid material supplied by

outside contributors.[26] Even some of the smaller East European sister papers have no fewer than some twenty people in
their foreign news departments, even though the relatively
modest space available is mainly filled with communiques,
agency tape and texts of speeches, already carefully edited and
'packaged' by the national news agency or the press section of
the Central Committee.

Nevertheless, the entire mechanism of 'instructional conferences' is subsequently repeated at all levels from top to
bottom, with the information available becoming gradually
less authentic. Communist journalists scrutinise the foreign
and domestic news in their own countries, or those of the
bloc as a whole, not for the eloquent proclamations of peace-
loving intentions or for the seemingly important professions
of fraternal solidarity in the movement and monolithic unity
at home, but for the details and nuances that betray the policy
shifts or the real conflicts. In this sense, the regular conferences set the tone for the entire communication media. The
leading communicators give lectures themselves both for the
agitators and the intellectuals, thus acting as one of the main
'legal' channels for spreading information through the 'word-
of-mouth-system', rumours and evaluations, often officially
inspired, thus get passed on to the population at large. Such
tested methods were applied in the Soviet Union after
Khrushchev's fall, during the high points of the confrontation
with the Soviets in Romania and on the eve of the massive
price increases in the summer of 1979 in Hungary.

Apart from the oddities of Communist jargon, does this
way of supplying the media with information really differ
from the systems of informal briefings and off-the-record
interviews, non-attributable leaks, 'deep background', etc in
the West? To hammer home the point once again, the basic
difference lies in the place and function of the media and the
journalists in the context of these single-party ideologically
structured systems. They are representatives of a special kind
of journalistic advocacy as distinct from investigative reporting and critical comment. They are briefed only to 'sell' and
to explain in a more efficient and optimal way, but not to
question the basic party and government policies.

History has provided ample proof that freedom to attack

basic policies, to question ideological legitimacy or criticise leading personalities is incompatible with the Communist system of government. Leaving value judgments aside, realistic students of Soviet and East European affairs must agree on this cardinal point with the ideological spokesmen of the régimes themselves.

Consider, for example, Hungary where the press played a crucial role in the period of the post-Stalin thaw and contributed to the emergence of a revolutionary situation in 1956 which, primarily through the blunders of the Soviets, escaped control from above. The exhilarating period of genuine press freedom lasted only four to five days, albeit producing no fewer than seventeen different papers. Some of the most active journalists, including Miklós Gimes, one of the most erudite commentators, paid with their lives; scores were imprisoned and some four hundred removed from their jobs. During the later phase of the Kádár régime, most of the journalists who had been persecuted, compromised or disciplined were allowed to work again and even to travel abroad. But neither the rulers nor the media have forgotten the experience of 1956. This ever-present awareness of the limits on the part of both sides constitutes a vital part of what some call the 'Hungarian miracle'.

In Czechoslovakia, the muzzling of the mass media was in fact one of the main aims of the Soviet-led invasion. During the period of the so-called 'normalisation' after Dubček's final fall, between April 1969 and the beginning of 1972, over 1,500 members of the Journalists Union were expelled, a measure equivalent to the removal of their livelihood. In contrast to the policy in Hungary, there has not been even a limited reconciliation. Many of the journalists in the Czech lands were not even allowed to find jobs in libraries, institutes or even as white-collar workers. One of the most courageous and ablest commentators, Jiři Lederer, was sentenced to three years in jail and, on his release, allowed to emigrate.

Yet there is at least one leading reformer and former Central Committee secretary under Dubček, now in exile, Zdeněk Mlynář, who in hindsight regards the abolition of censorship in June 1968 as one of the major errors committed by the leadership. In a memorandum, written while he was still in Prague in February 1975, he criticised the lifting of all restraints on freedom of expression, which allowed the mass media to become the main vehicle of the reform, and regrets the failure to set certain limits on the media during the subsequent months.[27] This issue is likely to be long debated, but Mlynář's words highlight the unresolved dilemma of how to grant piecemeal freedom of the press without whetting the appetite for more. In the event, the journalists, reporting fully and freely after decades of censorship, ended up as convenient scapegoats both for the victors and the losers.

In a sense, it is the Yugoslav example which confirms most convincingly the impossibility of a free press even under the régime which has been the mildest and most daring internally and the most truly independent externally of all Communist governments. During the ascendancy of the liberals and the peak period of political and cultural experimentation, the Marxist philosopher, Svetozar Stojanović, expressed the optimistic view: 'Journalistic independence is possible if the party is run on a decision model which assures minority rights of dissent and tolerates differences of opinion.'[28]

Alas, ten years or more later, this model is as far away as ever. If anything, the position of the Yugoslav media has become much worse. Both the Press Law of 1973 and the new Constitution of 1974 entail a more restrictive interpretation of press freedom than before. Worse still, the extensive political purges, in the centre and in the republics, also removed some three dozen able editors and commentators and reimposed strong restraints on political reporting of domestic developments. 'Socially responsible journalism' in 'the spirit of socialist self-management' means once again that the press has to support the party line unconditionally, that political leadership or individual politicians can only be criticised once they have been attacked or sacked by the top party and state bodies, and that, on the whole, the press has to stay clear of controversial political subjects. The free-wheeling, internationally respected scholarly journal *Praxis* was banned and eight leading Marxist scholars, including both Mihailo Marković and Svetozar Stojanović, were ousted from the faculty of Belgrade University in 1975.

Even so, the Yugoslav papers are not only better written, laid-out and presented than their counterparts within the Soviet bloc, but also contain much interesting and straightforward information about world politics and economics. Front-page headlines in the Belgrade *Politika* actually reflect daily news and not the progress of the wheat harvest in Southern Serbia. To sum up, the readers of most Yugoslav papers are informed more quickly, more correctly and more comprehensively about what is going on in the world than those Soviet bloc inhabitants who lack access to confidential information bulletins. This does not, however, mean that they are always told of everything that happens in Yugoslavia itself.

This is why the Yugoslav media, where editors have much greater autonomy in decision-making and there is wider and more truthful reflection of international developments, is not included in the following account of how far political, economic and general information is subject to deliberate manipulation, systematic distortion and detailed censorship in Eastern Europe.

The overall historical, political and ideological background, described on the preceding pages, is not a comprehensive study, but should serve as an essential guide to the following chapters, which show that what at times appear to Western observers to be editing or interpretative 'slips' are in fact integral features of the Soviet bloc's own 'information order'.

2 What is Newsworthy – and What is Not?

BOTH SOVIET AND WESTERN media experts, scholars and journalists have been long debating the criteria and standards for judging what is 'newsworthy' in the countries of 'real socialism' where, so the theory goes, the very nature of society is the best guarantee for 'responsible, comprehensive and objective reporting'.

Critics of the Western media, particularly of the major agencies, often single out as weak points in the international flow of information the tendency to over-represent the rich industrialised countries, to present events in personal terms and, last but not least, the disproportionate stress on 'negativism'.

The charges of ignorance and wrong priorities in reporting on both current events and long-term developments in the Third World, in the lesser-known European countries and in the Soviet bloc are not without foundation. Criticism, how-ever, should be related to substantive matters and not moti-vated by transparent political interests. There is no reason to disagree with James Reston's self-critical assessment:

> We are pretty good at reporting 'happenings', particularly if they are dramatic. We are fascinated by events, but not by the things that cause events . . . We are not covering the news of the mind as we should. Here is where rebellion, revolution, and wars start. But we minimise the conflict of ideas and emphasise the conflicts in the streets without relating the second to the first.[29]

The priorities of Soviet information policy have of course always been different. As an American student of Soviet political indoctrination and communication methods suc-cinctly put it: 'What is news? In the Soviet context basically anything which can be used to illustrate current party policy or economic progress is considered worthy of publication and almost anything else is considered unimportant and unworthy.'[30] This is naturally a somewhat oversimplified picture since it ignores the so-called 'grey area'. Reporting on many major political events, particularly in crisis situations (the Cuban crisis of 1962, Czechoslovakia in 1968, the overthrow of the Idi Amin régime in Uganda, the revolution in Iran 1978–79, or the intervention in Afghanistan), is often effected by delaying tactics, sometimes subtle, sometimes crude. These are intended to gain crucial time to prepare, first the propaganda apparatus, and then the general public, for news which has eventually to be released.

The sensational defection of the Bolshoi Ballet star, Alexander Godunov, on 22 August 1979 while on tour in New York, may well rate only a footnote in the works of future historians. Yet the case produced not only a temporary crisis in US-Soviet relations but also an illuminating insight into just how the Soviet media work. After Godunov's disappearance, his wife, Lyudmila Vlasova, who had also been performing with him at the Lincoln Centre, was put on the next Aeroflot plane to Moscow. The American authorities, however, blocked the departure of the plane for three days until the ballerina personally told US officials that she was returning home voluntarily.

For our purposes the main point is not the inept handling of the case by the State Department, nor the personal feelings of the ballerina, but the simple fact that the massive anti-American propaganda, accusing the US of hypocrisy, inhuman behaviour and Cold War strong-arm tactics left the Soviet public in the dark about the factual background. Thus it was not until Sunday morning, the 27th, that Radio Moscow identified Vlasova as a Bolshoi ballerina. On Monday, for example, Belgrade *Politika* carried on its front page under a banner headline a report by its Moscow correspondent that the Soviets had sharply protested in the case of the blocked Aeroflot plane. However it also added in a three-column subtitle that 'the Bolshoi soloist, Alexander Godunov, Vlasova's husband had asked for asylum in the US.' But it was not until after the plane had departed that *Pravda*, in a lengthy, sharply worded piece – *End to a provocation* – indicated a reason for all the fuss. It informed the readers that 'Vlasova did not want to find herself in a situation similar to that of her husband, Bolshoi ballet artist A. Godunov, who had disappeared earlier under circumstances which are not yet clear.'

Not surprisingly, the way the Soviet media treated the sensitive affair which was of course widely known in the East through international radio broadcasts, served as a model for the entire communication apparatus east of the Elbe. The East Germans were, as so often, over-zealous. Twelve days later the East Berlin weekly, *Horizont*, published a whole page attack against the 'incitement and hate campaign launched by the West German bourgeois media' over the Vlasova affair. The article rebuked the West German media for acting according to the principle 'truth is what harms the Communists and socialism'. The only thing the self-righteous weekly forgot to mention was the defection of the ballerina's husband.[31]

The Soviet and East European coverage of a major topical news story confirms that the observations of a former TASS director general, and erstwhile head of the Moscow University Faculty of Journalism, N. G. Palgunov, are as valid today as they were some twenty-five years ago:

> News should not be merely concerned with reporting such and such a fact or event. News or information must pursue a definite goal: it must serve and support the decisions related to fundamental duties facing our Soviet society, our Soviet people marching on the road of gradual transition from socialism to Communism. . . . In selecting the object of information, the author of an informative report must, above all, abandon the notion that just any fact or just any events have to be reported in the pages of the newspaper. The aim of information must be to present selected facts and events . . .

One might think that this kind of reasoning at a so-called theoretical level is no longer in fashion, but only quietly practised. A short more recent quote from an authoritative

Pravda article dispels such assumptions: 'The press should not provide a simple photography of facts, an account of what happened, but a target-orientated description of events, phenomena and novelties.'[32]

Nothing would be more misleading than to always look for some sinister exercise of censorship or political motive behind the often slow release of information by TASS or other Eastern news agencies. The delay is very often due to simple inefficiency, poor organisation or slow distribution. In February 1950, for example, when the Sino-Soviet pact was signed in Moscow, all Western news media immediately reported this significant event. However, in Hungary and elsewhere in Eastern Europe, everyone was waiting in suspense for the release of the text from Moscow. TASS finally began to cable the material twenty-four hours later: the morning newspapers never reached their subscribers. Two decades later, the publication of the Soviet Journalists Union itself revealed, among other examples, how the tradition of slowness hit the largest circulation newspaper in the city of Gorkiy with 1.2 million inhabitants (250 miles east of Moscow): the picture of a *Soyuz* space ship and its crew arrived only three days after the actual launching.[33]

But delaying tactics, or genuine mishaps which are after all not a privilege of the Communist media alone, pale into utter insignificance compared to the most striking and apparently immutable characteristic of the Soviet and (with the partial exception of Hungary and Poland) East European media as a whole. This is the total indifference to, and frequent suppression of, major news and reports of significant events that occur at home or abroad. This practice flagrantly contradicts Lenin's oft-cited statement: 'The state gets its strength from the consciousness of the masses. It is strong when the masses know everything, can pass judgment on everything and do everything consciously.'

These words were also quoted in the most comprehensive and, by all accounts, most important Central Committee decree adopted since the twenty-fifth Party Congress in 1976, on political indoctrination, communication policies and the mass media. Its main points were discussed at an ideological conference where none other than M. A. Suslov himself, the seventy-six-year-old guardian of orthodox ideology delivered the (unpublished) keynote address. Certain formulations in the resolution about the 'fierce offensive of the imperialists, assisted by the Peking chauvinists and aggressors' who seek, with the aid of 'the most refined methods and modern technological means' to 'poison the minds of the Soviet people' were clear indications that the Kremlin is increasingly worried about the widespread audience for the Russian-language broadcasts of *The Voice of America*, the BBC, *Radio Liberty* and *Deutsche Welle*.

Faced with the problem of a widening credibility gap, the Central Committee resolution was obviously on the right tack when it bluntly stated: 'It must become a rule that no question agitating the working people is left without an answer'; adding, 'where there is a lack of open airing of issues in public affairs, direct harm is done to the activities of the masses.' The resolution even spelled out in detail which party committees, institutions, ministries and other organisations have to report on the implementation of the decree by December 1979 and then again by December 1980. However, some recent developments do not augur well for the future.

The criteria for what is not 'newsworthy' and what must be kept out of the papers have not been altered. At any rate, the media treatment of two serious accidents in August 1979, that is more than three months *after* the publication of the resolution and the ideological-propaganda conference, shows no change for the better. In some ways it reflects an even greater contempt for the people's right to know.

The traditional way of informing the domestic public about a disaster, be it natural catastrophe or industrial accident, if a complete 'blackout' of the news proves impossible, is the announcement of the event itself, always with one additional sentence, that the 'competent authorities have started an investigation.' If the communique says that the government and the party organs expressed their condolences to the families of the victims and promised measures to help them, then this is an unmistakable sign that there were many deaths and injuries. But we must, however, stress the fact, repeatedly confirmed by private Soviet sources, foreign correspondents and diplomats, that what gets known or reported of disasters is only the tip of an iceberg.[34]

Consider, for example, the treatment of one of the biggest accidents in Soviet aviation history, the mid-air collision of two passenger aircraft on Saturday 11 August 1979, somewhere in the Ukraine. The first oblique hint of the accident in the central Moscow press was a two-line announcement on Tuesday in *Izvestia*, at the very end of a short report about the nineteenth round in the first division of the Soviet soccer league, that the match between *Dynamo* (Minsk) and *Pakhtarov* (Tashkent) had been postponed. In the meantime rumours had already been circulating in the Soviet capital that two airliners were involved, with the *Pakhtarov* team on board the aircraft flying from Tashkent in Uzbekistan to Minsk in the Belorussian Republic.

On Wednesday the 14th, TASS, in a brief communique, announced that two passenger airliners, one from Tashkent bound for Minsk and another, on its way from Chelyabinsk, east of the Urals, to Kishinev, the capital of Soviet Moldavia, had collided, that all passengers and the crew of the two aircraft had been killed, including the members of the soccer team *Pakhtarov*. The communique stated, as usual, that the reasons for the collision were being investigated by a special commission. Thus, with a delay of four days, TASS at least reported the accident itself. However it still gave no information about the number, age or profession of the victims, their nationality, the location of the accident, the time of day, the weather conditions or any other pertinent details normally reported by papers not only in the West, but also in Hungary, Poland and, of course, Yugoslavia.

After numerous phone calls to ministries, local authorities and republican newspaper offices, Western correspondents managed to find out that two twin-engined TU-134 jets had collided in bad weather and poor visibility near Dneprodzerzhinsk and that the death toll had been about 150 (one subsequent report put the number of dead at 173). It was also learned from sports circles in the capital that many school children, returning from a vacation camp, had been on board one of the aircraft. The local papers in Minsk, Kishinev and

Tashkent printed already on Tuesday brief notices about the crash, with messages of condolence from the government and the party's Central Committee.

On Friday 17 August, TASS reported that 'thousands in Tashkent had attended the funeral of the *Pakhtarov* team members who had perished in an air disaster', adding that, in their speeches, the Uzbek party secretary Salimov and the deputy chairman of the Soviet sports committee praised the achievements of the deceased players. In addition to the local party paper, *Pravda Vostoka* in Tashkent, the sports journal, *Sovietski Sport*, also reported on the funeral. Both papers were very concerned about the fate of the Uzbek team, consoling the fans with the news that the '*Pakhtarov* team will not be left alone' and that players from other clubs in the first division were already being transferred to Tashkent to help to form a new team.

What, however, the tens of millions of readers of *Pravda*, *Izvestia* and other major central papers still do not know is what actually happened on that fateful Saturday. Who were the victims? What were the causes? The largest circulation Soviet papers did not even publish the nine lines of the TASS communique. The worst aviation accident in Soviet history did not even rate a news item in the central press. TASS, the local Tashkent papers and the sports paper would also probably have ignored the disaster altogether, had not one of the best Soviet soccer teams been on board.

For once even *Neues Deutschland*, normally a strict follower of the Moscow propaganda line, was out of step. On the day of the funeral in Tashkent (totally ignored in the Moscow press), the East Berlin party paper carried on its front page a telegram, signed by party chief Erich Honecker and Premier Willi Stoph, expressing their condolences both to the Soviet leaders and 'to the families of the victims and of the crews, who perished in the air accident of two Soviet airliners.' As the *Frankfurter Allgemeine Zeitung* ironically remarked, through the publication of this telegram, the disaster had now at least really taken place – if only in the eyes of the public in one socialist state. On a more serious note, the influential Frankfurt daily also noted that in this particular case, the East Berlin paper had behaved more decently and humanely than the Soviet press and had given Soviet information policy a well-deserved lesson.[35]

In many ways, this tragic air collision could provide ample material for an instructive case study of what is still not considered as a legitimate news story by those in charge of Soviet media. When Robert Kaiser, the *Washington Post* correspondent in Moscow in the early seventies, asked the head of *Pravda*'s Information Department, Mrs Irina Kirilova, technically in charge of the coverage of such things as plane accidents, why the press did not mention plane crashes, she replied that 'the reader must know something new and good.' After recalling the story of a plane with a jammed front landing gear, which nevertheless landed safely due to the skill of the pilot and ground crew precautions, Mrs Kirilova declared: 'If there is a connection with heroism, courage or overcoming a great risk, then we write about it.' 'What about unluckier occasions, when planes crash?' her visitor asked. 'What's the point of writing about every one? It happens that accidents occur for technical reasons – that doesn't interest us very much,' she replied.

We shall later see in detail what *does* interest Soviet media, but at this point we may as well recall the two previous disasters which had induced the American correspondent to raise the matter in the first place. In late 1972, an *Aeroflot* jet flying from Leningrad crashed in a muddy swamp outside Moscow, killing 176 people, among them thirty-nine foreigners. The news was buried as a forty-two word item on *Pravda*'s back page, most probably only printed at all because of the foreigners involved. In June of the following year the mid-air explosion of a Soviet supersonic jet transport, in front of television cameras and thousands of spectators at the Paris air show was the major news of the day in most of the world's newspapers. In *Pravda* it was tucked away as a twenty-seven word item at the bottom of page six, its back page.

One might of course speculate that this was an effort not to upset airline passengers, and to avoid adverse publicity for *Aeroflot*, the national carrier with worldwide operations; and that the concern is limited to air transport. Is the silence, or minimal reporting of air disasters perhaps motivated by sensitivity over anything which might imply lower technical standards in the Soviet Union? Not if the following story of a train disaster is anything to go by.

The Moscow correspondent of the Norwegian daily *Aftenposten*, and other Scandinavian papers, heard of a dramatic railway disaster which occurred in Lithuania on 4 April 1975. The date and the fact that there were fatalities was announced by the republican government in a brief communique in the local paper, *Sovietskaya Litva*. As usual, condolences were expressed and it was stated that a government commission had been set up to investigate the causes of the accident. Subsequently, eyewitnesses told the correspondent that a fully-laden passenger train had crashed into a military train made up of petrol tankers which were set on fire by the impact. Flames soon engulfed the passenger train. Many people were trapped in their carriages and burned or suffocated. Local sources estimated that several hundred persons may have perished in the flames. This disaster was, again, of no interest. Not a word about it was carried in the Moscow central papers. When, a week later, a Norwegian parliamentary delegation headed by the Speaker visited Lithuania, what appears to have been the worst accident in national history was not so much as mentioned by their hosts.[36] Thus, it is evident that it is not only plane crashes which are sensitive subjects. According to many informed sources the censorship regulations forbid any mention of domestic plane, train and bus accidents.

A second example of a major accident which also happened *after* the party resolution's call for more candour and 'prompter, more understandable and more concrete reporting', is taken from industry. TASS and Radio Moscow reported on 11 August 1979 that a methane gas explosion had taken place the preceding day at the *Molodogvardeiskaya* mine in the Donbas coal mining region in the Ukraine, causing death and injuries. The report did not give figures for the dead and injured. The accident must have been serious, however, for the Soviet media to report it at all. Statistics on industrial accidents, as on so many other subjects, are secret and accidents in industry are rarely, if ever, mentioned in the press. The last major accident to be reported before this was divulged in

February 1978, when an unknown number of miners were killed in a copper mine in Kazakhstan. Some six months later *Trud*, the newspaper of the trade unions, published an item about the condemnation of several mining engineers found guilty of neglecting safety precautions and thus causing the death of three miners.

This time, the government and the Central Committee not only sent letters of condolence, but also announced measures 'to help families and to eliminate the consequences of the accident.' Yet nothing was revealed about the number of the victims nor about the circumstances and consequences of the explosion. It is strange that a country whose propaganda handouts always claim that no other state does so much to protect the health and safety of its workers, should be so secretive about industrial accidents.

The mine where the latest explosion occurred happens to be situated near the pits where Vladimir Klebanov, who founded the Free Trade Union for the Defence of Workers' Rights in the autumn of 1977, was employed. Poor working conditions and the neglect of basic safety measures were the original reasons that sparked off his public rebellion. Klebanov, a miner himself, protested against 'gross violations' of the Labour Code, complaining that unrealistically high production targets often forced miners to work twelve hours a day underground. At the mine where he worked, accidents killed twelve to fifteen persons a year and injured 600 to 700, he said. Klebanov was arrested, put into a psychiatric hospital, and most of his associates were jailed.

Such issues as industrial accidents and inadequate safety measures are not regarded as suitable subjects for debate in the media. Only specialist Soviet journals are said to admit that safety precautions are inadequate and the level of mechanisation is low. According to a Western source, a 1978 survey revealed that two-thirds of the deeper mines in the Donbas basin were 'highly dangerous' and recommended the introduction of degassing techniques adopted in the West about thirty-six years ago.[37]

To go back to Mrs Kirilova's point about heroism, the point seems to be that good news is news – bad news is not really news at all. Or not so far as the public at large is concerned, though for the recipients of confidential bulletins it may be a different matter. To dispute this attitude is to be guilty of 'Western sensationalism', which pollutes moral standards and undermines responsible journalism.

Perhaps the most potent argument against this kind of reasoning, which makes the systematic suppression of unpleasant news an indispensable tool in protecting the population from 'bourgeois' selection criteria, is the example of other East European countries whose leaders had the courage and intelligence to break, albeit only partially, with a ridiculous and – even from the régime's point of view – counter-productive practice.

For example, two months after the accident in the Donbas mine, another explosion took place, this time in a coal mine in Poland. There, the authorities announced, after a delay of twenty-seven hours, that thirty-three miners had died and others had been injured. This was the second serious mining accident reported in Poland that October; the first had killed seven miners and severely injured three. Hungary, too, regularly reports every major mining accident or train disaster. In contrast to the Poles, with their detailed censorship guidelines (which will be discussed later), the Hungarians have no compunction about free reporting even of murders and hold-ups and other crimes, and they provide detailed annual crime statistics, both in the regular account presented by the Attorney General to Parliament and in their Annual Statistical yearbook.

In free-wheeling Yugoslavia the kind of information policy still prevailing in the Soviet Union, Bulgaria or for that matter in Romania, is regarded as a ghost from the distant past, even as something of a joke. Bogdan Pešić, now retired, who edited the most influential Yugoslav paper *NIN* after the war, recalled in an interview how, in 1952, he published a news item in *Politika* about the hijacking of a Yugoslav plane to Italy by three armed men and the subsequent return of the plane and passengers. In those days the report was a sensation and eventually led to Pešić's replacement as Editor-in-Chief. What is fascinating, however, is his account of debates with the 'leading comrades in the party' and the letter in which he set out his main arguments against restrictive and 'paternalistic' news filtering. More than twenty-five years later, it is worth quoting some of his words, now openly published in the mass circulation weekly.

> Ever since I worked in the daily press as a journalist, I have never agreed with the practice that newspapers should be the last to report on some events, particularly when those events are generally known, commented on and discussed by the masses. Information usually comes first from Radio London, which in this way has unfortunately acquired great prestige as a very well-informed station among our citizens, who listen to it regularly. We journalists find ourselves in a very curious situation when we are asked from all sides, by both well- and ill-wishers, whether we know about this or that event and if yes, why we have not written about it. This was the case for a long time with train accidents and natural disasters. Although it was generally known that this or that train accident had taken place, the daily paper did not write anything about it for some days and in this way the public was led to believe that there had been some kind of outrage or sabotage, that there had been twice as many victims . . .

Finally, Pešić concluded that the press is often reproached for sensationalism, although it is often very difficult to draw a line where objective information stops and sensation begins. Even in Yugoslavia, a quarter of a century after Pešić's letter, the debate about the permissible limits of free criticism continues. For example, *NIN* itself was recently reproached by party functionaries in Belgrade for having deviated, once again, from the correct line in economic, national and cultural policy and accused of printing 'too dramatic and misleading headlines'.[38] How can one balance financial and organisational media autonomy with 'responsible reporting' and proper 'socialist orientation', as defined by the politicians who arrogate the right to speak on behalf of public opinion? This remains a permanent bone of contention in a multinational country based on self-management where the media is, of course, also used by the various republican lobbies. But for all these restrictions, the Yugoslav media are at least free to report as quickly as any Western paper on crime, accidents, epidemics and natural disasters.

It is sometimes argued that the ingrained tendency to

suppress 'bad' and 'very bad' news in the Soviet Union is facilitated, and even stimulated, by the enormous distances in that vast country, which covers between one-sixth and one-seventh of the total surface of the globe and is almost three times the size of the United States. The observation, made by foreign visitors to Czarist Russia, that the government always treated the people as minors, not truly fit to look after their own affairs, is another factor which has long shaped the pattern of information policy. The tradition of secrecy lingers on in many profoundly characteristic ways. How else can one explain the fact that, in most cities and towns apart from Moscow, it is still practically impossible to get hold of a city map; that the first telephone directory to appear in fifteen years listing private phone numbers in the capital was printed in 1973, in an edition of 50,000 copies for a population of eight million; or that even the chief of the Soviet negotiating team at the SALT I talks, deputy Foreign Minister Vladimir S. Semenov, was kept in complete ignorance of such elementary information as the number, size and location of the strategic weapons deployed by his own government?[39]

In *A World Restored*, Henry Kissinger wrote:

> The memory of states is the test of truth of their policy. The more elementary the experience, the more profound its impact on a nation's interpretation of the present in the light of the past. It is even possible for a nation to undergo an experience so shattering that it becomes the prisoner of its past.[40]

This observation is not only true of Russian attitudes towards arms and diplomatic negotiations, but also of Stalin's heritage, in turn built on the Czarist traditions, in all matters concerning communications between the rulers and the ruled.

Perhaps nothing could better illustrate the unbroken tradition of secrecy as the treatment of the earthquake which hit Ashkhabad, the capital of Turkmenia in October 1948. According to the latest edition of the *Great Soviet Encyclopedia* it was one of the strongest earthquakes registered in history, completely destroying the city, which in that year had a population of 200,000. The disaster took place at 4 am when most of the inhabitants were still asleep. The *Encyclo-*

pedia lists the deaths caused by other quakes from Japan to Turkey; but thirty years later the number of dead in the Ashkhabad earthquake is still a secret. This case was related by the exiled Soviet biochemist Zhores Medvedev in his book on the Soviet nuclear disaster of 1957, to convince the sceptics that in the Soviet Union the number of victims is never revealed, even if the disaster took place three decades ago.

The nuclear accident which occurred in the Kyshtyn area, between the industrial centres of Chelyabinsk and Sverdlovsk in the Urals, was kept secret by the Soviets for almost twenty years. Medvedev, who first reported it in 1976, regards the accident as the worst nuclear disaster ever.[41] It is only against this background that the apparently illogical Soviet reporting of the recent accident at the Three Mile Island nuclear plant near Harrisburg in the US can be understood. In contrast to the usual dramatic treatment of technological failures and major accidents in the West, and their attribution to the profit-seeking capitalist instinct, the Soviet media was noticeably reticent in reporting, let alone analysing, an event which caused world-wide concern and gave a new fillip to anti-nuclear protest movements in Europe.

The Three Mile Island story rated in *Izvestia* only forty words two days later (30 March 1979). *Pravda* and Moscow Television blamed the monopolies in very brief reports on the accident on 2 April. The party organ followed this up on 3 April, with a lengthy article on the large 'Lenin' nuclear power plant, whose safety system renders 'absolutely impossible' any increase in the accepted radiation level or any danger whatsoever to the environment. Further comforting statements followed in an interview with the head of the State Committee for Environment in the mass circulation weekly, *Literaturnaya Gazeta*.

In view of the all-out programme throughout the Comecon area to build a string of nuclear power plants, which by 1990 should meet about one-third of the total demand for energy, nuclear safety is a major concern. As in all essential matters, so also in this sensitive field, the governments laid down priorities and took decisions behind closed doors, without consulting the public, let alone allowing the publication of dissenting views. Once again, Yugoslavia was the sole significant exception. There, popular pressure has caused the construction of a second nuclear plant on the Adriatic island of Vir, near the port city of Zadar, to be cancelled and the project moved to another site.

The issue of nuclear safety has split parties and families, caused the defeat of a democratic government in Sweden and, in Austria, led to a referendum which prevented the commissioning of an already completed plant. But in the Soviet Union it has not been permitted to cause a ripple on the smooth surface of public opinion. But then, as a German scholar aptly observed, in the Soviet Union 'propaganda replaces public opinion because it is the only opinion published.'[42] In this highly sensitive area, not even the 'word of mouth' system, the deliberate dissemination of information through party channels, has so far been applied.

In the autumn of 1979 two Soviet scientists were allowed to refer to the possible ecological and safety hazards of nuclear power in the authoritative party monthly, *Kommunist* (circulation: 947,000 copies). This may represent not only increased concern among Soviet scientists but, above all, more candour in the discussions. However, contrary to press reports, this was not the first time that either the two authors concerned or other Soviet scientists had warned of nuclear hazards and advised the building of nuclear plants in more sparsely populated regions. But such references, always oblique, are scarcely equivalent to the public discussion of a crucial subject.[43]

The more sophisticated Hungarian approach to communications is also evident in the nuclear debate. For example, the widely-read Budapest cultural and political weekly, *Élet és Irodalom* carried a leading article over three full columns on its front page (29 June 1979) under the provocative headline: 'Do we need a nuclear power plant?' The author described the world-wide unease and recent dramatic protests, and also admitted frankly that there was a crisis of confidence over nuclear safety which could not be ignored since it had also reached Hungary. Though he bluntly stated that the anti-nuclear attitude is a 'reactionary phenomenon', public concern and the need to deal with it was repeatedly stressed. It would be, of course, totally inconceivable, even in Hungary, to publish any substantial article in a widely-read journal spreading actual doubts about nuclear power and safety precautions while the country was engaged in erecting a large nuclear plant. Indeed, raising the matter so candidly the article cleverly responded to popular concern, without even remotely raising the basic question of the wisdom of erecting a plant in a densely populated area.

Yet even such guarded comment would be unimaginable not only in the Soviet Union but also in neighbouring Romania, a country which illustrates the point that the application of Soviet standards of 'news-worthiness' is not necessarily a function of size or of specifically Russian historical factors. An imaginative and occasionally even flamboyantly independent foreign policy has considerably enhanced the country's international prestige. Romania is, after all, the only Warsaw Pact state which has repeatedly defied the Soviet line over such vital issues as the Moscow-Peking conflict, the Middle East imbroglio or military spending. Much less, however, is reported in most Western papers about the gradual estrangement of key social groups and the slow but inevitable erosion of the leadership's moral authority in the wake of its proven inability to cope with the problems of deplorably low living standards, housing, health care and elementary services. Rumblings among the intellectuals and the two million-strong Hungarian minority have been occasionally reported, with the attention of the Western media primarily aroused by the personal courage of individuals, such as Paul Goma, the noted writer, or Károly Király, a former high-ranking Romanian party official of Hungarian stock, who publicly condemned the violation of human rights.[44]

Yet it was also in Romania that in the summer of 1977 some 30,000 coal miners in the Jiu valley organised a powerful protest strike against a controversial draft law on miners' pensions and demanded an improvement of their working conditions. They resumed work only when President Ceauşescu himself appeared on the scene and publicly promised the repeal of the law and the satisfaction of their grievances. Several ministers and high officials in charge of the mines were sacked soon afterwards. According to rumours reaching Western journalists and Amnesty International in London, hundreds of the most active organisers were later detained and deported to other areas of the country.

The local media has never reported on the potentially most dangerous workers' conflict since the Communist takeover. The fact that Western radios, including Radio Free Europe in Munich, informed the entire Romanian population about the labour conflict, did not induce a nervous leadership to discuss the subject publicly.

Silence is again the rule rather than the exception, when it comes to disasters. A few months before the trouble with the miners, on 4 March 1977, a strong earthquake hit Romania, with the industrial and residential areas in Bucharest being particularly severely damaged. Speaking at the end of March, President Ceauşescu announced that the death toll was 1,570 with 11,300 injured, 854 of whom were still receiving medical treatment. Yet, filing from Bucharest four months after the disaster, Sidney Weiland, a senior Reuter correspondent with many years of experience in Eastern Europe, reported that it was generally thought in Bucharest that the death toll was at least 3,000. He added that many people had apparently been buried under the rubble. The authorities never disputed the accuracy of these figures, nor have they corrected their own earlier statements.

One year later, in April 1978, Western sources heard rumours about a powerful explosion in the chemical plant at Piteşti, causing widespread destruction with twenty to sixty people injured. While no statement was issued about this alleged accident, a laconic communique on 1 November the same year announced that on the previous day an explosion in the same chemical complex had caused nine deaths. This time, too, Western diplomats heard rumours of much higher figures.

Nothing could better illustrate the bizarre treatment of accidents by the Romanian leadership than the fire which broke out in August 1978 in the National Theatre, next door to the Hotel Intercontinental in the heart of Bucharest. The fire, witnessed by scores of foreign correspondents covering the visit of the Chinese Premier, Hua Kuo-feng, raged for several hours during the night, destroying the stage and parts of the auditorium. More than one year later reconstruction was not yet completed. Yet the Romanian media neither published the news nor gave any subsequent details about the causes and damage. It would be somewhat difficult to imagine a similar accident in London or in Paris with the Old Vic or the *Comedie Française* on fire (even without the visit of a Chinese Premier), and the British or French press remaining mute.

Finally, there was the case of the fire that broke out in the Victoria department store in Bucharest in April 1979. Many hundreds of shoppers and the sales staff were trapped in the building. Rumours spread quickly, causing general anxiety. It took fourteen hours before *Agerpress*, the national agency, issued its first report, eight or nine hours after Western radios had already broadcast the news of the catastrophe. The agency said that three people died and hundreds were treated in hospital. Western agencies and local sources put the fatality count at between fifteen and forty.

The examples are taken from the past few years and even for that period are far from exhaustive. What they show is that the Romanians, for all their clashes with the Soviet leaders over foreign policy and trade, not only repress intellectual and national ferment as ruthlessly as their neighbours, but also apply the same criteria to what is not newsworthy.

Who, then, would be surprised to hear that Romania's southern neighbour, Bulgaria, the most faithful Soviet ally in the East, does exactly the same in the face of a natural disaster? On 8 November 1978, Radio Sofia broadcast a brief communique to the effect that on the previous day 'several people were drowned when a pontoon bridge at Boleslav, some twelve miles east of Varna, collapsed into the sea.' The government and party expressed their condolences to the families of the victims and also dispatched a deputy Prime Minister to lead an investigation on the spot. Western correspondents who happened to be in the capital a few days later were told by several sources that the collapse of the bridge had been in fact a major disaster. According to unsubstantiated rumours it may have caused up to one hundred deaths.

Apparently, many people returning from the festivities marking the anniversary of the Russian Revolution in Varna had rushed across the bridge trying to catch a train. In any case, no more details were officially released and the real death toll will probably never be known.

The tendency to minimise as far as possible the impact of a disaster, even if it has nothing to do with the social-political system prevailing in the country concerned, was also painfully evident in the coverage of the March 1977 earthquake. Along with Romania, adjoining areas in Bulgaria were also hit. The official communique listed eighty-three dead. Five weeks later a speech by Prime Minister Stanko Todorov casually referred to 125 dead.[45]

These then are some of the many reasons why many educated newspaper readers, television viewers and radio listeners in the Soviet bloc regard the output of their own media with deeply entrenched doubts. Information via the word-of-mouth system, more often than not originally based on news disseminated by foreign radios, is often cited as 'the most reliable source' in private conversations and even in secret opinion surveys (carried out, for example, in Hungary). As we have seen, there are considerable differences in the degree of candour and sophistication in the treatment of 'non-news' items between the individual Soviet bloc states. These are also reflected in *what* they publish, *how* the news is presented and what they regard as newsworthy. Thus before turning to an analysis of the Communist world view and the basic political message common to all the ruling parties, it may be instructive to compare typical recent issues of *Pravda*, *Neues Deutschland*, *Népszabadság* and *Scînteia*.

President and Secretary General Leonid Brezhnev complained at the plenary meeting of the Central Committee on 28 November 1978, that newspapers, TV and radio broadcasts were 'overloaded with general phrases which do not give anything either to the mind or to the heart.' The same line was taken in the Central Committee resolution, already cited, the following May, which mentioned, as being among the cardinal sins of the media, 'frequent formalism, verbal twaddle, propaganda clichés, grey official style of materials, mechanical repetition many times over of general truths instead of their creative interpretation.' It even implied that the organisation of information and ideological work was just not up to the higher educational and cultural standards of the Soviet people.

A scrutiny of *Pravda* of 1 October 1979, should help to judge whether this shattering indictment was fair. What are the main news items, published on the same day, in the *International Herald Tribune* in Paris and the German *Frankfurter Allgemeine Zeitung*? Both Western papers feature, as the main news story on the front page Pope John Paul II's appeal for peace in Ireland on the eve of his flight to the us. The *Tribune* also reports on the front page the purge of the armed forces in Iran, the talks between the us and Mexico about compensation for the oil spill, the Washington-Bonn vow to press dollar support, a Chinese official accusing Russia of encroachment and, under a four-column headline, an interview with the Soviet foreign affairs spokesman, Georgi Arbatov. The main political news stories on the following pages deal with Bokassa, the deposed Emperor, having killed students in the Central African Republic; President Carter's consultations concerning the attitude to Soviet troops in Cuba; the execution of Macias Nguema, the former dictator of Equatorial Guinea and indications that Senator Kennedy will run as a candidate for President. Apart from topical domestic political controversies, the Frankfurt paper carries on its front page, as third lead story, Carter's efforts to produce proof of the presence of Soviet troops in Cuba, followed by stories on the West German Defence Minister's trip to Washington, a half-page feature on the Pope's activities in Ireland, a two-column analysis of Greek Premier Karamanlis' journey to Moscow, the Mexico-us talks and many other short political items.

What, then, did *Pravda* report on the same day on its front page? Two full columns out of eight are taken up by an unsigned editorial, calling for higher standards in political and economic work, firm action against indiscipline and the utilisation of all reserves in order to 'succeed in the great overall cause of building Communism.' The main news item

in the right upper corner, under a two-column headline, is
'Harvest completed', a report about the successful work of
the *sovkhoz* (state farm), 'forty-year Kazakh SSR', in the
Oktober region of Kazakhstan. In the centre of the front page
two photos are grouped together: on the left, three outstanding young workers from the Odessa oil refinery; on the right,
the factory hall of a ball-bearing plant in Moscow. Three brief
one-column items about geological explorations, agricultural
experiments and new ships on Lake Baikal, and a long four-
column interview with the Minister of Power about new
methods being applied in a power plant going up in Rjazan,
occupy the centre part. And what is the foreign lead story?
Under a two-column headline 'Important factor', a report
from Vienna, quoting Franz Muhri, Chairman of the Austrian Communist Party about the 'importance for Austria of
trade and co-operation with the Soviet Union and other
socialist states, in particular in the fight against unemployment and for the stabilising of its energy supplies.' One
wonders which, if any, of *Pravda*'s readers know that in the
1979 Austrian general election Muhri's party received less
than one percent of the vote, that the Communists have not
been represented in parliament since 1959 and that, on top of
that, Austria has had full employment for many years.

The second main foreign news item is an account of the
situation in the Central African Republic, quoting the critical
comments of the French Communist daily, *L'Humanité*
about the dispatch of French parachutists. A brief, low-key
telegram sent by the Soviet Council of Ministers and the
Presidium of the Supreme Soviet (no names are given) to the
equivalent Chinese bodies on the thirtieth anniversary of the
founding of Chinese People's Republic is the politically most
important report. Finally, at the bottom of the front page,
readers are informed of the arrival of the Greek Prime
Minister, Konstantin Karamanlis, together with a brief biog-
raphical note.

The following pages are mainly taken up with long pieces
by a deputy chief engineer of the Jaroslavski iron plant and a
book-keeper from a *sovkhoz* in Minsk about the year of
political indoctrination and the application of Lenin's teachings;
reports about the situation in the 'Dimitrov' *kolkhoz* in

the region of Novgorod and the contact between science and production in the city of Volvograd.

A cultural feature, describing how young poets respond to the challenge of building Communism, is followed by a critical assessment of management practices. A long piece about China, stressing that the Soviets have always been willing to forge good-neighbourly and friendly relations and that it is up to the Chinese to give up their 'hegemonistic' policies, is followed by an article reproaching Western writers for falling prey to cheap anti-Soviet political propaganda.

The overall picture would not be complete without three short reports about 'fraternal parties' from Hanoi, Tokio and Geneva, and an item about the reception of a Socialist International delegation by Brezhnev. A picture of a smiling Mongolian girl from a factory in Ulan Bator strengthens the stamina of the reader before he turns to Page Five, where the correspondents of *Pravda* and TASS report on the state of the world. At the top of the page, under a banner headline 'Fight for justice', two separate dispatches grouped together, report how 'Americans are outraged by racist and political repression', and on mass demonstrations and protest meetings in Newark and Philadelphia (it is noted that in the latter city between 1970–78, 469 people were killed by the police without trial and investigation). In Canada, the economic situation is deteriorating even further, in Australia, US capital takes over the economy and in Britain, the Conservative government brutally violates human rights, by not allowing the unification of families from Asia and Africa. In the world of socialism, in Havana, East Berlin and Sofia new production records and educational successes are achieved; in Cambodia the second congress of the United National Front draws a positive balance sheet of normalisation and in Afghanistan the (progressive) government will issue new passports.

The last page of the newspaper is, not without reason, regarded by the readers as the most interesting. There, they find the TV and radio programmes, weather reports and sports news; on 1 October there were also long reports on the performance of the Soviet participants at the water-skiing world championship in Toronto and on an international chess torunament. Nevertheless, the lead story on this page is a lengthy feature about the geographical museum in Vladivostok.

This, then, is the detailed content of *Pravda* on a normal day. It is not only completely different from the two Western newspapers cited earlier, but also ignores the main news story of the previous day in the 'non-socialist' world, namely the Pope's dramatic appeal against violence in Ireland. Scrutinising a copy of *Pravda*, there is no reason to doubt the unanimous view of every new Western correspondent in Moscow, after an obligatory visit to the newspaper's offices, that when the editorial board conference in the morning begins, the following day's paper is already complete and ready for the printers except for a few small spaces left blank for late-breaking official announcements or a story expected from overseas. The editorial staff is in fact putting the final touches to a paper which will only appear two days later. No wonder that reports of events that actually occurred the day before, at home or abroad, make up only some ten to fifteen percent of the paper's content.

A comparison of *Pravda* of 1 October 1979 with the issues of the two previous days, shows that the main articles and features are on the whole interchangeable; they could appear any day or any week, and in many cases even in any month or any year. Thus the editorial on 1 October could have been printed at any time in the past, provided a quote from Brezhnev was replaced by one from Khrushchev, or even Stalin, and the reference to the twenty-fifth Party Congress by an earlier one. The main point is that *Pravda* and most Soviet and East European papers are put together, controlled and read like official gazettes in disguise – newspapers without news.

As a Western media executive put it, 'the purpose of the news is simply to inform. The purpose of propaganda is to influence. Propaganda is most effective when it slips into the stream of information in the guise of news.'[46] It would of course be fascinating to ascertain, through representative surveys, the percentage of those Soviet subscribers who actually read any part of the newspaper apart from the essential information about weather, TV and radio programmes plus sports on the last page, and whether propaganda in the 'guise of news', so turgidly written and presented in such a boring form, can have any appreciable effect? Even the few published, and therefore evidently carefully censored, statistics about readership preferences, indicate that many Soviet people may have reached saturation point in their exposure to politics.[47] In a sense, the most convincing proof of the growing indifference of the educated Soviet public to the exceedingly dull diet offered by the media, and its susceptibility to audio-visual penetration from abroad, was provided by the Central Committee resolution which called for higher professional standards. Yet the resolution itself was a prime example of the turgid and old-fashioned propaganda style.

At this point, a few words about the use of television in the selection, interpretation and, above all, transmission of political messages may be appropriate. The tremendous implications of the Soviet régime's capacity to reach tens of millions of viewers in a vast country and exert a politically welcome 'narcotising effect', becomes evident if one notes the rapid growth of TV sets, from twenty-seven million in 1969 to 55.1 million by 1975. The best guide to an assessment of television as a tool of political persuasion is a brief glance at the main political newscast. Called *Vremya*, it is broadcast at 9 pm every evening and repeated the following morning at 8 am. Let us take 14 April 1979, a Saturday during the Easter weekend, with nothing extraordinary happening either in the Soviet Union or abroad. Here is the complete list of the items in the order they were shown:[48]

> The Central Committee issued its annual sixty-eight slogans for the 1st of May celebrations, published in all papers on the front page.
> On 21 April, Lenin's birthday, a *subotnik* will be staged, workers and farmers in the whole country will work free of charge on this day.
> Film about a textile plant in Kirgisia showing the ever faster and better production; an outstanding female labourer who overfulfilled her norm is interviewed.
> Leningrad. Brezhnev sends greetings to a scientific conference discussing the 'new socialist man'. A speaker quoted Lenin's

words about the quality of labour. Pensioned miner talks about plan fulfilment. Film about an oil refinery with reference to co-operation with East Germany in this branch of industry.

Reports from the world of labour. A car plant in the Urals increases production, more vegetables harvested in Azerbaijan, a film about new methods, with women harvesting cabbage.

The first Bulgarian cosmonaut and his Soviet colleague receive decorations.

Moscow. Report about a conference on 'science day', with an Academician talking about science in the service of industry, agriculture and the Communist party.

Tiflis. Meeting of the Communist Youth Union on Lenin square.

Vienna. US-Soviet talks about satellites.

Sofia. Bulgarian President Todor Zhivkov receives unionists and speaks with them about disarmament.

Hanoi. Vietnamese note handed over to the Chinese. New accusations against Peking leadership.

Damascus. Protest meeting against the Egyptian-Israeli peace treaty.

Beirut. Palestinians protest against Sadat's 'capitulation line'.

Teheran. Premier Bazargan predicts further successes in the reconstruction of Iran.

Islamabad. According to a report by the *New York Times*, American citizens involved in 'counter-revolutionary' conspiracy against the Afghan Government under Premier Taraki.

Rome. Film about the election campaign. The 'conservative bourgeoisie and the monopolies' place their hopes on anti-Communist propaganda.

Nicaragua. Opposition against the Somoza régime increases: successes of the guerillas.

Kampala. Calm in Uganda's capital, new Premier Lule sworn in. Western agencies report that Idi Amin still has some support in parts of the country.

Addis Ababa. Ethiopia recognises Lule's government in Uganda.

Stockholm. Protest demonstrations in Swedish capital against unemployment. Film about a typical crisis symptom in a capitalist country.

Delhi. Chinese 'bands' stir up unrest on India's borders.

Moscow. First night performance of the ballet *My Vietnam* in the congress palais in the Kremlin.

During the following two days of the Easter weekend the TV news continued to focus on 'positive' items about the Soviet Union and her allies and on a negative picture of the

West this time with films showing mass demonstrations, in Rome for 'peace and disarmament' and in New York against youth unemployment, as well as reports on terror in Northern Ireland and fighting in Nicaragua.

Politically most revealing is the treatment of the Third World countries, both in television and in the central press. Thus the weekend newscast did not say anything about the background to the rebellion against Amin or about the dictator himself. Amin had been, during his rule, on very good terms indeed with the Soviets, between 1971–1979 the Kremlin provided Uganda with massive deliveries of heavy weapons. Nevertheless Soviet press reports about the dictator were always low-key, on account of his poor image in the rest of the world. In view of *Pravda*'s sharp attack on Britain's 'inhuman treatment' of the immigrants' families cited earlier it may be instructive to recall that on 15 August 1972 *Izvestia* supported Amin's expulsion of at least 50,000 Indians holding British passports, on the grounds that Uganda was quite capable of solving its domestic problems without 'imperialist interference'. During the war with Tanzania in 1978–9, Soviet media gave the public no background information whatsoever, and a TV commentator on 29 March 1979 restricted his remarks to the classic phrase that 'fighting could only benefit foreign reaction'. By the end of April 1979, however, *Pravda* discovered that the 'forced wholesale expulsion of 70,000 Asians' had created an acute shortage of skilled labour, thus also reversing the previous line of tacitly supporting Amin's anti-Asian policy.

While *Novoe Vremya*, the international affairs weekly, still spoke mildly on 20 April about the 'former government's serious administrative errors'; *Pravda*, nine days later, had discovered that 'thousands of people had disappeared inside barracks and prisons without trial.' Finally, after three more weeks, *Izvestia* called Amin a 'dictator' and told its readers that 'more and more new facts are being learned about the overthrown régime's bloody crimes.' During the eight years of Amin's rule approximately 300,000 people are said to have been killed.[49]

The treatment of Amin sheds a characteristic light on the Soviet model of 'objective, responsible and comprehensive

reporting' as admired by Unesco experts. As long as Amin
was in power and on the whole amenable to Soviet interests,
albeit personally unpredictable and therefore sometimes
embarrassing (for example when he wanted to erect a statue of
Adolf Hitler), one could have searched in vain with a
magnifying glass for a single critical analysis of the situation
in Uganda. The world's press had for years been reporting
Amin's murderous régime in great detail, but *Pravda*, which
according to its previous Editor, Mikhail V. Zymanin (now
Central Committee secretary), is different from all bourgeois
papers because 'it writes nothing but the truth', discovered
the 'bloody crimes' only at the end of April 1979. By then,
Tanzanian forces had occupied the whole country and Amin
had been forced to flee. Thus for eight years the Soviet media
were either ignorant of the events in a 'friendly' country – or
had simply lied for reasons of state. This is the only possible
conclusion.

An even more circumspect approach was taken towards
Russia's powerful and rich Iranian neighbour. As long as the
outcome of a power battle in a Third World country is
shrouded in uncertainty, the Soviet media use a vague and
seemingly unspecific language, often relying on tendentiously
selected quotes from Western and Third World publications.
During the first period of the anti-Shah movement, the press
and TV tended to blame the convenient, ever present
'imperialist' scapegoats for the trouble; primarily the US and
occasionally the British, rather than the Shah himself. When
the Kremlin began to consider the overthrow of the Shah as a
distinct possibility, more and more space was given to
reporting on the anti-government riots. The press, however,
was still primarily relying on quoting Western sources and
withholding sharp and direct criticism. In mid-December
1978, *Izvestia* mentioned that 'the entourage of the Shah is
resorting to any means possible to protect the anti-popular
régime'. Quoting a statement by Khomeini in Paris, it
identified the Ayatollah as a progressive force. By the end of
December the Shah was already mentioned in Radio Moscow's Persian language broadcasts as a target of violence – but
he was still not personally attacked. It was only in early
January that *Pravda* began to print anti-Shah slogans in

dispatches from Teheran. As soon as the Shah had left the country, he was repeatedly and savagely attacked for cruelty, corruption, parasitism and subservience to American interests.[50]

The East European countries, which the Shah and his wife had visited in 1966, 1970, 1973, 1977 and 1978, were also placed in an embarrassing situation. Radio Warsaw's commentary on the Shah's last visit to Poland (15 August 1977) was in many ways characteristic of bloc assessments. It praised his 'far-sightedness' and 'broad pragmatism', calling him a 'great social reformer' and father of the so-called 'white revolution'. In Prague, in the same month, the Shah was awarded the Order of the White Lion with Chain, the country's highest decoration for foreigners. Charles University conferred honorary doctor's degrees in law and philosophy on the Shah and his wife respectively.

The Poles and the Czechs, the Hungarians and Bulgarians (even as late as May 1978), were hailing the visiting Shah, vying with one another in complimenting him and praising the good bilateral relations between their countries and Iran. For example, President Husák noted 'a broad identity of interests' in mutual relations and 'identical or very close views' on most world issues. The talks were, as could have been expected, marked by 'cordiality and a constructive spirit'. Once the Shah fell, Radio Prague celebrated the 'great victory of the massive anti-monarchist movement'. The armed people seized the main jails, in which 'Iranian patriots have been kept and tortured for decades.'[51]

The turbulence in Iran still continues to subject even seasoned Communist commentators to verbal acrobatics which are unlikely to enhance their reputation. For example, during the Easter weekend telecasts cited above, Moscow television broadcast Khomeini's anti-Western and anti-American outbursts, but kept silent about the numerous executions in Iran, and the resignation of the Foreign Minister. In September 1979, difficulty in sticking to the same line produced a rare plurality of views: *Nedelya*, the weekly supplement of *Izvestia*, carried a report by Alexander Bovin, a well-known commentator, accusing the rulers of Iran of violating civil rights and disappointing the hopes of the people for the success of the revolution. But another dispatch from Teheran, published a week later in *Izvestia*, praised the 'anti-imperialist policy' followed by the government which enjoys 'the broad support of the people'. This was of course not the harbinger of a diversity of views among Soviet columnists, but simply the reflection of different and changing assessments of the fluid situation within the Soviet leadership, with shifts in the 'general line' getting confused in the cumbersome bureaucracy in charge of information and censorship. The surprise was such that Western agencies reported something which would be quite normal in any other country, namely that two journalists happened to have different views about the interpretation of political trends in another country. The stir that this censorship mishap caused was in itself a telling proof that Soviet newsmen are regarded solely as the voice of their political masters.[52]

The Soviet invasion of Afghanistan not only marked a watershed in East-West relations; it also provided the latest stunning examples of what an American analyst has called 'the brutality of the lie' in Soviet propaganda. Thus Moscow did not admit publicly that there were any Soviet troops in Afghanistan until three days after the coup of 27 December 1979 which overthrew President Hafizullah Amin and installed Babrak Karmal as his successor. After months of fierce, if sporadic, fighting, and the presence of some 80,000 Soviet combat troops of which thousands have been killed or wounded, the Kremlin still maintains silence over the scope of the military operations and casualties in Afghanistan. The official line is that 'a limited military contingent' was requested by the legitimate government of Afghanistan under imperialist threats and that it will be withdrawn as soon as an end is put to 'outside interference'.

A glance at the sequence of events shows, however, that the Soviets have been forced to resort to the tested mechanism of outright and grotesque lies to produce a semblance of legitimacy for the occupation of a neighbouring and, nominally at least, non-aligned country. At the time of the Soviet invasion, described by the Kremlin as a response to Afghanistan's appeal for help, the country's President was Hafizullah Amin. Yet he was killed during the Soviet takeover, denounced as a 'Stooge' and later as a CIA agent. Subsequently, Soviet propagandists, and Karmal himself, claimed that the Soviet government had received fourteen requests for military assistance in 1978–79, four in December 1979 alone. Such statements have done little to clarify the mystery of the removal and execution of the man who was supposed to have asked for Soviet help.

It is doubtful whether a 'CIA agent' would have issued repeated appeals to Moscow for military assistance. Amin had been deputy Premier and Foreign Minister in the Marxist government since May 1978, became Prime Minister in March 1979 and finally, after the murder of his predecessor Taraki, took over as President in September 1979. The Soviet leaders congratulated Amin and only four days before his ouster *Pravda* praised his role in fostering good Soviet-Afghan ties based on mutual co-operation and non-interference in domestic policies. How was it possible that an 'imperialist agent' could occupy such important positions and enjoy the confidence of the Kremlin for so long?

Today Soviet bloc media condemn Amin's rule as a 'regime of terror and persecution'. But when West German, French and American newspapermen in the autumn of 1979 reported the methods of torture applied in Kabul's prisons, the Soviet and Eastern European press remained either silent or even complained about the 'slanderous campaign against the patriotic revolutionary forces in Afghanistan'. As to the role of Babrak Karmal, who at the time of writing is the head of the party and the state, he was flown by the Soviets into Afghanistan from his exile in Eastern Europe after the coup that ousted Amin. 'Radio Kabul' which announced the news of the coup was actually a Soviet transmitter at Termez in the USSR. At the very time when these prerecorded broadcasts were put on the air the genuine Radio Kabul was broadcasting 'normal' programmes.

Karmal himself has, in the course of recent months, begun to present a series of increasingly bizarre explanations of the role of Amin. Thus he told the German news magazine, *Der*

Spiegel, that Amin had already been a CIA agent in 1955 when he was a student in the US, that he had been forced by the majority of the leadership to call in the Russians even before 27 December and that he, Karmal, had at that time been 'in the underground in Kabul but in contact with the anti-Amin majority in the government and the Central Committee'. Such absurd lies have not been heard since the days of the Stalinist show trials. No wonder that Soviet bloc propaganda concentrates on the alleged imperialist, Chinese, Pakistani, Zionist, etc, threats to Afghanistan and the friendly relations between Soviet servicemen and ordinary Afghan citizens, while downplaying or ignoring the fantastic tales concocted by the embattled and isolated Karmal régime.

Though Hungary and Poland were much more restrained in their expressions of support for the Soviet move and in the coverage of developments in Afghanistan than the Bulgarian, Czechoslovak and East German régimes, they too have had to accept the official version about the coup as the truth. Neither the condemnation of the Soviet invasion by a vote of 104 to 18 in the UN General Assembly on 14 January 1980, nor the flight of over 700,000 refugees into neighbouring Pakistan and Iran, coupled with world-wide reports of the continuing fight by the rebels against the Soviet occupiers and their local stooges, produced a change in the mechanism of lies and half-truths once the basic line was laid down by the Kremlin. The manipulation of the media and other control mechanisms has so far allowed the Russians to operate without significant domestic dissent. The lack of Western, and particularly NATO, consensus on the US-sponsored boycott of the Moscow Olympics has helped to cushion the blows to Soviet prestige. As far as the average Soviet citizen is concerned, the impact of the direct or indirect criticism of the Kremlin by the Yugoslav, Romanian, Italian and Spanish Communist parties was overshadowed by the success of Soviet propaganda in whipping up national support for a move which is depicted as an effort to forestall an imperialist plot to turn Afghanistan into a forward base against the Soviet Union. Things are, of course, different, and hence also more difficult for the media, in the smaller East European countries, where the ruling parties are painfully aware of the high political costs of increased military expenditure.*

The effort to imitate the Soviet system of indoctrination is perhaps nowhere so evident, and yet so ridiculous, as in East Germany. If we take, for example, *Neues Deutschland*, the central party organ, of 1 October 1979, it reads more or less as a German-language *Pravda* with slight local variations. There are, however, two differences. Firstly the paper announces, under a four-column banner headline on the front page, that a Soviet party and government delegation led by Brezhnev will arrive in East Berlin on 4 October for an official visit to mark the thirtieth anniversary of the founding of the German Democratic Republic (*Pravda* kept its usual silence until the actual arrival of Brezhnev four days later). Secondly, in contrast to its Soviet sister paper, *Neues Deutschland* reported on the Pope's trip to Ireland and to New York, even if only in six lines tucked away at the bottom of the front page, preceded by such 'foreign briefs' as the arrival in Austria of a peace bicycle rally from the Netherlands and the South African bombing of Angola.

On the whole, however, *Neues Deutschland* conveys the same world view and the same stereotypes about a happy population, prospering citizens and a powerful economy as *Pravda* does. The lead story on the front page, side by side with the announcement of Brezhnev's trip, is a report with a picture about a visit of Enrico Berlinguer, the Italian Communist leader, to an exhibition in Rome of the achievements of the GDR. Page two is dominated by a major news story about the opening of a diary and meat plant and page three by a glowing three-column review of party leader Erich Honecker's book on the role of the trade unions. Who, then, could be

*For a good summary of Soviet press treatment and chronology of events in Afghanistan see *The Global Significance of the Occupation of Afghanistan by the USSR*, published by the US International Communication Agency; Mark Heller, *The Soviet Invasion of Afghanistan* in *The Washington Quarterly*, Summer 1980, Volume 3, Number 3; see for Soviet media coverage especially RL Research Reports 17/80, 62/80 and 113/80. For Babrak's grotesque statements see *Der Spiegel* No 14/80; *Frankfurter Allgemeine* 8 February and 19 April 1980.

surprised that, apart from the pieces about China, demonstrations in Newark, Portuguese unions and the rest, already familiar from *Pravda*, *Neues Deutschland*'s main foreign report is a long illustrated account of an international cycling rally 'against the arms race and for peace' from Amsterdam to Bonn, Prague and (by plane!) to Moscow?

Of course, what makes the eight million copies of *Neues Deutschland*, and the thirty-eight other dailies produced in East Germany, so unique is that they are written and edited for by far the best-informed population in the Communist world. All East Germans can listen to the news bulletins of the West German radio stations and eighty percent can also receive TV transmissions from the Federal Republic. Nowhere in the Soviet bloc is the state's monopoly of information so thoroughly undermined as in East Germany. According to reliable audience surveys, only seven to ten percent of the viewers see the main evening newscast of the East Berlin TV, while the two main news programmes of the West German networks are seen regularly by twenty-two percent and forty percent of East Germans. When there is a crisis, such as the assassination of prominent personalities by terrorists or the hijacking of a Lufthansa plane to Mogadishu, up to eighty-seven percent of the East Germans watch Western TV newscasts.[53]

Rarely, if ever, can one observe such a Kafkaesque situation: some seven thousand journalists turn out thirty-nine dailies, thirty-one weeklies (8.7 million copies) and 517 periodicals (17.8 million circulation) as well as about 650 factory papers (two million copies) – admittedly a much higher circulation per head than in the Federal Republic. At the same time a vast apparatus of about five thousand people produce nineteen hours of TV programmes daily on two channels, costing the state 650 million Ostmark annually. Yet the political messages are not really read, nor seen and heard and, above all, not believed.[54]

Telecasts from the West threaten to create insurmountable problems of credibility for a régime which, alone in the Warsaw Pact, also lacks a national basis. Despite the recognition of the GDR by 127 states, seventy-five percent of young people between sixteen and twenty-five described themselves as Germans rather than as 'citizens of the GDR',[55] according to an opinion survey institute. Though Western penetration via the TV screen and the radios alone cannot become a major threat to domestic stability, it does promote a climate of heightened social tensions, by accelerating the changes in values and cultural choices, and influencing the life style of the young and the cultural élite.

The East German media executives are faced with insoluble problems. Their political output is eminently dull. In order to attract at least some audience, their programmes must either copy Western trivialities such as thrillers and revues, or purchase series shown years earlier in West Germany, thus discrediting their claim of seeking to 'shape a new socialist man'. Even technically good documentaries using Western cameramen and newsreels to show the darker and seamier sides of West German capitalism backfire in the end because they consist mainly of reports about right-wing extremist groups, the unemployed and people excluded from civil service jobs because of their Communist beliefs. The propaganda is so overdone that even ordinary people can recognise the exaggerations.

Take, for example, the astounding statement made in a recent commentary in *Neues Deutschland*, under the title 'Between Dream and Reality,' that 'the standard of living in the GDR is higher than that in the Federal Republic.' Even leaving aside manipulated statistics, it is not only the daily television programmes, but also the encounters with 7.9 million relatives and friends from West Germany who visited the GDR, in 1978 alone, and, above all, the number of applications for exit permits, which indicate the impression such blatant propaganda must make on normal people. The Communists had to erect the infamous Berlin Wall in 1961 after an annual average exodus of 225,000 Germans between 1950 and 1960 threatened the very existence of the 'first German socialist state'. Currently, between 8,000 and 10,000 people leave legally each year and it is estimated that, despite adverse consequences, some 120,000 people have tabled applications for exit permits.[56] Last but not least, there are still hundreds willing to risk death, serious injuries or, at the very least, long years in prison just to get out of the GDR.

Nowhere in the Communist world is it so evident that journalists have to produce newspapers not to provide information, but solely to try and stabilise the society, even if it involves publishing patent untruths. Insensitivity to the impression such crude propaganda makes is a basic precondition of work for journalists in the make-believe world of East Germany.

Communist Romania faces no such problems in communication policies. Its criteria for what is 'newsworthy' are even more straightforward: anything related in any way to the life and activities of Nicolae Ceauşescu, head of state and Secretary General of the Romanian Communist Party, generally referred to as 'the most beloved son of our nation', and, on festive occasions, as 'the most genuine popular leader to emerge in the entire history of the Romanian people' or 'the most remarkable statesman of our modern history'.

For the past ten years or so the propaganda apparatus has been partly directed by the former Editor of *Scînteia* and Central Committee secretary Dumitru Popescu who, at the eleventh Party Congress, surpassed all the other functionaries in his praise of the supreme leader:

Since here and there Western newspapers express astonishment at the fact that the name of Comrade Nicolae Ceauşescu is so often on the lips of the Romanian people, and that his merits are praised with such warmth at our great public gatherings, I will take the liberty of giving such possible wonderers the answer in advance. . . . People love and extol their leaders because they quench their own thirst for perfection, for the perfection to which man ceaselessly aspires, no matter how inaccessible it may be. In the past, they had Julius Caesar, Alexander of Macedonia, Pericles, Cromwell, Napoleon, Peter the Great, Lincoln. We had Mihai, Stefan, Cantemir, Brincoveanu, Balcescu and Cuza. . . . Now we have Nicolae Ceauşescu: for ten years he has been our shepherd – as our chronicles called the nation's leaders. The eulogies we address to him are not invented. They are indeed true. So why should we not extol him? In fact, my conviction is that the full greatness of his role in Romanian history will be understood only by our descendants, who will undoubtedly be even more generous in their praise.

It is easy, and always highly entertaining, to watch the transition from one cult to another. Thus, for example, Ceauşescu himself warned, about three years after his predecessor Gheorghe Gheorghiu-Dej's death in 1968, that: 'We do not need any idols. We do not need to turn people into standard-bearers, Marxism-Leninism has rejected and continues to reject any such concepts that are alien to the ideology of the working class.'

Ten years later, the adulation of this modest leader not only far surpasses the cult of Gheorghiu-Dej, but, in sheer volume of praise, it may even have overtaken the cult of Stalin. Ceauşescu's sixtieth birthday in January 1978 could certainly stand comparison with Stalin's seventieth for the length and variety of praise that it elicited. For over two months telegrams, poems, drawings and photos of paintings, marble busts, tapestries and pottery images of Ceauşescu filled the columns of all Romanian papers.

His frequent trips abroad and his tours of his own country are major events in the media. First there will be an interview with the President, sometimes several on the same day, followed by reports from the capitals concerned about the suspense and anticipation with which governments and people await the great emissary from Romania. Often his arrival coincides with the publication of the appropriate translation of one of the fourteen volumes of his speeches. All the speeches, receptions, toasts and activities during his visit are fully covered, event by event, hour by hour, by television and newspaper reporters, filling half to two-thirds of the newspapers and telecasts, regardless of whether the leader goes to the US, to Gabon or to neighbouring Bulgaria. After his return, the special correspondents report on the enormous press coverage in the countries he visited. At the same time hundreds of telegrams pour in filling the columns of the newspapers for at least a week, sometimes two.

The situation in Romania cannot be grasped without some examples. Thus at the end of April 1978 *Scînteia* and all other papers carried a seven-column headline: 'Recognition and Thanks for Indefatigable Work in the Service of Our People and the Fatherland' and – in smaller type – 'Working People from Town and Country Express in Messages to Comrade

Nicolae Ceauşescu their Great Satisfaction with the Out-
standing Results of the Trip the President of the Republic
Undertook Together with Comrade Elena Ceauşescu in Eight
African Countries'. A sample message, from the Ministry of
Machine Building, stated:

> In our thoughts, and with unbounded respect, we were at your
> side during this whole mission of extraordinary, historic and
> political importance, following with great interest every moment
> of this voyage, replete with eventful phases of the greatest
> significance for the relations of co-operation and solidarity with
> these countries. Spurred on by enthusiasm through your won-
> derful example, we convey our fullest approval for the results of
> these visits.

The party committee of Covasna saw:

> . . . with unlimited pleasure and special satisfaction that you,
> highly esteemed, beloved Comrade Nicolas Ceauşescu, an out-
> standing political personality of our days, an indefatigable fighter
> for the noble ideals of freedom, independence and social prog-
> ress, peace, friendship and co-operation with other nations, were
> received on African soil with great enthusiasm.

Twelve other lengthy telegrams expressed the same feelings in
basically the same phrases, always adding a promise that the
party committee, factory or enterprise concerned, stimulated
by the President's lofty example, would do its best to achieve
even better results in its field.

As the Romanian leader undertakes dozens of trips abroad
each year, such telegrams have become an integral part of the
newspapers. In January 1979 the sixtieth birthday of Elena
Ceauşescu was also celebrated with unprecedented pomp, the
letter of the party's Political Executive Committee extolling
her merits as a party leader, chemical scientist and wife of the
'highly esteemed and beloved leader'. Laudatory articles and
speeches dominated the front pages of the papers for three
days.[57] Three weeks later, Ceauşescu's sixty-first birthday
was celebrated at a dinner given by the party leadership. The
speeches, photos and yet another congratulatory letter from
the Executive Committee, together with a whole page of
congratulatory telegrams from all parts of the country filled

three of the four pages of *Neuer Weg*, the German-language daily, on 28 January 1979. The messages praised the President's brilliant example of devotion and selflessness', his 'decisive role' in foreign and domestic policies. All the messages 'respectfully congratulated and thanked him for the particular attention' paid to their problems and advice given by the President.

Another typical example is *Scînteia* of Sunday, 23 September 1979 with three full pages out of six devoted to the Ceauşescu's visit to the President's native Scorniceşti for the celebrations marking four hundred years of documented history of the village. Eleven pictures of the presidential couple, accompanied by their son Nicu who is already secretary of the Communist youth union, underlined the significance of the event. The paper also published his interview with Mexican television and two telegrams sent by him to other leaders. What the Ceauşescus do in public is invariably the lead item on the main evening news programme. If Ceauşescu leaves (even on a domestic tour) or arrives back in the capital, the entire leadership is gathered to greet him and the announcer will read the name of every single high-ranking comrade who shows up. If Mrs Ceauşescu receives a visitor on her own, or carries out some engagement, her full title – 'Comrade, Academician, Doctor, Certified Engineer Elena Ceauşescu' is always mentioned. She is also a member of the ruling Politbureau, director of a chemical institute, chairman of the party cadres commission, Chairman of the Scientific and Research Council, with Cabinet rank, and, since the spring of 1980, First Deputy Prime Minister. No wonder that the activities of the couple often take up three to five minutes of a ten-minute broadcast.

The space remaining in the newspapers is filled with the same sort of economic, social and protocol reports as *Pravda* or *Neues Deutschland*. There are major differences only in foreign news reporting: as stressed earlier, Romania conducts an independent-minded policy on some major issues. This means that coverage of, for example, the Middle East, China or events in Afghanistan, is more balanced than in the other Soviet bloc papers. Basically, however, the function of the media is exactly the same as in the Soviet Union.

Finally, a glance at the Hungarian media may be worthwhile, since the Kádár régime it widely regarded currently as having the highest degree of domestic relaxation, within the Soviet bloc albeit always within politically safe limits. Here too the most authoritative daily, the central party paper, *Népszabadság*, must be scrutinised, although there are great differences in candour and quality between the voice of the party and some political and literary weeklies or monthlies.

The issue of 4 October 1979 was typical. The one-column editorial on the front page dealt with the need to improve the look of houses and streets, and the main lead story was about the competition among enterprises in seeking to fulfill their obligations to honour the next party congress and the thirty-fifth anniversary of the liberation, both due the following spring. The Pope's speech at the UN was given front page treatment and, in general, treated in a more realistic and balanced fashion than in *Pravda* and *Scînteia*. But the reporting and comment on China, Vietnam and Cambodia was as one-sided as in *Neues Deutschland* and the Soviet paper. Domestic political and economic pages were dominated by such items as problems of political indoctrination in higher education, the Budapest meeting of the 'socialist solidarity committees with Vietnam, Laos and Cambodia' (with Romania significantly absent), efforts to produce better quality wheat and the concluding part of a series on the great successes in fraternal East Germany.

Yet a feature about how a middle-aged, upper-grade bureaucrat left his wife for a young woman may well have touched a raw nerve in many functionaries faced with similar problems. It is in this field of human relations, behaviour, morals and life styles that *Népszabadság* is more outspoken about the many contradictions in a supposedly socialist society than perhaps any other Soviet-bloc party organ. On this day, five out of its sixteen tabloid pages contained advertisements, small and large, placed by individuals wanting to sell a flat or plot of land, and companies seeking to employ labour. The state travel agencies often use the party organ to lure customers with lists of organised tourist excursions both to the East and West, including trips to North and Latin America (costing the equivalent of five to eight months average salaries!). The weekend editions even deal with such subjects as new men's and women's fashions, often with sketches, advice about cooking, interior decoration or the quality of various consumer durables (unimaginable in *Pravda*).

In the final analysis, however, *Népszabadság* merely provides a more useful service within its own terms, which are, on the whole, not so different from *Pravda*'s scale of values and political priorities. A Hungarian communications expert recently wrote in the lively cultural-political weekly, *Élet és Irodalom*, a highly revealing and very pertinent article about the basic dilemmas of communication policy under the title 'Hidden messages'. He complained that the platitudes of communiques about international or inter-state negotiations are 'hidden messages' which can only be deciphered by the initiated: 'The only way to inform the public about foreign political and internal events is to democratise the communication about them.'

As concrete examples, he mentioned one of .the routine communiques announcing that the planning and finance commission of Parliament held a meeting chaired by X, and discussed and approved the draft budget. Nine MPs participated in the debate. 'Everything is correctly reported, yet the text is completely irrelevant because we learn nothing at all about the budget or the views of the deputies. This news item (and the many similar items which appear every day in every paper) provides only the framework and form of the event. But within the hard, outside shell of the happening there is in fact nothing'. A similar, even worse, example according to the writer was the discussion a few years ago of the draft for a new constitution. 'Nothing was published about the substance of the debates, but merely about the formal aspects: how many people spoke, their names, etc. As a result, the publication of the full and revised text just one week before its adoption in Parliament, was in fact pointless, because the public had no adequate information, above all with regard to the changes between the old and the proposed text.'

The Hungarian critic went even further and bluntly warned that the majority of people simply do not read long articles and statements. 'In such cases the method of communication acts against the reception of the communicated message, the original intention turns into its opposite: through the long communiques the people become not better, but worse informed! Instead of printing long monotonous communiques in all the papers, shorter texts should be carried and also adapted to the special interests of a special readership,' he concluded.[58]

The deadening barrage of political messages directed at the ordinary people from East Berlin to Irkutsk, reflects the cardinal weakness of Communist propaganda methods. What should all these messages convey to the readers and listeners? A world view dominated by a picture of capitalism and the West as periodically shaken by structural economic and social crises; haunted by growing unemployment, uncontrollable inflation and a rising tide of protests, strikes and demonstrations; ridden with crime and corruption; and last but not least, ruthlessly repressing Communist and other progressive, peace-loving forces.

On the one hand, the NATO countries are split among themselves, their differences continuously sharpened by domestic contradictions, popular pressures and conflicts of class interests. On the other hand, they are ignoring the series of peace-loving propositions made by Brezhnev on behalf of the Soviet Union and the 'socialist community', and stubbornly carrying on with, the arms race, assisted and even abetted by the Chinese great power chauvinists. On the other hand, preceding trips by Brezhnev, Kádár or Husák to West Germany, France and the US, or on the arrival of a Western Premier or President in Moscow, Budapest or Prague the local Communist media will suddenly paint a brighter picture of the state in question; the mutual advantages of economic co-operation are stressed, always indicating that the Soviet (or Comecon) orders provide jobs for so and so many people.

Now contrast the unstable mire of rapacious capitalism and imperialism with the calm confidence, steady progress and full harmony between state policy and public interest radiated by the 'world of socialism', and above all by its leading power, the Soviet Union! The leaders of these countries are firmly united and share the common concern for peace and the well-being of their people. Petrol problems, natural disasters or common crimes can only momentarily disturb the general progress towards an ever higher standard of living and the birth (or further perfection) of the socialist man who cares for the community first and only second for himself. Though the special conditions under which socialism is being built may vary from country to country, the common features – the leading role of the Marxist-Leninist vanguard, the means of production in public possession and no compromises with the foreign and domestic class enemy – prevail elsewhere. The adherence to a firm party political line and the careful application of the generally valid laws of building socialism provide everywhere for law and order, growing prosperity and the happiness of those lucky people already living under socialism. Last but not least, public opinion in the socialist countries realises the importance of strengthening the defence capacity of each country, and of the entire socialist community, for as long as imperialist circles harbour expansionist plans and turn a deaf ear to the constructive proposals of the Warsaw Pact.

It is probably impossible to reform, or even modernise, the Communist mass media without a comprehensive blueprint imposed from above. The analysis in the next chapter of the attitude to 'information as privilege' and the mechanism of censorship should give an idea of the institutional barriers which neither pious resolutions from above nor intelligent suggestions from below can eliminate without political reform.

3 Censorship, Secrecy and the Special Bulletins

THE VISIT of Pope John Paul II to Poland from 2 to 10 June 1979 was an unprecedented event of great national significance in Polish history, symbolising the unbreakable bond between the Catholic Church and the Polish nation. It was the first time that a Pope had been to a Communist-ruled country. The fact that this Pope was Karol Wojtyla, who only nine months earlier, as a Polish Cardinal and Archbishop of Cracow, had been intimately involved in efforts to enlarge the scope of religious freedom and civil rights, lent a dramatic note to the unique occasion. It is now known just how deeply Communist rulers, and not only in Warsaw, but also in the Kremlin, Budapest and Prague, were worried by this challenge to the legitimacy of the régime of the largest and most populous country in the Soviet sphere of influence.

At the same time, the sentimental journey by the youngest and most personable Pope on record to his native country was generally seen as a TV spectacle and media event even more gripping than his trip to Mexico. Scores of TV and radio teams and some 1,200 journalists were accredited in Poland to report the great event. In countries with large Roman Catholic populations, such as Austria, Germany, Italy and Spain, there were special daily telecasts, sometimes lasting three to four hours, and a considerable part of the normal evening news programmes on TV and radio were devoted to the colourful and – often even for non-believers – very moving scenes. ORF, the Austrian TV station, transmitted forty-two hours of special reports on the Pope in addition to regular commentaries on TV and radio.

The Pontiff spoke to perhaps six million people, delivered

some thirty public addresses and sermons and was seen world-wide by an audience estimated at between 700 million and a billion viewers. Both Polish and foreign observers agreed that no other leader had ever succeeded in so captivating audiences in Poland, mobilising vast masses without coercion or any advance propaganda, in the way Pope John Paul II did.

How did the East European, and above all the Polish, media deal with this momentous event? The great exception to the generally low-key treatment by the Soviet bloc was, as usual, the Yugoslav press. Though Yugoslav Catholics are concentrated in the Western republics of Croatia and Slovenia, not only *Vjesnik* of Zagreb and *Delo* of Ljubljana, but also *Borba*, *Politika* and the news magazine *NIN* based in Belgrade carried short items and long reports. *NIN* even printed special reports in three consecutive issues, and included photos showing the Pope addressing the crowds. 'The Church is a Great Force – Millions of Believers on the Streets', 'The Church Has Become More Powerful than Ever', these and similar headlines reflected the generally fair Yugoslav reporting.

What a startling contrast to the coverage in Hungary, where Catholics account for seventy-seven percent of the population. On Sunday 3 June *Népszabadság* printed a thirty-five line item on the Pope's arrival in Warsaw, and his talks with the Polish leaders. The story was about the same length, but less prominently placed, as reports on the Berlin-Hamburg motorway, and allegations of secret US contacts with Bishop Muzorewa. Radio Budapest carried the news as the third item on its midday news report. Throughout the entire visit, the media carried only brief news items, concentrating on the arrival and departure of the Hungarian Cardinal Lékai and the final departure ceremony at Cracow. In accordance with the Agit-Prop guidelines, issued at the bi-weekly meeting with the editors only one daily (*Magyar Nemzet*), one weekly (*Magyarország*) and of course the Catholic weekly, *Uj Ember*, were allowed to publish commentaries. Party speakers at the closed media conferences expressed sympathy with 'the Polish comrades who find themselves in a rather embarrasing situation'.

Yet even this minimal Hungarian coverage was consider-able compared to the perfunctory attention paid to the Pope's visit by the Czechoslovak and East German media. Though seventy-seven percent of the Czechoslovak population are estimated to be Roman Catholics, on 4 June *Rudé právo* devoted seventy words based on a CTK dispatch to the Pope's arrival. A few days later, during the Pope's three-day stay in Czestochowa, a report appeared in the paper on the modernisation of the town. The story contained no reference to the Papal visit whatsoever, and on the following day *Rudé právo* reported on the growth of the Polish party!

In neighbouring East Germany (with less than ten percent Catholics), the weekend edition of *Neues Deutschland* did not even mention the Pope; its first brief reference was in Tuesday's issue. The East Germans, along with the Bulgarians and Romanians only reported on the Holy Father's arrival, his speech in the Auschwitz camp and his departure.

Needless to say, the Soviet coverage was also minimal. Two points however may perhaps merit some attention. In Auschwitz the Pope paid special tribute to the sufferings of the Jews, in addition, of course, to those of the Poles, and also mentioned the role of the Russians in World War II. Radio Moscow devoted nine lines to the visit to the concentration camp, mentioning the Pope's tribute to the Soviets, but omitting his words about the Poles and the Jews. Next day, *Izvestia* reported the Auschwitz visit in three paragraphs, again leading with the reference to the Russians, but also noting the Pope's words about the Poles. There was no mention of the Jews. The other point worth recalling is that those in charge of the media took almost two weeks to give the green light to an extremely cautious and basically non-committal eight-minute commentary by a TASS political cor-respondent in Moscow Radio's 'Questions and Answers' features programme. The relief felt by the Kremlin that the 'Polish circus', in the words of a Soviet observer, 'was at last over', found a muted reflection in the statement that, in spite of the predictions of the 'reactionary press' in the West, the visit had been 'on the whole quiet. . . .'

The most intriguing question of all is how did the Polish media cope with this unparalleled event in national history?

Basically, the régime sought to combine four things: to present the visit as a merely religious event, yet also as a symbolic recognition of 'People's Poland's achievements at a time of the fortieth anniversary of the Hitlerite aggression'; to provide a seemingly 'generous' coverage by the standards of an 'atheistic socialist state', yet also to eliminate virtually all the crowds and all signs of the enormous upsurge of enthusiasm among the population.

Polish radio and television nationwide covered only three events: the arrival and the reception at Belweder Palace by the state and party leadership coupled with the Mass and wreath-laying ceremony at the Tomb of the Unknown Soldier in Warsaw; the visit to Auschwitz; and the departure ceremony at Cracow Airport. All other events were only shown on local or, at best, regional TV with the time given varying according to the type and place of the event. The same restricted coverage was provided by sound broadcasting stations. On the average, Polish television devoted about fifteen minutes a day to the visit, with extended time for special occasions. What made the Polish media a worldwide laughing stock was the way in which the camera angles showed the Pope apparently surrounded by trees, clouds, nuns, choirs and clergy, with an occasional shot of old people, but never showed the immense crowds which often ranged from hundreds of thousands to millions. The difference, for example, between the live coverage, which often relied on Polish camera work, and the film taken by Western camera teams and shown later, were quite breathtaking. When the Austrian network transmitted several hours of comment and translation by its special correspondent, Alfons Dalma, on the religious and national symbolism and the background to the mass at Gniezno and Czestochowa, stressing that millions of people were listening and applauding, the Polish cameras conveyed the idea that the Pope spoke only to a relatively small, ageing crowd. At Nowy Targ, for example, an enormous crowd of over one million people was made to appear as one of the smallest.

The Communist media not only sought to minimise the audio-visual impact of the Pope's visit, but also to prevent the people from hearing what he actually said in his sermons and statements. His plea for more religious freedom and respect for human rights, his assertion of man's right to own land, his warnings against materialism and conformism, etc, were ignored completely, as were some of his improvised messages, for example those 'to his Czech children' and those who could not cross the border. (Before and during the Papal visit, Czechoslovak banks either stopped, or restricted to a minimum, the sale of Polish currency to Czech and Slovak citizens who had intended to go to Poland.) Heavily doctored summaries of the day's events in the evening radio and TV newsreels generally occupied only the fifth or sixth place in the news. Even the microphones were placed in such a fashion that they recorded only the voice of the Pope and cut out the response and enthusiasm of the applauding, singing crowds.

According to some reports, television coverage was particularly poor and scanty in the eastern and northern parts of Poland, where broadcasts can be picked up in Western Belorussia and Western Lithuania; and the Bialystok station was temporarily 'out of order', allegedly as a result of Soviet pressure.[59] Apart from the official speeches delivered on the first day by the Pope, the Head of the State Council, Henryk Jablonski, and party leader Edward Gierek, the press subsequently printed only PAP bulletins with a minimum of substantive information, citing certain politically acceptable portions of the Pope's sermons about the value of and respect for work or the importance of national unity, but ignored many other more important statements. None of the dailies, except for the organ of the pro-régime Catholic PAX movement, *Slowo Powszechne*, and none of the numerous weekly periodicals, except for the only genuinely independent-minded Polish paper, the Catholic weekly *Tygodnik Powszechne*, provided anything resembling a reasonably comprehensive coverage or the type of reporting found in both the serious and popular Italian, Austrian, German, French, Swiss and Spanish dailies.

Nevertheless, both the Polish public and East Europeans in general were kept thoroughly informed because the Western radio stations, above all the Munich-based Radio Free Europe, seized the exceptional opportunity to demonstrate their irreplaceable role in filling information gaps in the Communist world. As for the Western press, the hundreds of foreign correspondents were on the whole able to work freely, and the initial ploy of levying a $300 charge for accreditation was subsequently scrapped by the authorities after widespread criticism, though special fees for certain services still yielded some badly-needed foreign exchange. Occasional interruptions on the lines to Vienna or Cologne tended to coincide with live interviews of prominent dissident figures – and were evidently not accidental.

In fact the world soon learned that nothing, literally nothing, had been left to chance as far as the Polish media were concerned. Long before the Pope arrived, the propaganda experts of the Central Committee of the party drew up a ten-page draft of instructions for local coverage. Smuggled out of Poland and first published (in an abbreviated form) in *Time* magazine[60] three weeks after the Pope's departure, the document provides a rare insight into the murky depths of a state-controlled press. Western journalists had to cover a fast unfolding story; improvising, ad-libbing and revising their reports on what the Pope himself described, in his farewell address at Cracow Airport, an 'unprecedented event' and 'an act of some courage on both sides'. But their Polish colleagues faced no problems from the unexpected.

Both the packaging and the content of their reports, including the number of accompanying photographs, were laid down in every detail weeks before the event by the political bureaucrats in charge of the media. Though the document may have subsequently been amended, and though there were also references to other memos, the main points of the draft instructions were definitely put into practice.

The text informs the recipient that reporting will be centrally supervised and approved. Stories and news material directly and indirectly linked with the visit will be approved and controlled by two five-man teams working round the clock from 8am to 2am the following day. Some journalists will be assigned to supply foreign correspondents with 'correct information' on Poland's problems, as well as to accompany those Western newsmen 'who show a hostile bias towards us'.

No detail was too small to be ignored. 'On the opening day of the visit, the morning and afternoon press will publish a picture of the Pope, the news of his arrival, a profile and a commentary to be distributed by PAP' (the Polish news agency). The party newspapers 'will publish no photographs, only a news item, a biography and a commentary provided by PAP'. (As a matter of fact, *Trybuna Ludu*, the central paper, did carry a photo on its front page.) Both the voice of the party and the second most important Warsaw daily, *Zycie Warszawy*, were given permission to publish their own commentaries, as were some weeklies, always subject, of course, to 'normal' censorship. Even the articles and photos of the nominally independent religious press were to be 'supervised according to the censorship regulations in force', the draft noted. Everything had to be cleared in advance.

The flow of information was to be channelled exclusively through PAP, even down to such details as the provision of headlines. All photographs had to be submitted to the press department. After the Pope departed, according to the draft, illustrated magazines could 'publish several pictures (two to four)', and all other publications should step up their coverage of international events ('to be outlined in a separate document') 'especially with regard to the forthcoming signing of the SALT II treaty'. The wording implied that no time was to be lost in refocusing the population's attention on what the régime regarded as really important secular matters.

In addition to the 'political line' and 'professional instructions', the draft dealt with the rules of accreditation and foreign press access to the available communication equipment, transportation, etc. Despite some minor changes in the prepared script the performance of the Polish media conformed closely to the plan. Thus on 4 June the morning dailies all had virtually the same story of the Pope's arrival in the same place on their front pages with the same photograph of the Pontiff meeting Gierek. Instructions for television and radio coverage were probably laid down in other draft papers. At least one Polish cameraman admitted that he was under orders not to show the huge crowds. In one case, TV cameras had to remain fixed on the Pope's hovering helicopter for several minutes to avoid any crowd shots.

In retrospect, the draft document which reached the West confirms that the entire domestic mass media had been pre-programmed to suppress or distort information and to blot out the impressive manifestations of a genuine popular enthusiasm never previously witnessed in a Communist-ruled country. Western observers correctly stressed the remarkable potential for public mobilisation in support of religious causes and Church activity. There can be little doubt that the régime went to such lengths to downgrade the impact of the Papal visit because it had a not unjustified fear of what might happen were the people, in whose name it ruled, to manifest their will.

As a postscript, two final points should be remembered. Firstly, the millions of Poles who welcomed the visitor, spending hours listening to him and singing with him, demonstrated to the whole world the power of the Church and their profound attachment to religion despite thirty years of anti-religious indoctrination. Though the position of the Church is different in Hungary and Czechoslovakia, let alone in Lithuania and Romania, the strength and unbroken faith in the future displayed by both the clergy and the believers in Poland constitutes long-range encouragement of both Catholics and other Christians in other East European countries.[61] Secondly, modern communication technology has proved once again that censorship is unable to seal off the citizens of the Soviet bloc from news even if events take place within a Communist country. Experts in Austria and Germany estimate that some 2 to 2.5 million people in Western Hungary and well over a million in Czechoslovakia can receive Austrian and German television programmes. Thus it is reasonable to assume that hundreds of thousands of Hungarians, Czechs and Slovaks (in addition to many Croats and Slovenes in Yugoslavia) will have watched at least some of the unforgettable scenes of the Pope's pilgrimage to his native land. Paradoxically, this means that Hungarians and Czechoslovaks living near the Austrian and West German borders gained a more powerful impression of the trip than the Poles themselves.

The journalists are victims of a system that often treats them as cogs in the vast propaganda machine. But any criticism can only be circumspect. Writing before the last congress of the Polish Journalists Union, Kazimierz Kozniewski, a respected journalist of the pre-war generation, noted that to be a journalist is not a popular profession because there are . . .

> the most delicate, ticklish, sometimes drastic restrictions imposed upon one's creative freedom in the name of ideological reasons . . . The journalist is the least independent and the greatest proletarian among all creative professionals since the press is, among the cultural superstructures, the biggest field and the most attractive and successful propaganda instrument. The centralisation of the press has reached an intensity that – let us be frank – is not propitious to a creative pursuit of journalism. . . . This multiple dependence of the journalist's profession . . . also creates many difficult, even ticklish moral situations, it becomes a source of ideological and political conflict. Many a time, a journalist must give in, adapt to various demands and censorships, must work and make creative efforts in situations and under systems imposed upon him.[62]

But, only a few days later, a speech delivered at the congress by the party secretary in charge of propaganda, Jerzy Lukaszewicz, confirmed the party's view of journalists as its 'close and unfaltering allies'. The tasks of the mass media are simply 'to help people understand the meaning of the party's policy, to popularise efficiently the party line, to show the achievements in socialist construction, to pave the way for new trends and play an important role in combatting backwardness and anything else inconsistent with socialism.'[63]

It was a speech that could have come from any functionary; such statements and such office-holders are interchangeable. Reading such speeches and the lengthy statements periodically released by the various ruling parties on ideology, press, the arts and literature, brings to mind a devastating article written before the 1956 October uprising by the late Gyula Háy, a Hungarian playwright, erstwhile underground Communist and, subsequently, an emigré in Moscow. As one of the leaders of the writers' movement, Háy wrote the most quoted indictment of the faceless functionaries, whom he called 'Kucseras'.

Kucsera knows nothing, consequently he meddles in everything and only on an executive level. For Kucsera this goes without saying. On reading these lines not only does he take offence: he fails to understand what I want of him. I bet he thinks I am out of my mind. After all, are his activities not confined to the giving of directives? And only theoretical directives at that. About anything. At any time. How on earth, then, can I expect him to know? . . . If Kucsera has any claim to reliability, it is not for his part in any revolution but for his stake in the joint interest of those who, without knowing a thing 'theoretically direct' anything. This is especially striking in the field of art and literature. The Kucseras have still not reconciled themselves to the very existence of such things since these are so difficult to regulate, to codify, and to administer. Hence any artist or man of letters is, to them, unreliable from the very first. That is why governmental and other organs connected with art and literature are full of functionaries possessed by the spirit of Kucseras – in other words, men who, instead of knowledge, can boast of hatred for the arts. These men then, are incredibly 'reliable', since their immunity is complete: they are left stone cold by any literary or artistic effect, no matter how great. With this they merit such influence and boundless confidence in Kucseran circles as eunuchs in a harem. That we, writers and artists don't like the directives of these Kucseras is, perhaps, not altogether surprising.[64]

What a difference in tone and in candour between the carefully formulated complaints of the Polish journalist and the anger of the Hungarian writer! Alas, in the Poland of 1978 there could be no hope of a basic change; but the cutting edge of Háy's satire was, in 1956, directed against a crumbling system, swept away by a popular explosion two weeks later. Yet whether one calls these officials 'Kucsera' or Winston Smith, who in George Orwell's *1984* is employed by the Ministry of Truth to censor the past, there are still tens of thousands of them from East Berlin to Moscow, from Prague to Bucharest, reading, probing scrutinising, assessing, controlling, searching and opening literally everything from articles and book manuscripts to galley proofs and book parcels from abroad.

The names of the men at the very top and those of their most prominent victims may have changed, but the system of supervision has essentially remained everywhere the same.

With a handful of exceptions, the institution of censorship has survived all the upheavals of the 1950s and 1960s. It was accurately noted by an astute Czech observer, that even where censorship exists as a formal bureaucratic institution, it ranks at the bottom of the hierarchy of control and supervision.[65] Yet neither the Soviet Union nor most other Soviet bloc states (with the partial exception of Hungary) can give up this ancient, if crude, method of control, which completes the elaborate structure of party supervision and self-censorship sketched out in the preceding chapters.

As Hannah Arendt noted in her comments on the 'terror-sustained lying fictions of totalitarian régimes' it 'takes power not propaganda skill . . . to teach a whole nation the history of the Russian Revolution in which no man by the name of Trotsky was ever commander-in-chief of the Red Army.' Who would have imagined, for example, that even twenty-five years after Stalin's death his successors would still refuse the pleas of Yuri Larin, the son of Nikolai Bukharin, for the rehabilitation of his father, sentenced to death by Stalin and shot as a traitor in 1938? Bukharin, whom Lenin once called 'the favourite of the whole party', is not mentioned in any of the Soviet reference books and as far as the present generation of Soviet people is concerned he might never have existed. The son, who learned his real surname only in 1956 when he was twenty years old, has mobilised a number of West European Communists and Socialists – in vain. In a letter written to Enrico Berlinguer, the Italian Communist leader, Larin related that the chief of the secretariat of the Control Committee in Moscow read a statement to him on the telephone confirming that 'the criminal charges on the basis of which Bukharin was sentenced have not been withdrawn.'[66]

What does this mean in practice? Are Bukharin and all Lenin's other comrades-in-arms who were executed in 1936–38 still considered spies for Hitler, guilty of organising sabotage of Soviet industry, of participating in the murders of Kirov and Gorki and of attempting to kill Lenin himself? The tacit withdrawal of some of these charges in some reference works is not tantamount to a legal rehabilitation. Despite the promises made by Khrushchev in 1962 to Bukharin's widow, all those guilty of rightist or leftist deviations are still officially regarded as being 'objectively' traitors. Yet in a preface to an authoritative work written by five French Communist intellectuals, commissioned and approved by the French party leadership, Trotsky and Bukharin are mentioned as 'two great personalities who have not been rehabilitated in the USSR' but who represent important currents, as do Rosa Luxemburg and Gramsci, in the workers' movement. Subsequently a senior party official, writing in *L'Humanité*, confirmed in late 1978 that the French party had undertaken several attempts to secure Bukharin's rehabilitation, 'a humanitarian act of justice', the more so since the thesis of a conspiracy is 'no longer upheld officially' in the Soviet Union.[67]

But the Kremlin is still clinging to the original fiction, however absurd, because, after much soul searching and sharp internal debates, Stalin's successors have time and again concluded that the complex of the trials cannot be 'safely eliminated without wrecking the whole structure of systematic lying' concerning the Stalin era.

What does the fate of Bukharin or the others have to do with our subject? Communist propagandists would describe this historical diversion as a 'provocation' intended to divert attention from the 'real live issues of our day'. But the old Stalinist lies and half-truths are still very much alive. It is the permanent task of propagandists and censors to fend off any attempts to question generalised propaganda slogans – even if they were originally coined on the basis of lies which have had to be quietly shelved. The spectre of the great purges of the thirties and the heritage of Stalinism haunts not only Soviet and Western European Communists. The fact that Bukharin and his comrades have still not been cleared of the 'crimes' for which they were executed over four decades ago causes problems of credibility and embarrassment to the ruling parties in both Hungary and Poland. Since the 1956 upheavals both countries find it more difficult to turn lies into truths by destroying the facts which existed before.

Consider, for example, the fate of the first major political biography of Béla Kun, the leader of the short-lived Hungarian Soviet Republic (1919) and an internationally known functionary of the Comintern in the 1930s, until he too perished in Moscow in the Great Purge. Written after ten years of research by an established historian and published in 1979 by the party's publishing house, 10,000 copies of the biography were printed. Prepublication interviews with the author and a glowing review by another well-known Communist journalist in a radio programme drew attention to the publication which was timed to coincide with the sixtieth anniversary of the Soviet Republic. The book, however, never reached its prospective readers; before the first copies could be put on sale, they were called back. An authorised biography, sponsored by the Central Committee's Institute of Party History, written by a Communist historian of the workers' movement and specifically controlled and approved by the editor of *Népszabadság*, a member of the Politbureau, had to be destroyed after sharp protests from unidentified 'Soviet comrades', probably alerted by Kun's daughter and son-in-law who felt that Kun had been treated 'shabbily' by the author.

The most likely explanation of the book's withdrawal is that the author dealt in a factual way with the great figures of Soviet Communism. Trotsky, Bukharin, Zinoviev, Radek, etc, were frequently mentioned and the book even included pictures of some of them. The text scrupulously avoided any value judgment about the Soviet purges, which merely provided the background to Kun's personal history and final tragedy. But even so, this was a far cry from the silence or studied vagueness of the Soviet-type reference books, and came dangerously close to a truthful account both of the events and the terrible atmosphere of the 1930s.[68] Compared to Khrushchev's famous secret speech at the Twentieth Soviet Party Congress, the Kun biography was mild indeed. But then Khrushchev's shattering indictment has never been published officially – it was 'only' read in the spring of 1956 at tens of thousands of party meetings all over Eastern Europe. There were similar problems with the *Memoirs* of former Foreign Minister Endre Sik, an International Lenin Peace Prize winner and, until his death, a celebrated figure in the world peace movement. The book described his thirty years in the Soviet Union and was published by the Army Publishing house. It was recalled and destroyed in 1971 within weeks of publication.

Even making the most generous allowance for Soviet sensibilities, national pride and ideological pretensions neither book could be described as violating the 'state secrets' of either the Soviet Union or Hungary. In fact, the disappearance of a scholarly study, after much pre-publication publicity, could only engender even more cynicism and undermine what credibility remained to Communist historiography. The confiscation and destruction in 1972 of a collection of documents about the first post-war years in Hungary, merely because some letters and reports referred to the occasional 'excesses' of the Red Army (witnessed by the entire population of Central and Eastern Europe in 1944–45), was further evidence that the hands of Hungarian scholars and commentators are tied even if they seek to deal with events which have no direct political relevance today.[69]

The fact that the books got as far as they did is evidence of a slackness in dealing with dangerous subjects which would of course be impossible in the Soviet Union, where for many years the Main Administration for the Preservation of State Secrets (once called *Glavlit*) has been ensuring that everything is excluded from newspapers, books, TV or radio which could in any way clash with the official propaganda line. Even in the editorial offices of *Pravda*, every single article has to be stamped and signed by the censor as 'allowed to be printed'; the first copy is once again subject to the same procedure and the presses must wait until the first copy is stamped 'allowed to be released',[70] before they can be set in motion.

Despite the existence of a formal censorship apparatus the touchy subject of Soviet history also continues to cause headaches in Poland. The quarterly 'green bulletins' regularly issued to censors by the Central Office of Press, Publications and Spectacles (COPPSC) in Warsaw contains a special section called 'Censor's Oversight' which includes fragments of deleted texts with an analysis of the mistakes committed by the censors themselves. The issue 74/1 (February 1974) contains a four-page analysis of A. Czubinski's book: – *The Soviet Union: Years of Battles and Victories*. Permitting the publication of the book was regarded as a mistake because the author mentioned Trotsky, Bukharin and others. A typical paragraph from the report reads:

> Czubinski devoted large parts to the differences of opinion within the Communist party, the emergence and liquidation of factions, the growth of the cult of personality. . . . These dramatic events, described in a concentrated form, have a particularly strong impact on the reader. For example two pages of information about the trials in 1935–38 is packed with details, the names and number of the party, state and military leaders sentenced. As the author brings factual information without appropriate commentary, he raises even more question marks.[71]

Thus the fate of Stalin's victims continues to involve not only the families of those concerned, not only Soviet officialdom, but also any publisher, scholar, commentator and printer in other East European countries who dares to deal with the skeletons in the Soviet cupboard. The same applies to an event as amply documented as the Soviet-German pact of August 1939. Forty years later it was remembered, analysed and, above all, justified, in newspaper articles in Moscow and elsewhere in the bloc. But none of the commentaries referred to the Secret Additional Protocol of the pact which envisaged 'spheres of influence' and a 'territorial rearrangement' in Poland and the Baltic States of Estonia, Latvia and Lithuania, as well as containing the expression of Soviet 'interest' in Bessarabia. Nor was there any mention of the joint German-Soviet communique about the carving up of occupied Poland and the agreements signed by Ribbentrop and Molotov in Moscow in September 1939 with their additional secret protocols about a final 'rearrangement' concerning Lithuania and Poland.[72]

These are only the most recent examples to illustrate the general proposition. The problem of information in the Communist countries has never been one of finding out state secrets, but rather of winning the right to write and broadcast what everyone knows. For Soviet journalists, insult was added to the permanent injury of censorship in May 1979 when their political masters passed a resolution on propaganda and ideology which rapped them over the knuckles for failing to openly discuss 'topical questions of our public life'. In the spring of 1977, these same leaders removed the head of state Nikolai Podgorny and demoted him from all of his top positions, yet no explanation of the 'topical question' of Podgorny's fall was ever given, and no journalist would have risked discussing it openly.

But the list of subjects permanently ignored by Soviet and most East European newspapers goes beyond major political and historical issues, or natural disasters and their fatality counts. It includes the number of illiterates or drug addicts, the crime and accident statistics, the privileges of athletes, and the range of top salaries. There is no mention of disagreements with East European or Western Communist parties; no meaningful comparisons of social services or purchasing power with other countries; and, last but not least, no admission of errors. In sum, the Communist press, like the party on behalf of whom it speaks, projects an image of infallibility.

Thus, it would be inconceivable to admit that a representative collection of President Tito's speeches, published in Moscow in 1973, omitted his politically most important statements between 1948–56, or that three years later the East Germans even censored Tito's major address on the fiftieth anniversary celebrations of the Yugoslav party, eliminating the crucial parts about the conflicts with the Comintern and Stalin and his condemnation of the purges and the 1968 intervention in Czechoslovakia.[73] In September 1968 *Izvestia* furiously attacked the Czechoslovak Foreign Minister, Jiři Hájek. The Soviet paper implied that he was a Jew who had changed his name and collaborated with the Nazis. These allegations were patent lies – and proven as such. The mistake, with its anti-semitic echoes, caused world-wide indignation, with Western Communist papers publicly rebuking *Izvestia*. The Moscow paper has never retracted its false denunciation of Hájek – nor, of course, has *Neues Deutschland* which slavishly reprinted it.

It is only in a rare moment of acute personal or official crisis that the outside world glimpses the thoughts and emotions of the bureaucrats working in one of the myriad subsections of a national censorship institution. The deputy chief of the second subsection of *Glavlit*, the Soviet censorship office, a forty-eight year-old man called Andrei Sokolov was the central figure of a celebrated episode which could have happened only under a totalitarian system. Sokolov's story conveys the flavour of a system which has only become bearable for the individual through a curious mixture of inefficiency, corruption and sheer bungling.

Comrade Sokolov worked for fifteen years in the department which has to examine all foreign printed matter. As imported books are subject to censorship and as many books of the most popular Russian writers are unavailable, or have never been printed at all, novels or poems by Bulgakov, Hemingway and Kafka are highly-prized items on the semi-illegal black market. The equivalent of up to half a month's salary can be asked and received for a book which is in demand. Publications smuggled into the country, for example Solzhenitsyn's books in the original, are even more expensive and it takes longer to get hold of them. But, like everything in the so-called socialist states, it is all a question of money and connections.

Sokolov's department had confiscated thousands of books over the years, stamping them 'to be destroyed'. In the meantime more and more books turned up on the black market; in one instance a university professor bought from a street vendor the very same books which had been confiscated from him a few months earlier. The unusually large turnover on the black market engendered suspicions, which finally led to the unmasking of Comrade Sokolov. The material he classified 'for destruction', he later channelled, through middle-men, to the black market. With the proceeds, he managed to have two flats in Moscow, to keep two women, fly several times every year to the Black Sea for a vacation, and in general to live at a level few Soviet citizens can afford. In a secret trial Sokolov was sentenced to seven years forced labour, a sentence generally regarded as extremely mild and probably influenced by his 'past services'. The chief of the second department was sacked for 'lack of vigilance'. Such cases are naturally never reported in the Soviet press, since any information relating to censorship itself, its organisation and working methods is a state secret. But the Sokolov affair had such dimensions and produced such widespread repercussions that the details became known in dissident and press circles.[74]

The case of the Polish chief censor Lazebnik was of a totally different character. It was not the greed for money, but the general upsurge of demands for press freedom during the high point of the post-Stalin 'thaw', after the Poznan riots and before the 'Polish October; which undermined the sense of discipline and mission among the Polish censors in the summer of 1956. They undertook an initiative unprecedented in the annals of the Communist-controlled mass media. Infected by the dynamics of the de-Stalinisation campaign, the Polish censors voted for a resolution urging their own dissolution as an institution. With tears in his eyes chief censor Lazebnik read the motion aloud at a stormy meeting of journalists in Warsaw.[75]

However, as we have seen, the institution is still, two decades later, highly active. The chief censor was sacked soon after his emotional public self-criticism – but the censorship is as powerful as ever. One of the wittiest Polish columnists, Stefan Kisielewski, who normally writes for the Cracow-based Catholic weekly *Tygodnik Powszechne*, observed that 'censorship is a preventive and protective activity, employed by the state with precaution and precision, using all the means at its disposal'. And, in a bitter outburst: 'Censorship ruined my life, made it intolerable. It prevented me from becoming a political commentator, which is my profession. Censorship falsified, twisted, corrupted ninety percent of what I have written.'

Where was this indictment published? Not, of course, in the Cracow weekly – but in a quarterly opposition review, called *Zapis*, which publishes works of Polish authors either eliminated by, or not even submitted to, censorship. One of the most baffling features of the current Polish situation is the blossoming of some thirty typewritten or mimeographed publications, which began to appear during the past four or five years. Their circulation is estimated at 40,000 copies, less than 0.1 percent of the total for all publications in Poland. They are different from the Russian type *Samizdat* (literally self-publishing) publications, written, produced and distributed furtively. It is rather an opposition press beyond the grasp of the censorship, representing various strands of the Polish intelligentsia ranging from Marxist and liberal left to Catholic and nationalistically-minded groups, with specialised publications also appearing to cater for students, farmers and the workers. The name and address of the Publisher or the Editorial Board is invariably given in the publication. Needless to say, these opposition organs are not printed or produced in many thousands of copies. They appear irregularly and their size also varies considerably. Their tenuous existence depends on the general political climate, the balance of forces and the survival of the present weak, discredited, and at the same time relatively moderate leadership, at the time of this writing headed by Edward Gierek.

The same is true of the activities of various opposition groups. Their most prominent spokesmen are from time to time arrested, beaten up or harassed in different ways. The secret police know the location of the mimeograph machines and the editorial offices of these opposition sheets as well as the addresses and movements of most leading dissidents. It is beyond the scope of this study to deal with the deeper reasons behind the different methods applied by the Polish and the Czechoslovak régimes in dealing with intellectual dissidents. Evidently, the combined fear of the Catholic Church and of the working class, which toppled the leadership in 1956, 1970 and 1980 and twice (in 1970 ad 1976) humiliated the party by forcing it to abandon price increases, together with the ever-present possibility of a Soviet intervention, have produced a political atmosphere which allows – temporarily at least – the operation of such groups. Always provided they remain within limits judged by the authorities to be politically bearable and avoid confrontation with the régime.

But such toleration can be reversed at any time, the machinery of censorship, like the secret police themselves, is ready if and when more rigour is needed.

The most deadly revelations about the Polish censorship were provided by Tomasz Stryzewski, who defected to Sweden at the end of 1977 taking with him 600 pages of priceless documents. Stryzewski was the first censor from a Communist country to flee to the West. The documents, he smuggled out were almost immediately smuggled back to

Poland where some seventy pages of highly secret 'Directives' and 'Recommendations' periodically issued by the chief censors were published by the opposition Social Self-Defence Committee. Later all the documents were printed in Polish in two volumes in London. The subsequent direct quotations are from the original documents whose authenticity the régime has not even tried to deny.[76] As noted by Leo Labedz, the astute observer of the East European scene, the documents for the 1974–76 period show that there is no room in an elaborate totalitarian censorship of the Polish type for a Lamoignon de Malesherbes. The French liberal chief censor between 1750–53 advised the King 'to seek remedy not in severity but in tolerance'. The Polish censors evidently cannot adopt Malesherbes' further advice: 'Tolerate many small abuses in order to avoid the larger ones.'

The material available consists of various directives issued by the Central Office of Press, Publications and Spectacles Control (COPPSC). Most important are the 'Directives and Recommendations' which contain all the regulations, including the new ones that are added each day in the form of 'notes of information'. These include all new items to be kept out of the media, warnings on current issues and cancellations of old regulations that are no longer in effect. There are other publications, all in different colours, such as the fortnightly *Informations* in red, reproducing censored texts, quarterly *Bulletins* (brown) describing 'main tendencies in the material withdrawn from all the mass media in the country' during quarterly periods. A special bulletin (yellow) deals with censored material from the Catholic press. They also provide statistics on the censors' interventions and the amount of material partly or fully withdrawn. The readers are unaware of the cuts because every newspaper has an iron reserve of non-political or absolutely safe editorial material ready at all times to replace any text deleted by censorship.

Consider first the statistics for overall interventions. The fortnightly *Information*, marked as 'confidential' ZL-051/10/74 of May 1974 provides the following statistics:

Time	Number of interventions	Number of items eliminated
March 1–15	616	125
March 15–31	620	57
April 1–15	463	44
April 15–30	531	57
May 1–15	584	63

Then follows a separate statistical break-down on the subjects concerned: a hint of plan fulfilment by the censors!

Subjects	Number of interventions Period 1–15 May 1974	In %
Social-political	268	45.9
Social-economic	85	14.6
Cultural-historic	70	11.9
Religious	36	6.2
Total	459	
Protection of state secrets	125	12.4
Grand Total	584	100.0

Five articles which were negative and satirical in their criticism of the television programmes [with the names of the papers also listed].

Considerable cuts were made in sixteen articles dealing with environmental problems. Information about the pollution of the air, earth and water, about the growing ecological damages, the wrong location of industrial plants which would accelerate the pollution process, the direct endangering of human health and the irreversibility of the damages, have been deleted.

The close picture of how the mechanism of totalitarian communications control works is composed of innumerable and profoundly characteristic details. They allow an insight into the assessment of the popular mood by the censors and also indicate the enormous range of subjects affected by censorship. These vary from obituaries and marriage announcements to the annual coffee consumption and river pollution, from licence agreements to the blacklisting of the Polish-born political scientist Zbigniew Brzezinski (along with many other persons he 'may not be mentioned in any way'). The instruction concerning Brzezinski was immediately cancelled when he was named President Carter's National Security Advisor.

The following verbatim quotes may give the flavour of the directives, but it is important to remember that they represent only a small fraction of the actual instructions:

In school No. 80 in Gdansk a harmful substance emitted by the putty used to seal the windows was noticed. The school has been temporarily closed. No information whatsoever may be published about this subject.

All global figures on labour hygiene and accidents in the sectors and branches of the economy are to be withheld.

Information about the endangering of life and health of human beings caused through ˙chemicals used in industry and farming have to be deleted.

Banned is all information about food poisoning and epidemics affecting larger groups of people and especially in important plants, furthermore food poisoning in factory canteens, holiday centres, summer colonies.

Information and descriptions with instructive character should be eliminated from materials about thefts, burglaries, plane hijacking and other terror outrages. *This directive is also to be applied to strikes*, forms and methods of their organisation [Italics in the original].

All obituaries, advertisements and announcements about meetings in cemeteries, at monuments and memorial sites planned by former soldiers of the Home Army and other right-wing organisations which participated in the Warsaw Uprising are to be withheld.

Without consultation with the direction of COPPSC no criticism of the Article 13 of the Customs Law, nor of the relevant activity of the customs offices (confiscating some foreign parcels with books, periodicals, etc) is allowed. Same ban to be applied on criticism of the Polish Post Office for not delivering such shipments to Polish recipients.

There should be no disclosure about the pollution of rivers flowing from Czechoslovakia, if the pollution is caused by economic activity on our territory. On the other hand, information about the pollution of these rivers can be released if this is caused by economic activity on Czechoslovak territory.

A book by Adam Schaff on *Structuralism* will be published by Ksiaska i Wiedza, publishing house. All reviews and comments must be cleared with the COPPSC before publication.

Concerning the death of Antonin Slonimski [one of the greatest Polish poets – P.L.] the press may publish only the communiques of PAP; one daily may publish the obituary signed by the Minister of Culture and only one official commentary. The literary press will publish only articles authorised by the Central Committee and all editorial reminiscences and commentaries must be approved by the Central Committee.

No information is to be disclosed about the special pensions granted by the Prime Minister to certain persons.

No information should be published about the corruption affair in Sandomierz.

No information may be published about the additional purchase of potatoes [at prices set by the state – P.L.] which are intended for export.

No reference concerning the sale of meat by Poland to the Soviet Union is allowed.

No criticism of Soviet oil drilling equipment used in exploration in Poland may be published. Any reference to suggestions of purchase of such material from other foreign sources must be eliminated.

No information, written in an approving, tolerant, understanding tone about hippies in Poland may be published. Only unequivocally critical references are allowed.

No information should be published about the annual coffee consumption in our country, in order to eliminate all possibilities of calculating the amount of coffee which is re-exported.

All criticism of income and social policies, including wage claims, is forbidden. This also refers to social services such as pensions, grants, leaves of absence, health care, etc.

These are some of the most revealing instructions from a much longer list of prohibitions and recommendations concerning the domestic scene. The items prohibited formally mention such seemingly trivial ones as the five prizes awarded by the Polish Pen Club, reviews of thirteen selected films or the names of twenty-eight intellectuals, ranging from architects and mathematicians to chemists and art historians.

The central censorship office receives a detailed list of guidelines from the party leadership every week. But the tasks of the censors include many trivialities. For example: on 14 October 1975 a certain Tadeusz Ratajski, the vice president of the central office, wrote to the censors that no decision had yet been made as to whether 9 May should be a holiday and that therefore in the 1975 calendars, the words 'Victory Day' next to 9 May *may be* printed in red. Three days later a coded telegram was sent to the censors instructing that the printing of the words 'The Thirtieth Anniversary of the Victory over Fascism' in red was now *obligatory*.

The chief target however was evidently the church with all favourable references to religion being banned. One censor, for example, suggested that a Polish Catholic journal should replace the phrase 'All men are sinful' by 'We Catholics are sinful.' Again, 'No information must be published on demands for construction or renovation of churches and chapels.'

Another vast field affected by the censor's trade consists of matters relating to foreign countries, above all to the Soviet Union and the rest of the bloc. The instructions reveal an almost desperate anxiety not to displease the Soviets:

> In reports of the Polish Exhibition staged in Moscow on account of the thirtieth anniversary of the Polish People's Republic, one should avoid expressing excessive satisfaction with the successes of particular exhibitors, since this may suggest that some Polish products created a furor in Moscow and were not previously known on the Soviet market.
>
> Information concerning price changes of some goods must be deleted from all materials concerning the protocol signed in Moscow about next year's trade exchanges and payments arrangements.
>
> Information concerning Comecon must be free of any criticism of the usefulness and the principle of co-operation among socialist countries or of indications of divergencies of opinion among the member countries. No criticism of the standpoint of any members may be permitted.
>
> All information about Romania's initiative with regard to membership in the movement of non-aligned states is forbidden.

The censorship office also carefully and characteristically outlined the way in which references to the Katyń massacre, the murder of 15,000 Polish officers in 1940 by the Soviet secret police, were to be treated. No one in Poland, or among serious and impartial historians in the West, has any doubts about the responsibility for this massacre which Stalin and the Great Soviet Encyclopedia attributed to the Germans. But the directives of COPPSC repeated the few lines in the Soviet reference work about Katyń, and continued, 'The former practice consisted of the elimination of all references to Katyń as a place where Polish officers were killed during World War II'. But, the latest instruction added, information corresponding exactly to the interpretation given in the Soviet Encyclopedia, may be permitted, Vice-President Ratajski nevertheless qualifies this with the ominous advice that: 'it would not be advisable to treat the Katyń case extensively in historical works, let alone in the press.'

This was the last straw for thirty-two-year-old Tomasz Stryzewski. In an interview given in Sweden after his defection, he related that his own grandfather, a Captain in the Polish Army, had been among the victims, and as a censor in Cracow he had to make certain that the list of the victims was never published in Poland. Thus, the tragic family involvement of a Polish bureaucrat with the great taboo of Polish-Soviet relations led to sensational revelations about censorship, the abolition of which became a key demand during the upheaval in the summer of 1980.

There is no reason to think that, if a Soviet, or Romanian, or Czech censor should defect, his revelations would be very different from those made by Stryzewski. The Polish system was originally based on the Soviet pattern and as the Soviet media in general are visibly much more tightly controlled than the Polish press, there is no reason whatsoever to regard the revelations of Stryzewski as something uniquely Polish.

As a foreign correspondent in Warsaw pointed out, the revelations of the censors' directives and the narrow limits to free expression engender a certain respect for the local newsmen who often manage to write interesting and even critical pieces. And few, if any, observers would prefer the Bucharest papers to those in Warsaw, even though Romania formally abolished censorship in 1977!

In one of his periodic bursts of hectic activity, President Ceauşescu, perhaps spurred on by the repercussions of the Goma affair and its echo in the West, announced with great aplomb at a writer's conference in the summer of 1979 that censorship would henceforth be abolished and replaced by self-administration and control in publishing. *Scînteia* praised the decision as a search for 'new democratic forms'. The Committee for Press and Printed Matter, the censorship institution, was formally dissolved. The former censors however entered the new managing councils of newspapers, publishing houses and theatres and the previous chief of the censorship office became secretary of state at the Council for Socialist Culture and Education. It is in fact the council which now acts as the supreme censorship body in fact if not in name, with political and ideological responsibility for publication, imports and control of the 'lists of data and information supplied to papers which according to law are not permitted to be printed.' The council has also the power to confiscate the offending issues prior to legal proceedings, to allocate paper, to appoint journalists and to control their activity.[77]

A year later an assistant professor and representative of the younger generation of Romanian writers, Ion Coja, challenged the official line with almost suicidal candour, and ripped off the velvet glove concealing the iron fist. Speaking at a literary conference in Cluj in May 1978, he quoted comparative figures about the publication of books per head of the population in Eastern Europe, concluding that on that basis even Albania printed more books than Romania. He concluded:

Romania is today by and large the most backward country in Europe as far as its book output is concerned. On the other hand, we occupy the first place in Europe, if one takes the number of written and unpublished books. Similarly dramatic is the situation with regard to theatre plays. I know of more unperformed plays of my colleagues than of those which were produced on the stage. Even sadder is the fact that the not-produced plays are not only greater in number but also better than those performed.

. . . and now to the second general issue: to the censorship. It was abolished a year ago. This is what the Secretary General of the party decided. I ask those present here who have the opportunity, to inform the party leadership, that the censorship in Romania has not been abolished, but on the contrary has become even more stupid. Out of fear, over-eagerness, or as a consequence of the incompetence of those people who are paid to carry out the policy of the party in the literary field? I do not know.[78]

It is something of a miracle that this speech was published, even if only in the very small circulation monthly of the Writers' Union. Though George Macovescu, President of the Writers' Union since 1977, and a former Foreign Minister, promised that all the statements and papers presented at the Cluj conference would be printed in full, warnings by Hungarian and Romanian literary figures against excessive nationalism were not allowed to be reproduced. A footnote in small print informed the readers that it was not regarded as right to print statements going beyond the 'strictly literary character of the gathering'. It was also significant that the double issue for July-August only appeared in October, that is, five months after the conference. The attack by the literary critic and playwright on censorship practices was probably published as a concession in exchange for deleting the most controversial references to the (officially 'long resolved') national question. Furthermore Coja cleverly combined his outburst with a party-minded, albeit ambiguous, declaration:

> . . . we writers are those who apply the party line in literature. And one should take note, that the censorship already functions, functions well – in our brain. In our consciousness. A censorship which no one can ever abolish.[79]

If one accepts the definition of censorship as 'the process whereby restrictions are imposed upon the collection, dissemination and exchange of information, opinion and ideas'[80] by a governmental or party authority by means of obligatory pre-publication notification of a special office, then there is no censorship in neighbouring Hungary. The direction and control of the printed and broadcast media, as well as that of the arts, is based on the credo spelled out by Ion Coja; on a well-functioning system of self-censorship.

Thus the man ultimately in charge of the entire publishing and ideological sector, György Aczél, Deputy Premier and Politbureau member, could claim in a recent address to party activists that in Hungary, 'the creative workshops are independent', and that editors 'do not need any kind of special resolution' 'to be able to decide whether something should be published or not.' How could someone acquire authority for himself if he cannot or dares not decide to accept the consequences of his decision? 'It is well known that there is no censorship in Hungary. But the directors of the publishing houses, the editors of the papers and the chiefs of film studios who enjoy the confidence of the party, state and people have also their moral and material responsibility.' In other words, it is up to those 'responsible' persons in charge of publishing to strike a balance in every case between granting what Aczél called 'creative freedom' and the 'correct use of the right to decide'.[81]

In reality of course, the mechanism of self-censorship is already in motion before the material even reaches the editors or reviewers of manuscripts. A Hungarian underground publication with the title of *Profile* published in a typescript of 1,000 pages extracts from the manuscripts submitted by thirty-four different authors in the previous ten years and rejected by the various periodicals. The title was taken from the customary rejection formula used by the publishers: 'Your contribution is not in accordance with our profile. . . .' Privately, the explanations offered also contained such hints as 'your article is interesting, but publication at this particular moment might endanger the fate of an even more important book or essay.' An examination of the manuscripts indicates that the subjects ranged from anything remotely critical of the Soviet Union – for example the hair-raising reminiscences of a former Hungarian prisoner of war in Russia – to a penetrating study of urban poverty in Budapest and a fascinating interview with 'a high-class prostitute' supposedly a species extinct in a society which calls itself socialist.[82]

It would however be misleading to assume on the basis of this volume that the Hungarian press, above all the weeklies and sociological and literary monthlies, are as monotonous as the media of other Soviet bloc countries. Except for certain taboos (the Soviet factor, the party dictatorship, personalities) articles and essays deal with many burning issues, from alcoholism and juvenile delinquency to Jehovah's witnesses and the strength of religious feelings. In writing about such subjects, the journals do not confine themselves to individual examples and case histories, but make use of statistics which give an overall picture and would certainly be banned by the Polish censors.

This appearance of freedom is the reason why the editor of

the short stories and essays published in *Profile* stressed the 'subtle mechanism of censorship': the reliance on 'self-censorship through blackmail'. Or what another dissident intellectual, in a comment on a British debate on censorship, called 'the mythology of personal responsibility [i.e. self-censorship] supported by an all-pervading paternalism' of the state. He even went so far as to prefer the existence of 'a theoretically controllable, reasonably precise criteria' to the Hungarian situation which in the final analysis leads to 'an unlimited, uncontrollable censorship.' Talking to Hungarian intellectuals who share this view, one has a sense of *déja vu*, an echo of the language of the 'New Left' in Germany, France and the US in the late sixties and perhaps early seventies, of Marcuse's scathing account of the 'repressive tolerance' of bourgeois liberal societies.

Under such a sophisticated system of 'persuasion', informal constraints acquire a great importance and the tendency to eliminate in advance passages likely to be crossed out by the editor may operate more efficiently, from the official point of view, than clumsy repression. A high degree of repression could in fact be regarded as a measure of failure in a totalitarian system. The main danger seen by the leftist intelligentsia in Budapest is apparently that the intellectuals may have come to *want*, or at the very least to accept, what they have.[83]

The tacit compromise in Hungary has so far not been placed in jeopardy because in some way even most dissident intellectuals have been absorbed by the prevailing *laissez faire* atmosphere. There are, for example, a handful of writers and essayists whose works have appeared in the underground publications, but who have nevertheless had less controversial works published through the normal channels. Aczél's personal role in keeping the channels of communication open to virtually every critical intellectual should also be stressed. The main argument, repeated and whispered in countless variations, is that any attempt to go beyond politically safe limits would provoke both the Russians and the domestic hardliners, endangering the very substance of Kádár's middle-of-the-road policy, which is the maximum Hungary can hope for under its international and geographical circumstances.

When all attempts to keep the lid on fail, two other tactics (also used elsewhere) are brought into play: a controversial work can be delayed, or published in a relatively small edition. Thus 30,000 copies of a collection of essays by Hungary's greatest living poet, Gyula Illyés, now aged seventy-seven, were produced in 1978, but distribution was stopped and at the time of writing, eighteen months later, there is still no sign of publication. The paperback includes hitherto unpublished works on the sensitive subject of the tragic fate of the Hungarians in neighbouring Czechoslovakia and Romania. Though the party leaders deeply respect Illyés, they seek to control the pressure of public opinion, an effort not made easier by the blatant discrimination to which Hungarians are subjected in Romania.

This is in fact one of the major bones of contention between many intellectuals and the Hungarian leadership. 'Informal constraints' and self-censorship are therefore very much in evidence in the field of relations with neighbouring countries. Consider, for example, the publication of a two-part series by Illyés about the Hungarian nation and the treatment of minorities in the Budapest daily, *Magyar Nemzet*. Although Romania was not mentioned, the inference was clear. Illyés was rudely attacked in a Romanian paper by a leading party official. His response, a cautiously worded article, was, however, vetoed by the Hungarian leadership. Instead, a Communist historian defended the great poet and gently rebuked the Romanian critic in the party paper in Budapest. In other words, not even this outstanding literary figure can do or write what he wants if important state interests are at stake. It is the 'paternalistic' Politbureau which decides the best way to defuse an international controversy.

This leads us to the subject, everywhere taboo, of controversies and conflicts between ruling Communist parties. It is not only the Polish censorship which, as we have seen, bans references to differences of opinion among Comecon member states. It is for this reason that economic conferences, even relatively unimportant and specialised ones discussing, say, what kind of paper-making machinery or marine engines should be primarily manufactured in which country, are shrouded in secrecy. Disputes about the location of an aluminium plant, a rolling mill or interest on investment

credits become fateful issues simply because countries that
call themselves fraternal cannot confess selfishness and profit-
seeking at the expense of another partner. Can a Communist
country be imperialistic? Can territorial disputes make
enemies of two Communist countries? Can a Communist
state discriminate against a national minority associated with
another country? All this is inconceivable, yet it continually
happens, not only between the Soviet Union and the small
countries but also among the smaller Communist states
themselves. As all Communist countries are, by definition,
'brothers', they must conceal differences that would be
considered perfectly natural among non-Communist countries.

Once a ruling party refuses to recognise that there is only
one centre authorised to define the 'universal' truth and the
vital interests in any situation and at any given moment
ideology ceases to become a binding element and becomes a
factor that makes action and compromise more and more
difficult. It also becomes, increasingly, a fig leaf, for the
'brothers' must hide the recurring conflicts among themselves
under ideological formulas.

At the same time, the ruling parties never really explain the
roots of past public disputes or the reasons for a new
reconciliation to their subjects, who must profess unshakeable faith in the infallibility of the leadership. This in turn
pollutes the political climate, both within the country and in
its relations with its neighbours. By pushing the real issues
below the surface instead of dealing with their causes, Soviet
domination and Communism have erected new barriers
rather than dismantling the old ones. Aside from the issues of
black marketeering, speculation in the guise of tourism and
mutual exploitation of the unrealistic exchange rates of non-
convertible Eastern currencies, the East Europeans are sepa-
rated from one another more than ever by a curtain of mutual
ignorance, envy and suspicion. This is a direct consequence of
the tight supervision of reporting about other Communist
countries and the changes in their foreign and domestic
policies. Relations with Yugoslavia constitute, as ever, a
touchstone for the willingness and ability of the East European parties to face up to past sins. The censoring of Tito's

speeches and other incidents related earlier show that the exchange of visits and anniversary articles, as well as other friendly gestures are merely political tactics. In theory, at any rate according to the still valid party programme of the CSSU adopted in 1961, 'the programme of the League of Communists of Yugoslavia is the fullest embodiment of the ideology of revisionism.' None of the attacks against Yugoslavia in the Soviet reference books have ever been officially revoked. Since the issue has not been dealt with in Moscow, every ten years the Hungarian press publishes long pieces about the merits of Rajk and his comrades, hanged in 1949 as 'traitors in the pay of Tito's gang and the imperialists', and subsequently rehabilitated without any explanation of the real background to the purges in Eastern Europe, which were ordered and directed by Stalin and his henchmen.

Such constraints also affect the media in Yugoslavia. However, it must be stressed that in Yugoslavia no authority has the right to prejudge media content and apply prior censorship. Only after the publication of an article is prosecution possible. The decision to ban an issue can only be taken by the courts.

As mentioned earlier, the guidance of the Yugoslav media is based on the selection of 'politically responsible' editors and the replacement of those who at one time or another have been guilty of 'separatist', 'great nationalistic', 'anarcholiberal' or 'technocratic' deviations. There has however always been an exception throughout Yugoslavia's post-war history, namely the control from above over foreign news reporting if it relates to the Soviet Union and the bloc on the one hand, or the non-aligned countries on the other.

For example, as soon as relations with Czechoslovakia began to improve after the 1968 invasion, press reporting of what was really going on in Prague became muted, and subsequently non-existent. News coverage is an integral part of Yugoslavia's foreign policy vis-à-vis the Soviet bloc. As the latest Press Law and the 1974 Constitution specifically spell out that 'the endangering of friendly relations' with other countries is a cause for legal intervention, there is great scope for arbitrary interpretation. No Yugoslav paper has, to the knowledge of this author, ever been confiscated because of senseless, exaggerated reporting about the resurgence of 'neo-Nazism in West Germany', 'in Carinthia' or of 'neo-Fascism in Italy' (campaigns that were in tune with perceived Yugoslav interests). But the Zagreb District Court, in 1973, banned an issue of *Glas Koncila* because 'texts published in the issue could have adversely affected relations with Czechoslovakia and Romania.' In other words, the Zagreb Catholic paper dared to print the truth about the repression of religious activities in both countries. In 1978 the *Studentski List*, the Croatian student newspaper, was banned because it reprinted an article from *Le Monde Diplomatique* which 'could have harmed good relations between Romania and Yugoslavia'.

There is certainly a *de facto*, if not *de jure*, censorship concerning articles about Romania in general and about Czechoslovakia when relations with the latter are not too bad. As Romania is a close ally in the fight for autonomy and independence, and in the blocking of Soviet expansionist aspirations, and as Tito and Ceauşescu regularly met once or twice every year, there can be no question of writing anything remotely resembling a truthful account of the ally's internal situation. Things stand of course completely differently when it comes to Bulgaria. As the Balkan neighbour impudently refuses to recognise a Macedonian minority in the Pirin area and as it is not willing to accept the Yugoslav-Macedonian version of history, the Sofia leadership is not only suspected of territorial ambitions and expansionist dreams, it is also, according to the Yugoslav line, incapable of raising the standard of living and is faced with a very difficult economic situation. Though the real economic situation and living conditions in Romania are probably even worse than in Bulgaria, a similar comment about the policies of the Bucharest Government would be inconceivable in a leading Yugoslav daily or weekly. And when such an 'unfriendly piece' appears in 'marginal' religious or student publications, the issue is immediately banned. A classic case of double standards applied by the same journalists who like to lecture to the rest of the world on how to be 'objective' and 'constructive' in reporting on Yugoslavia itself.

Nevertheless, banning on account of foreign news reporting is relatively rare. Recently, *Vjesnik*, the Zagreb party daily, published a revealing record of confiscations on the basis of court judgments between 1969–79.[84] In this period, thirty newspapers were banned in the Republic of Croatia (the rest of Yugoslavia is ignored in the article). Twelve of the cases occurred during the tense period of national conflict in 1971, with nine of the judgments proclaimed before the purge of the national-minded leadership of the republican party had been carried out. The measures were applied to periodicals, calendars, etc. In 1974 *Studentski List*, the student paper, was banned. The reason was its support for the eight Professors at Belgrade University who were suspended in flagrant violation of the self-management rules. A popular magazine was banned because of a piece on homosexuals on Lesbos. In 1976 a serious periodical published by the mass organisation Socialist Alliance was banned because of a study of a large petrochemical complex, involving foreign partners, which raised ecological and economic questions. The court found that some of the facts quoted were 'economic secrets'. Apart from the confiscation over foreign reporting, the last ban on the student paper was pronounced because of an article about believers and polemicising against the banning of a book by a Belgrade court.

Interesting and revealing was the casual remark, made by the author of the *Vjesnik* piece, that the large proportion of youth papers banned was probably due to the 'inexperience of the editors'. Nevertheless the harassment and prosecution of Milovan Djilas and two other writers for publishing an 'illegal' mimeographed literary magazine called *Časovnik* (in about 800 copies of 200 pages) consisting exclusively of short stories and poems in the autumn of 1979, proves that while the Yugoslavs may hear, see and read an incomparably greater variety of news and opinions than the citizens in any other Communist state, the régime is as far as ever from anything resembling a constitutional government.[85]

Regardless of the forms and severity of censorship in Eastern Europe, the fate of individual journalists and newspapers time and again reminds the observer that 'the Stalinist political mind did not die with Stalin'. How could it, in movements whose leading personnel, not only in the Soviet Union itself, had been schooled in the 'Stalinist view of things' for a generation?[86] Within many East European, even Yugoslav, functionaries there lurks, consciously or subconsciously, a little Stalinist. They should reread the famous and far too quickly forgotten poem written by Yevtushenko in 1962: 'We carried him out of the Mausoleum. But who will carry Stalin out of the heirs of Stalin?'

Few people in the West know that – after foreign trips – it is not a car or a weekend house, but the regular access to information which is the greatest privilege in every single Communist country. As we have seen, the local press has very little to offer in the way of hard news. Information is a privilege, the amount and the kind of information one gets depends on rank and influence.

The following account of how the processing and distribution of the confidential press is structured and run may sound bizarre, even improbable, to a Western reader, accustomed to Western papers, TV and radio. Yet, east of the Elbe the production of confidential bulletins, accessible only to élite groups, is a routine matter, stemming as does so much else from the Soviet practice under Stalin. It is startling to observe how little the eerie world of special confidential bulletins has changed since 1949–51 when the author, as a young shift editor at MTI, had to select news for general distribution and for the confidential bulletins. Perhaps even more surprising is the discovery, made during the preparations for this study, that basically the same system is practised in all Soviet bloc countries. All that has changed is the technical side. Western broadcasts are no longer taken down in short-hand by translators as was the practice in the late 1940s and early 1950s, but are taped enabling translations to be prepared better and more rapidly.

A story related by a senior editor of a major Western news agency may serve as an introduction to the system. Some time ago two young journalists from an East European country visited him in his office. They wanted to collect information about the working methods of his agency. At the end of the conversation, the visitors asked their host whether they could pose an 'indiscreet question': 'If you don't want to answer, don't, we shall not be hurt'. His curiosity aroused, the editor told them to go ahead. 'What are your selection criteria for the news disseminated for the public at large, and the confidential information supplied only to the authorities?' asked the two East Europeans. When they were told that there is no such selection process at all, that the ministries, public authorities, banks, newspapers of every persuasion and the private subscribers receive exactly the same news items, they were stunned. The idea that the 'broad masses' are allowed access to the same type of information as the élite groups, seemed to them almost unbelievable;[87] so deeply imbued had they become with the system of confidential bulletins provided to what the Soviets call the *nomenclature*, the upper layers of the Communist élite in all branches of administration and economy.[88]

The compilation of special bulletins, containing full and unbiased information on world events, is perhaps the most important task allotted to the central news agencies in the Communist countries. Production and distribution is concentrated in a special department where everyone from managing editor to sub-editors deals solely with the preparation of the various editions of the mimeographed bulletins. The 'confidential desk' relies on news from the Western agencies, the Western press and the monitoring of Western broadcasts, in short all items the shift-editor does not approve for the general news wire.

This is however only one major source for the bulletin. Increasingly important are the special dispatches sent by the agency or newspaper correspondents abroad. Many people wonder what the numerous TASS and *Novosti* correspondents in the various Western capitals actually do when the Soviet press carries only sparse information about the countries concerned. There are, for example, currently seven permanent Soviet correspondents stationed in Vienna as well as representatives of all the major eastern bloc news agencies, not to mention a plethora of press attachés and the staff of various press bureaus. But one finds few items under a Vienna dateline in the eastern press. The same disproportion between the number of reporters and the amount of news published is also evident in the Soviet coverage of the US. In addition to the TASS bureau in Washington DC and New York, there are no fewer than a dozen editors working in the American department of TASS alone.[89]

All these people posing as journalists are, contrary to widespread beliefs, not spies (although many of them do operate also as full or part-time agents for their respective security services), but work primarily for the confidential bulletins. They transmit not just news reports, but also summaries of important articles from the local press often with a brief evaluation. At important press conferences with Premiers or Ministers, Soviet correspondents busily take notes or tape the entire session for the confidential bulletins.

A process of filtering and censorship is also applied to the distribution of this classified material. Before the war, a system of classifying the special TASS reports by colour was introduced in Russia. Thus in the Soviet Union the fairly innocuous foreign news, devoid of any overt anti-Soviet material, is available in the 'green' and 'blue' TASS reports to a relatively large category of recipients. The 'white TASS' contains much more complete information on what is going on in the world, including occasional news on difficulties or opposition in the various Communist countries. The 'red TASS' is even more confidential and goes to a much more select group, including only the editors-in-chief, ministers and their deputies, first secretaries of regional party committees and high-ranking officers in the army and the secret services. There is also a fourth, top secret, category about which no reliable information is available.[91]

As a tradition and a matter of courtesy, the East European ambassadors in Moscow regularly receive the 'white TASS'. The irascible Veljko Mičunović, twice Yugoslav Ambassador in Moscow, relates in his candid memoirs, how the confidential TASS bulletin once carried an American news report about alleged US aid commitments for Yugoslavia. He suspected (probably not without reason) that the story was 'leaked' by the Russians themselves and republished in the special bulletin in order to prepare the leading cadres for yet another policy shift vis-à-vis Yugoslavia.[92]

The danger of manipulation is as real as the power of those in charge of the Agit-Prop departments, who control the content and the distribution lists for each category of bulletin. The point is that the allocation of information is traditionally regarded by the Communist leadership as a vital political issue. Access to 'confidential information' is one of the most significant characteristics of membership in a privileged group. If we accept the estimate that the total of Soviet 'élite personnel' (including responsible full-time party, Komsomol, union and state officials, enterprise managers, the military, police, diplomatic service and prominent artists, intellectuals and scientists) in the early 1970s stood at about 227,000 (or one in just over every 500 employed), and that no more than 1,000 to 1,500 copies of the most confidential TASS bulletins (white and red) are produced,[93] we get a fairly good idea of just how important a privilege is access to sensitive information. As a Soviet colleague once put it to me: 'It's easier to get a *dacha* or a chauffeur-driven car than the 'red TASS'!

Fortunately we have even more detailed information on the system of special bulletins in the smaller East European countries, and there is reason to believe that it is much the same as in the Soviet Union. To start with, depending on the country, there are from six to ten different bulletins. Colours vary from country to country. For example, in Romania the most confidential bulletin has a yellow marking, while the red *Agerpress* bulletin goes to a wider circle and the green bulletin contains mainly economic articles. In Hungary the daily MTI 'special' has a red stripe, while the so-called 'C' or collection of articles, is produced three times a week with a green cover.

In the context of Soviet and East European societies, privileges, including access to information, are allocated on a strictly hierarchical scale. In this supposedly classless society, there are the following main layers: 'Royalty' that is the Politbureau members and Central Committee secretaries; next comes a kind of upper class consisting of ministers, secretaries of state, departmental chiefs at the Central Committee, first secretaries of city and provincial party committees, editors-in-chief of central papers and some important weeklies, high ranking general staff and police officers, senior departmental heads at the Foreign Ministry, a select group of top scientists and the directors general of a handful of state banks. Well-informed sources estimate that the 'red bulletins'

in Hungary, Romania and Czechoslovakia, the 'BTA summary' in Bulgaria and the 'white PAP' in Poland are each
received by only a few hundred recipients.[94] The next, much
more numerous group, may be called the middle class and
comprises several thousand people in each country. They
consist of middle-level *apparatchiks* in the party, state and
mass organisation apparatus, responsible scientific and editorial personnel, enterprise managers, etc. It must also be
remembered that there are also specialised publications with
restricted circulations, prepared either by the agencies or
various institutes, and devoted to economics, science, and
other subjects.

The way in which the distribution and the security aspect
are handled in each country also reflects the political climate.
In Hungary in Stalin's day, for example, the recipients got
their 'special bulletins' in closed manila envelopes delivered
by an armed courier. A receipt had to be signed and the
recipients were then responsible for secrecy. Within a certain
time limit, the bulletins had to be returned to the MTI. This is
still the practice in the Soviet Union and Romania. In the old
days, translators in Hungary were sacked if they lent a
Western magazine to a friend and could not immediately
produce it in a spot check. Today journalists give such
'subversive' illustrated magazines as *Der Spiegel*, *Time* or
Paris Match to their car mechanic or their hairdresser.

In the easy-going atmosphere of the early 1970s, for
example, MTI once sought to improve its income through a
publicity campaign for its 'C' bulletin containing translations
from the Western press. It is rumoured that in no time
circulation shot up from 1,050 to some 15,000 since every
collective farm chairman or co-operative director regarded
possession of the bulletin as a status symbol. The programme
was later stopped and it is now estimated that the 'green'
bulletin has some 2,200 subscribers. Nevertheless it is reckoned that the daily confidential report or collection of articles
is read by five or more people, so that the actual readership is
considerably larger than this cited figure would indicate.

The Bulgarian correspondent, Vladimir Kostov, noted in
one of his broadcasts, that the several thousand recipients of
the bulletin feel 'that they are judged according to their

merits, that they are privileged in relation to the nation as a whole.' And this feeling was even greater among the few hundred top functionaries: 'The sense of being privileged, of superiority over the rest of the people which is nurtured in these top officials through the glow of special information is very much stronger than that experienced by the several thousand propagandists and middle party cadres'.[95]

Who gets which bulletin depends solely on rank. The first sign a leading functionary gets of having fallen, if not into disfavour, then at least several rungs lower in the hierarchy, is when he receives a 'green' instead of a 'red' or 'blue' bulletin. It could be of course merely a technical mistake but is more likely the prelude to his fall. It is usually the Central Committee secretary in charge of Agit-Prop matters who deletes a name from the most exclusive list. If for example X loses his post as, say, Central Committee secretary and is appointed Minister of Transport, he automatically loses the privilege of receiving the most confidential bulletins. In Romania the control over access to the 'special bulletin' is so tight that even the Foreign Editor of a central daily does not receive the bulletin which contains translations of Western articles about Romania. Such a 'privilege' is reserved only for the Editor-in-Chief. While journalists who speak and read foreign languages are at least able to lay their hands on a Western paper, the average functionary has to rely completely on the 'specials'. This is of course particularly true of the top leadership.

The 'Royalty' at the tip of the pyramid of the élite receives, as do Western statesmen, the dispatches of the diplomatic service and the police reports. But they also get very special typewritten bulletins, at least once, sometimes several times daily, with particularly 'sensitive' material such as Western broadcasts or articles about the Soviet succession problem or a power battle in the leadership of the country concerned. In some cases, the reports are sent only to the dozen-odd Politbureau members. Sticking to the Soviet custom, the East European Ambassadors stationed in each other's capitals also regularly receive the daily 'red' confidential bulletins. The typewritten special reports however are not sent to the 'fraternal' diplomats; not even to the second rank of the élite.

Emigré publications abroad are evidently also regarded as 'extremely dangerous' material. They are purchased both by the Communist correspondents abroad and the press officers at the respective embassies not only for use in the confidential bulletins, but also for evaluation by the various secret services. It is understood that such material, published in separate bulletins, is accessible only to the top leadership and senior officials in the Foreign Ministries. In Hungary, for example, it is Mrs János Kádár, the wife of the first secretary who – working in the government's press office – supervises a monthly 'special bulletin' consisting of articles from Hungarian emigré publications.

In every Communist country, the leaders also receive every day a full monitoring report with extracts from important broadcasts. As all these various bulletins and reports amount to 200 to 300 pages daily, the First Secretary and other busy leaders obviously have no time to scrutinise them in detail. They are handed to special assistants who produce further extracts from the extracts, a process which, as noted by Jiři Pelikán, the former director of Czechoslovak Television, provides ample scope for manipulation. If the *apparat* wants to harm a particular functionary it is enough to drop the remark that Radio Free Europe spoke about him in a very positive way. Many case histories show that nothing can cement the position of a Communist functionary as much as attacks against him by the Western press as a 'hard-liner' and nothing can deal a more deadly blow to the reputation of a senior official than, say, *Der Spiegel* applauding his 'liberal' or 'nationalistic' feelings.

All this underlines the crucial role played by the functionaries in charge of information policy. In the all-pervading atmosphere of a personality cult, over-eager assistance can completely isolate the leader from real life. At the time of the mysterious, and abortive, initiative, launched at the Eleventh Party Congress of the Romanian Communist Party, for the election of Nicolae Ceaușescu as Secretary General for life, the German newspaper *Süddeutsche Zeitung* published a dispatch from Bucharest which noted that not even Stalin had entertained such a bizarre idea. Ceaușescu was not allowed to read such disrespectful remarks. His man in charge of the

Agit-Prop apparatus at the time, Central Committee Secretary Cornel Burtica, reasoned aloud that such a 'nasty piece' would only 'upset' the great leader and instructed the *Agerpress* editor on the spot to exclude the Romanian translations of the German article from the 'very special bulletin' prepared for Ceauşescu on the international coverage of the congress. This was seen as a particularly ominous sign by some highly-placed Romanian officials. Already fêted as an infallible genius at home, Ceauşescu was now to be protected even from foreign criticism of his policies.

It is often forgotten that while, in the West, a government is confronted with an opposition, independent unions, and critical comments from the press and can also avail itself of polls to assess the general political climate, a Communist ruling party has no such evidence of reaction to its policies. It can only get information about the popular mood through the appartus which it itself created: the Party, the Ministry of Interior and the security police. More than once, the East European upheavals have shown how unreliable an apparatus is when it feeds the leadership with what it wants to hear. The then Polish party leader Edward Gierek was said to have talked to every voivodship party secretary on the eve of the decision to announce steep price increases in June 1976. Each assured the First Secretary that everything would go smoothly. As is well known, within twenty-four hours Poland was on the brink of a civil war and the government had to beat a hasty retreat. To take another example: on 22 October 1956 a Hungarian party secretary, Károly Kiss, was warned at a party meeting in the large Csepel steel works in Budapest of the imminent 'danger of a counter-revolutionary action'. Kiss haughtily replied: 'We can liquidate such an action in thirty minutes.'[96] Thirteen days later the emerging multi-party system of a neutral Hungary had to be liquidated by a massive intervention of the Soviet army.

In short, the Communist leaders are always faced with the danger that they will become the victims of their own lies; they frequently are misinformed either because of the vested interests of the apparatus, or due to the gap between the party machine and an embittered population.

Under these circumstances, the Western media, including radio stations broadcasting to the people in the bloc in their native tongues, are in a sense sleeping partners in domestic politics. It is common knowledge in all Eastern bloc countries that the élite recipients read the 'special bulletins' with much greater attention than the local press. Neither the upper nor the middle groups rely on the domestic papers to tell them what they need to know about the world, or even about their own country. At the same time the atmosphere of mutual distrust is reflected in the rationing of uncensored news and comment, even within the party apparatus.

Yet this elaborate process was, and is, a gigantic farce, since the unprivileged masses can know just as much as the leader about world events if they have the patience to listen to foreign broadcasts and put up with the irritation of jamming. Any informed newspaper reader in the West can read material that is available in the East to only a few dozen, hundred or thousand people, according to the 'sensitivity of the content'. In short, almost all the 'highly confidential' information contained in the various 'white', 'red' or 'yellow' bulletins is readily available to any normal person in the West who reads a quality newspaper and listens to radio broadcasts. The same information is available to many in the East through their radio sets.

But the party activists, the middle and low-ranking functionaries who are not worthy of special bulletins are kept in complete ignorance. Occasional lectures cannot provide selected activists with the kind of solid and steady flow of information any listener can pick up from Western broadcasts. Thus, unless the functionaries themselves listen to Western stations, the scheme backfires, since the very backbone of the party is often incapable of countering 'western propaganda' or responding to simple questions about touchy subjects posed by a population which has relatively easy access to the flow of news from the West.

All this breeds an atmosphere of profound cynicism from top to bottom of the hierarchy. There are various theoretical ways to counter the dangerous availability of uncensored information to the population at large. But despite all the efforts of an enormous apparatus to prevent the man in the street from getting information, there is one area where the Communist régimes are unable to maintain total control over news and views: it is the world of international broadcasting which we shall consider in the next chapter.

PART II

The International Dimension

This universal, obligatory force-feeding with
lies is now the most agonising aspect of existence in our country – worse than all our
material miseries, worse than any lack of civil
liberties.

ALEXANDER SOLZHENITSYN
Letter to the Soviet Leaders

4 Western Broadcasts – A Lifeline of Information

'IF THE WEST believes in the power of its ideas, then additional transmitters and funds for broadcasting to the East are more important than missiles.' This is how, in the context of controversies about future resources for the BBC and President Carter's $25 million programme to increase the transmitter power of the Voice of America (VOA) and Radio Free Europe-Radio Liberty (RFE–RL), a Hungarian intellectual assessed the significance of Western broadcasts to Eastern Europe.[1] The statement may seem exaggerated to those unfamiliar with day to day life under Communism; but no one who has visited any Soviet bloc country for any length of time and read the works of Alexander Solzhenitsyn, Zhores Medvedev or Vladimir Bukovsky, is likely to dispute it.

International broadcasting to Eastern Europe and the Soviet Union provides an indispensable lifeline of information for close on 370 million people living in societies, which – as we have seen – still find it difficult to openly discuss natural disasters or major international events, let alone their current, thorny problems. As a consequence of the transistor revolution, radio is more than ever the principal means of nourishing the people in the East, who are fed a daily diet of selected, filtered, edited and censored information. The costly jamming operations (except in Hungary, Romania and East Germany) and the frequent, often almost hysterical, attacks against the 'espionage centres' and 'subversive instruments of imperialism' are telling evidence of the vital role the foreign stations play.

Foreign radio transmissions and, in East Germany, a part of Hungary, Czechoslovakia and the Baltic states, Western telecasts as well, breach the monopoly of information which is one of the main bases of Communist rule. The fact that this important medium escapes total monopoly, that any one can, by the turn of a dial in his own home, be exposed to ideas, information and a world view free of control and manipulation from above, is regarded, not without reason, as a serious and permanent threat to the single-party dictatorships.

The elaborate structure of control, manipulation and censorship in the mass media, sketched out in the previous chapters, as well as the Soviet concept of 'newsworthiness' is based on the premise that it is up to the governments of individual states to decide what their inhabitants may or may not receive by way of information. The Communists not only aim to exercise total control over their own mass media, but also claim the right to decide what news from foreign sources may or may not be broadcast to their citizens.[2] As we shall see in chapters on the Soviet counter-measures and the CSCE negotiations, this is the key argument for the double standard, which regards the dissemination eastwards of information suppressed or distorted by the controlled media, as an impermissible act of interference. In contrast, blatant and inflammatory intervention by Soviet bloc media in other countries' affairs is endorsed as righteous and justified.

As to the standard Communist charge of 'interference in the internal affairs of sovereign countries', a fitting answer was given by a Western diplomat in the negotiations about the Helsinki accords: '. . . any listener who finds news from Western sources uninteresting or offensive has a quick remedy – he can switch off.' But of course the régimes are haunted by the legitimate fear that, far from rejecting news from the West, their subjects welcome it.

Foreign broadcasting to Eastern Europe has become a new and extremely important, albeit often forgotten, dimension of Western diplomacy.[3] As Sir Michael Swann, the Chairman of the Governors of the BBC, remarked, the concept of providing unbiased world news and information 'acquired a most powerful impetus . . . during the war, when the Government assented to the notion that if you want to be believed when you are telling truths favourable to your own cause, you must also tell those truths that are *not* favourable to your cause.'[4]

Though, by and large, the BBC still enjoys the highest

degree of credibility, all major stations receive high marks for their fair and accurate reporting from East European listeners, who welcome above all the absence of overt propaganda. The fact that the Western broadcasts regularly report on political, economic and social crises in the capitalist world, on the youth revolt, terrorism, etc, convinces sceptical audiences that their newscasts and commentaries can be believed and trusted.

The rapid increase in the number of radio receivers has created a situation fraught both with short- and long-term dangers for the credibility and cohesion of the Communist system. The ownership of receivers (excluding loudspeakers connected to a wired broadcasting network) in Eastern Europe, including Yugoslavia, jumped almost fivefold in twenty years, from 20.2 million in 1955 to 59.7 million in 1965 and to 107.7 million in 1978. An equally fast growth was recorded in television sets: 24 million in 1965, 45.3 million in 1970 and 95.4 million in 1978.[5] A significant exception is isolated, maverick Albania with 180,000 radio and 4,500 TV sets (70 and 1.8 receivers respectively per 1,000 inhabitants, by far the lowest figure in Europe).

Though the national statistics do not distinguish between various types of receivers, from light, portable transistors to wired receivers and between locations (whether they are installed in cars, homes or public places), the proportion able to receive short-wave is believed to be two-thirds of the ninety-four million recorded sets.[6] Short-wave receivers are one of the few consumer durables easy to obtain, even in the Soviet Union, and any visitor to East European countries encounters many young people carrying transistor sets.

Before turning to the political aspects of international broadcasting to the East, we must distinguish four types of broadcasting and their audiences:

1. Available statistical evidence indicates that the short- and sometimes medium-wave broadcasts of such European stations as Radio Luxembourg and Vienna are extremely popular in Eastern Europe. No such surveys have been carried out on Soviet audiences. There is no reason to doubt, however,

the impressions of correspondents and temporary residents in Moscow that Soviet youth is as keen as the age group elsewhere on tuning in to foreign pop and rock music programmes. As one of the characters in Alexander Zinoviev's satire *Radiant Future* puts it, 'boredom is the essence of our existence'. With rare exceptions, the press, the radio, television and films in the Soviet bloc countries are so boring or so tendentious, and the light music programmes often so dated, that the young people and intellectuals are virtually forced to turn to foreign stations for entertainment. Thus it is estimated that in Czechoslovakia and Hungary fifteen percent of listeners above the age of fourteen listen to Radio Luxembourg's entertainment programmes, in Poland twenty-one percent, in Romania sixteen percent, in Bulgaria eighteen percent.[7]

2. A second group of listeners, partly of course overlapping with the first category, listens to the BBC European Service and Voice of America's English language programmes, the latter also has news bulletins in 'special English' (that is, in deliberately slow, simple speech). However, it is reasonable to suppose that the estimates in the audience and opinion research for BBC and VOA and the German stations, *Deutsche Welle* and *Deutschlandfunk*, refer primarily to those who listen to the foreign language services of those broadcasters. Radio Vienna is a significant exception. The fact that its audience is twenty-three percent of the listeners to all Western broadcasts in Czechoslovakia, but only eight to nine percent in Hungary and Poland, must also be ascribed to a greater command of the language.

3. East Germany is in a special and, as already noted, particularly difficult situation. The news and comment to which party secretary and head of state Erich Honecker objected in his conversation with Chancellor Helmut Schmidt in Helsinki 'as a continuing interference in the internal affairs of the GDR' was not carried in special services for Eastern Europe, but simply in the domestic service. With West German television reaching eighty percent of East German territory, and with radio broadcasts received everywhere, a permanent challenge exists to the basic ideological legitimacy

of the system. Honecker himself stated at the ninth plenary meeting of the Central Committee of the SED at the end of May 1973, that 'dozens of Western broadcasts can be received' and 'that citizens can switch West German air media on or off as they wish.'[8]

This statement was, of course, a belated recognition of the fact that methods such as asking primary school pupils whether their parents were watching Western telecasts, and redirecting roof aerials so that only East German TV could be received were in the end counter-productive, breeding even more contempt and hatred for the régime, without blocking access to West German media. All reports, including those based on information from defectors who had previously worked in East German opinion research and political science institutes, agree that over seventy percent of the East German TV viewers normally prefer West German programmes, that the RIAS, the US station in Berlin, is the most popular station in East Germany with three-quarters of the adult population listening to its broadcasts.[9]

It is against this background that the frequent attacks on ARD and ZDF, the West German TV networks, as 'the chief tools of persistent ideological aggression', and the frequent expulsion of West German correspondents from the GRD must be seen. The most vulnerable Communist régime must be, logically and inevitably, the principal propagandist against the Western radio stations broadcasting from West Germany, even though the Munich-based RFE and RL broadcast in languages other than German. This is also the reason why East Germany is more interested than any other Soviet bloc state in subjecting, not only broadcasts to the East, but also domestic mass media in the West, to a code of 'good behaviour' based on the criteria of 'peace, good neighbourliness and understanding between peoples', as of course interpreted and defined by the Communist side.

4. The fourth and most controversial category consists of Western broadcasts beamed to the East in Russian and other East European languages. Apart from the special case of East Germany, affected only by domestic German-language broadcasts, the Soviet camp regards these foreign broadcasts

as a major point of political vulnerability. Lenin described radio as 'a newspaper without paper . . . and without boundaries'. Due to the transistor revolution, any ordinary Russian, Hungarian or Bulgarian can switch on a news programme broadcast in his native tongue and can hear news or commentaries which are regarded by party officials as 'highly confidential'.

Political and technological factors have combined to produce a tremendous expansion of short-wave broadcasting, which has in turn led to a congestion on the short wavelengths and to interference. The importance that Communist régimes attach to the battle of the air waves is shown, incidentally, by the curious fact that tiny Albania, with the smallest per capita

External Broadcasting[10]

	Hours a week	
	1960	1978
Soviet Union	1,015	2,010
US	1,495	1,813
Warsaw Pact*	1,009	1,475
China	687	1,436
West Germany	315	780
BBC	589	711
Egypt		542
Albania	63	564
Netherlands		285
Australia		336
India		330
Cuba		321
Japan		259
Israel		204
France**	326	110

*Includes East Germany 331 hours, Poland 338, Czechoslovakia 254, Bulgaria 234, Romania 195 and Hungary 127.
**France stopped broadcasting to Eastern Europe from the end of 1974.

figures for radio and TV receivers in Europe, broadcasts 564 hours in foreign languages weekly, three times more than Italy and approaching the output of the BBC, which, though it held first place after World War II, now ranks only fifth among the major broadcasters. The USSR, the US and China currently broadcast between two and three times as much as the BBC.

Though the Soviet bloc increased its weekly broadcasts fourfold between 1948 and 1972 and currently broadcasts in eighty languages through extremely powerful transmitters which often manage to blot out other programmes on the same frequency, its spokesmen resort to the same basic ploy as in the arms controversies; they simply put the blame squarely on the other side. We shall deal with the Soviet counter-moves in detail later. At this point, however, a highly revealing Soviet complaint may be singled out:

> In 1947 only the BBC and VOA broadcast one hour weekly each in Russian. By 1956, their programmes were increased to 144 hours a week. Today thirty-five foreign stations broadcast daily 200 hours in twenty-two languages of the Soviet peoples. Thirteen of these stations express the standpoint of official imperialistic circles. There are furthermore nine church programmes and some so-called private stations. The latter belong to the so-called grey and black propaganda. They carry on a particularly reckless anti-Soviet incitement and know no restraints as far as the elementary norms of inter-state exchanges are concerned. Such stations are Radio Liberty, Radio Free Europe and others.

This is a quote from a Soviet book on the 'special role of radio in the service of imperialistic propaganda'. The author also analyses the Voice of America programmes and singles out the 'special character' of the *Deutsche Welle*. He particularly stresses that the latter, instead of providing information about political, economic and cultural developments in West Germany as laid down in its guidelines, concentrates on giving information about events in the countries to which its broadcasts are directed. Thus twenty-five percent of its Russian-language broadcasts are devoted to reports and commentaries on the events in the East European countries.[11]

This example reflects the major Soviet concerns: the simple

existence of Russian-language broadcasts, their growth during the last three decades and, last but not least, the implications of their reporting of what goes on in Eastern Europe.
This last factor is the reason why the Munich-based RFE–RL
are the prime targets of East bloc campaigns. The other
'imperialistic official stations' are not only lagging far behind
in programme hours and broadcast languages; their broadcast
content is shaped by their primary mission of projecting the
preoccupations of their own societies and the foreign policies
of their respective governments. We have to distinguish,
therefore, between the major Western broadcasters and the
Munich stations.

Until the Polish crisis in the summer of 1980, the three
most important Western official broadcasters, the Voice of
America, the BBC and *Deutsche Welle*, were not jammed in
the Soviet Union and Eastern Europe after September 1973,
with the partial exception of Bulgaria which stopped jamming
VOA only in 1975. The following tables show that in terms of
programme hours they are way behind the Munich stations.

Western broadcasts to the Soviet Union and East Europe

Hours per week[12]

	Soviet Union	Eastern Europe
Radio Liberty (RL)	462	–
Radio Free Europe (RFE)		555.1
Voice of America B(VOA)*	168	73.5
BBC*	34.7	86.7
*Deutsche Welle**	19.15	68.2B

*To Yugoslavia: VOA broadcasts one hour in Serbo-Croat and half
an hour in Slovene daily; BBC 16.25 hours a week in Serbo-Croat and
Slovene and *Deutsche Welle* 13.30 hours in Serbo-Croat, 3.35 hours
in Slovene and 1.45 hours in Macedonian.

In addition to these major Western broadcasters, there are
of course other stations regularly broadcasting to the Soviet
bloc: Radio Sweden (twenty-one hours a week in Russian),
Kol Israel, Vatican Radio, Radio Canada. And one should
not forget such erstwhile 'fraternal' transmitters as Radio

Peking and Radio Tirana. Though the Albanian broadcasts in Hungarian or Polish can be heard very clearly indeed in Central Europe, the effect of the revolutionary rhetoric of Enver Hoxha on the occasional listener in Budapest, Berlin or Warsaw is almost certainly nil.

Radio Free Europe, founded in 1950 and Radio Liberty, operating since 1953, but since 1976 merged into one unit with RFE, broadcast 150 hours daily in twenty-one languages to the Soviet bloc (except East Germany). The programmes vary from a twenty-four hour round-the-clock daily service in Russian to fifteen minutes in some Central Asian languages. In all, Radio Liberty broadcasts currently in Russian and fourteen other languages to the Soviet Union. Last year the Board decided to terminate broadcasts in Uigur, a twelve minute first-run programme repeated four times daily, because this ethnic group (about 175,000) was the smallest to which RL was broadcasting in its own language; all others are over one million. Furthermore it was more than 3,000 miles away from the transmitters. Ukrainian and Uzbek are regarded by the Board as the highest priority non-Russian languages of the Soviet Union.

Radio Free Europe broadcasts twenty and a half hours daily in Czech and Slovak to Czechoslovakia, nineteen hours in Polish, and Hungarian, thirteen hours in Romanian and eight hours in Bulgarian. The five East European and the Russian services account for three-fourths of the total programme hours and an even higher proportion of first-run (or non-repeat) programmes. Repeats are frequent because of jamming. Though not jammed in Romania, since 1963, or Hungary, since 1964, RFE–RL broadcasts are still jammed in the Soviet Union, Czechoslovakia, Bulgaria and, to a lesser extent, in Poland.

What irritates the Communist dictatorships perhaps more than anything else is that the Munich stations function as a sort of surrogate domestic radio for audiences otherwise dependent on state-controlled information. The programmes are strongly news-orientated, with ten-minute newscasts on the hour, morning newsreels, late evening summaries, feature programmes, and news analysis in depth accounting for one-fifth to one-third of first-run programmes in major language services. Press reviews, correspondents' reports, discussions and documentaries take a proportion of the time, with religious services, sportscasts and music-variety programmes completing the daily content

In addition to providing East European listeners with a full coverage of the West, not just of the US, but the whole of Western Europe, the Munich-stations broadcast not only *to*, but also *about* Eastern Europe. RFE and RL function as an alternative home service for national audiences in the sense that their primary objective is to furnish the listeners with objective, uncensored and up-to-the-minute information about the world and their own societies, and to fill in those information gaps which result from domestic censorship and government control over the local media. As formulated in the Statement of Mission adopted by the Board for International Broadcasting:

> RFE and RL are required by law to operate in a manner not inconsistent with the broad foreign policy objectives of the United States. . . While the Voice of America concentrates on presenting American society and institutions, RFE and RL reflect and project a diverse international awareness. Under American management and the statutory oversight of the Presidentially-appointed Board for International Broadcasting, the RFE/RL staff is composed of citizens of the United States, citizens of friendly European and other nations. Together, they seek to create neither 'American radio,' in the narrow national sense, nor 'exile radio', in the sense of organised political opposition, but international radio. It is international in the breadth of its coverage, its freedom from national or sectarian bias, its dedication to the open communication of accurate information and a broad range of democratic ideas. At the same time, it is 'local' in the sense that broadcast content is focused on the interests of the audiences.[13]

The management of the stations also issued lengthy Programme Policy Guidelines which, among other things, stressed:

> RFE and RL seek to identify with the interests of their listeners, devoting particular attention to developments in and directly

affecting the peoples of Eastern Europe and the USSR. In focusing on the special concerns of their audiences, they perform some of the functions of a 'home service' as well as of a surrogate press.

It is this aspect which lends not only a unique character to the operations of the two radios, but also involves great political and editorial responsibility. It is stressed that 'tone, language and manner of presentation are as important . . . as broadcast content'. Among the 'restraints' listed in eleven points which will continue to be observed, one finds 'avoidance of emotionalism, vituperation, vindictiveness, stridency, belligerency', etc, of 'inflammatory programmes', of 'any material which could be reasonably construed as incitement to revolt or support for illegal and violent actions' and last but not least 'the avoidance of any suggestion that might lead audiences to believe that, in the event of international crisis or civil disorder, the West might intervene militarily in any part of the broadcast area.'[14]

These and other editorial guidelines, as well as the control mechanism and the annual public reports giving detailed statistics about transmitter facilities, personnel allocation and the use of the operating budget (over $100 million in 1980) are the products of a turbulent history which culminated in 1969–71 in an acute crisis, threatening the very existence of the stations.

The radios began to operate at the height of the cold war and the fact, for example, that the station broadcasting to Russia was called Radio Liberation until 1959 reflected the spirit of the roll-back and anti-Communist crusades of the 1950s. When, in October 1956, the Hungarian Revolution erupted, RFE played a negative, harmful and irresponsible role. Most of the restraints listed earlier were blatantly violated and inflammatory and vindictive commentaries not only complicated the situation of the Imre Nagy Government, but also led the young insurgents and many embittered Hungarians, including numerous intellectuals, to believe that the West might even intervene militarily on the side of Hungary when the Soviet Army struck at dawn on 4 November 1956.

As Alexis de Tocqueville noted, 'in politics one must use

the same type of reasoning as in war and never forget that the effects of events depend less on themselves than on the impressions they give.'[15] This is the reason why the author, who was an eyewitness of the Hungarian tragedy, regards October–November 1956 as a stain on RFE's record. The disappointment after the suppression of the uprising, and the contempt felt for a West which used the crisis in Russia's East European empire to invade Egypt, combined to deal a serious blow to the station's credibility primarily in Hungary – but also elsewhere. Yet in view of the twenty subsequent years and the highly responsible way in which RFE covered the invasion of Czechoslovakia in 1968 and the Polish crises in December 1970 and June 1976, one is tempted to accept the explanation of an astute RFE executive that 'the mistake of Hungary was essentially one of inexperience rather than sinister machinations.'

Despite a far reaching transformation of the programmes and the replacement of veterans of the immediate post-war period, often with an extreme right-wing background, by new and younger emigrés more familiar with actual conditions in Eastern Europe, RFE and RL suffered world-wide damage to their image as 'privately funded radios' when, in 1970–71, the Administration had to admit that covert government support was channelled to the stations by the Central Intelligence Agency. Against a background of political turbulence in the US, cleverly abetted by a world-wide Soviet campaign, Senator William J. Fulbright, then at the peak of his influence, spearheaded the efforts to stop government funding for what he called 'relics of the Cold War' contrary to the spirit of détente. Fortunately, this politically naïve and in terms of East-West relations, downright foolish, campaign petered out. After a transitory period when special commissions studied the best way of creating an independent public corporation, the Board for International Broadcasting Act was signed into law on 19 October 1973. The Chairman and the other six members of the Board are nominated by the President and confirmed by the Senate. The annual grants are voted by Congress and the operations of RFE–RL, with its own board of corporate directors, regularly reviewed. Though all ties with the CIA were severed in June 1971, Soviet propaganda justifies electronic jamming with constant references to continued 'control by the CIA' and a staff dominated by 'former agents of Gestapo and Nazi intelligence services' as well as 'all kinds of renegades, who have sold their homeland.'

The CIA link was the result of the original belief that the stations 'would have greater credibility if they appeared to be privately funded'.[16] But with the CIA both under fire at home and abroad and with its admitted use of journalists for clandestine purposes, the international credibility of the Munich stations suffered greatly. With public funding, open administration by the Board, and an accurate, sober and responsible editorial programme, the problem of the radios' legitimacy has now been practically resolved. Suggestions that changing names might make a difference to Soviet and East European listeners may be well meant, but miss the point.[17]

The truth is that despite the debacle in 1956, and regardless of the past CIA links, RFE as a broadcasting station has been one of the great dramatic, though perhaps least known, success stories in the history of international broadcasting. Radio Liberty has had for a variety of reasons (severe jamming, inadequate transmission facilities, more competition by other Western broadcasters, and probably also a less responsive audience) a less impressive record. Another limiting factor may possibly have been the tensions in the Russian service between those who left before or during World War II, and the new arrivals – mainly Jewish – in the 1970s. Changes in the RL management, a continuing generation conflict, tinged with anti-Semitism, and last but not least the lack of qualified supervisory personnel for non-Russian languages of the Soviet Union, all openly admitted in the BIB reports, must have had an adverse impact on the effectiveness of the RL branch.

It is above all the attention paid to the domestic concerns of the Soviet and East European people, and the so-called 'cross-reporting', which contribute to the tremendous impact of the broadcasts east of the Elbe. At the same time one must also acknowledge the fact that rigid and counter-productive Communist information policy provides optimal conditions for a continuous breakthrough to listeners hungry for factual information. At a congress of Soviet journalists in 1966, the then Chairman, D. P. Goryunov, alluded to a recent accident which affected a TU 114 taking off from Moscow Airport which did not cause fatalities: 'It is also obvious that it would have been better if the Muscovites had learned about this accident from Moscow Radio and not from the Voice of America or BBC.' Yet as we have seen, the people in the Soviet Union and some other East European countries are still learning of such accidents and natural disasters only through listening to foreign broadcasts.

Cross-reporting keeps Russian listeners informed of protest movements in Poland and Czechoslovakia, while in turn the Poles and the Czechs hear immediately about similar events in the Soviet Union. Audiences in other countries learn of the Hungarian economic reforms, the controversies about Eurocommunism, Western credits extended to a given Communist state and so on. All Western broadcasts contribute to the growing domestic political role of foreign correspondents reporting from, say, Moscow about events not discussed by Soviet media. Western broadcasts feed such news back to the East, and sheer volume of programmes means that the Munich stations are the most likely ones to be heard.[19]

Some programme highlights from recent years might serve as the best illustration of the unique capabilities of the RFE–RL broadcasts. In December 1970 RFE was the first to report the Baltic workers uprising which ended the Gomulka era, and mass public protests against the food price increase in June 1976 in Poland might have also gone largely unreported except for RFE's detailed and quick coverage.

RFE's live broadcasts of the inauguration ceremonies of Pope John Paul II, and of the Nobel Prize ceremonies in honour of the dissident Soviet scientist Andrei Sakharov, show the possibilities of an 'international radio' as against the other major Western broadcasters. Speed is another important factor. RFE reported the election of Cardinal Wojtyla as the new Pope forty minutes before Warsaw Radio announced it.

An even more characteristic case was the devastating Romanian earthquake of 4 March 1977. President Ceauşescu was away on a foreign trip and for the first few hours Bucharest Radio was broadcasting serious music instead of meaningful and quick information for the public. It was RFE's Romanian service which provided continuous live programming. Many hours before Bucharest Radio, the Munich station informed listeners what had happened, what had been destroyed and transmitted information provided by seismologists and Western correspondents on the spot. More than six hundred Romanians telephoned the Munich newsroom and one in three of the calls came from Bucharest.

The station also provided, through its Washington bureau chief, on-the-spot coverage when President Carter visited Poland in January 1978. This enabled RFE's Polish service to report on the President's press conference in Warsaw live (with simultaneous translation) and also to cover Mrs Carter's visit to Cardinal Wyszynski and other events which local media largely ignored. In the same month, the Washington chief correspondent also accompanied US Secretary of State Cyrus Vance to Hungary, for the return of the Crown of St Stephen. As a result, RFE was the first to broadcast that Hungary would be granted most-favoured-nation status for its exports to the US. Such visits, as well as the coverage of various international events in Romania between 1966–74 by RFE correspondents, and last but not least the accreditation for RFE–RL special correspondents to report on the Belgrade CSCE review conference, are regarded by the Board for International Broadcasting and the RFE–RL management as perhaps the most effective answer to the 'outworn propaganda clichés' about the stations being 'subversive instruments of psychological warfare'.[20]

But no single piece of reporting in recent years could compete with the complete coverage of the historic visit of Pope John Paul II to Poland. How did the Munich station fill the information gaps and correct the distorted reporting by Polish and Soviet bloc media? The Polish service broadcast over ninety hours on the visit, including direct reporting. The programmes relied on special TV transmissions, two West German and one Austrian station plus the Vatican Radio's broadcasts. A special studio in West Berlin monitored Polish domestic TV broadcasts. The programmes also included international press reaction, colour stories, background reports, references to the poor coverage by domestic media and the complaints of Western journalists.

Once again the method of cross-reporting was particularly important. The Hungarian and Czechoslovak services broadcast twelve to thirteen hours in all, the Romanian, Bulgarian, Lithuanian and Russian language desks between two and four hours each, in addition to shorter reports in Belorussian, Ukrainian, Latvian and Estonian. It was in this way that Czechoslovak Catholics learned that during his mass at Gniezno the Pontiff noted a placard in the crowd calling on him to 'Remember, Father, your Czech children', to which he warmly responded: 'This Pope cannot forget the Czech children'. RFE also broadcast that Czechoslovak Cardinal Tomasek and Czechoslovak Catholics were again mentioned by the Pope at the mass at Novy Targ and that he prayed for those who could not cross the border from Czechoslovakia into Poland. The same selective attention to the visit was paid by the Lithuanian service. On two Saturdays and Sundays it doubled its normal programme from thirty to sixty minutes and especially stressed the Papal remarks addressed 'to our brothers, the Lithuanians'.[21]

The fact that the BBC and Voice of America sent special correspondents to Poland for the visit and that their broadcasts are not subjected to jamming should of course not be overlooked. In any case, the massive combined coverage of the visit showed the Western stations quickly, and even brilliantly, availing themselves of the exceptional opportunity to demonstrate their vital role as an alternate 'home service' bloc-wide.

The consistently high quality, undoubted effectiveness and professional skill of most RFE–RL programmes are partly due to a round-the-clock twenty-four hour central news division with a multi-lingual team of professional news writers and editors producing a daily news file of some 100,000 words from Western and Eastern news agencies, broadcasts and periodicals as well as RFE–RL's own specialised correspondents. There is, however, another key factor behind the entire operation – an impressive research service which was built up at RFE by J. F. Brown, a British scholar with an intimate knowledge of the diverse East European area, and at Radio Liberty by Keith Bush, a sophisticated observer of the Soviet scene.

Every day the RFE and RL research staffs evaluate several million words in over thirty languages, including broadcasts by forty-five Soviet and East European radio and TV stations, nearly a thousand periodicals, the entire output of Soviet bloc agencies and published reports and works of Western journalists and scholars. A library of some 100,000 books (more than two-thirds in the broadcast languages) combined with specialised archives and index files are at the disposal of the hundred-odd researchers – and of visiting scholars and students.

No other research institute is geared to produce the sort of information and analytical service which is a precondition for the high standards of accuracy in both reports and commentaries. According to an RFE–RL publication, the Czechoslovak research section alone has some 120,000 bibliographical cards and 65,000 subject cards. There are about 1,200 subscribers to RFE–RL research reports and publications, ranging from 108 US universities to the Bank of England and the Indonesian Embassy in Belgrade. However in the course of the institutional changes since 1971–73 there has been a certain tendency to underestimate the outstanding importance of the research sections (which at RFE cost a mere six percent of the operating budget) and to overrate the real significance of corporate and managerial reshuffles.

The pruning of personnel, the merger of the two radio stations and the centralisation of management and administration have reduced employees by twenty-six percent in five years – from 2,368 in 1973 to 1,730 by the end of 1979.[22] There is no doubt that the long period of uncertainty over the future of the stations and the cuts in staff have helped the infiltration of East bloc intelligence operators, details of which are contained in the next chapter. Unfortunately, the translation service of RFE, which in the past turned out English translations of East European articles verbatim, has been a victim of cuts. A somewhat curious phenomenon has also engendered reservations. In external broadcasts, 'editorial opinions' have to be 'clearly distinguished from newscasts and news analyses', but some of the research reports and longer specialised papers, mainly produced by us supervisory personnel or Western-trained senior research staff, are a mixture of facts and comments. This involves a potential danger, the more so because some of the journalistic recipients of the service as well as scholars not familiar both with the area and the languages tend to accept even controversial assessments at face value. But such concern only reflects the reputation for excellence these services have established!

How large is the audience for the Western broadcasts in the Soviet Union and Eastern Europe? According to data collected by the research and opinion institutes for RFE–RL, international broadcasting has an enormous impact, above all in Eastern Europe. Four out of five Czechoslovaks, three out of four Hungarians, Romanians and Poles, and one of every two Bulgarians are estimated to listen to Western radio. Predictably, RFE has the largest audience in the five East European countries: 31.5 million people, or forty-five percent of the adult population, tune in at least once a month, and 28.3 million at least once a week, to the broadcasts beamed by forty-six transmitters in West Germany, Portugal and Spain.[23]

Listening to Western Broadcasts in % of population over fourteen.
May 1978 – March 1979

	Western broadcasts total	RFE	VOA	BBC	Deutsche Welle or Deutsch- landfunk
Bulgaria	55	32	21	20	4
Czecho- slovakia	77	35	24	22	15
Hungary	66	49	20	19	9
Poland	77	50	20	25	14
Romania	.71	53	15	19	6

The picture is rather different in the Soviet Union. As noted by the BIB report, 'vast distances (not easily spanned by all present Western transmitters) as well as differences in political culture, national outlook and socio-economic levels have tended to limit the Soviet audience.' Though the estimates are less dependable, because based on even smaller or less representative samples than in the case of Eastern European listeners (research surveys are not permitted inside the Soviet bloc), they nevertheless tend to confirm earlier estimates of Western communication experts that 'about forty to sixty million people with varying degrees of regularity listen to foreign broadcasts'. According to a study comparing survey results for 1974–75 and 1977–79, there was a definite reduction of regular daily and weekly audiences. Thus, in the course of an average week in 1977–79, 50.4 million people listened to the four major Western broadcasters, down from an estimated 74.1 million four years earlier. On a typical day 15.3 million listeners tune in (as against 28.1 million earlier). According to the BIB report, there was a sudden increase after the jamming of Western stations (except for RL) was stopped in 1973. The audience subsequently levelled off, but still remained at higher levels than before 1973. It is also thought that severe jamming was a major factor in Radio Liberty's slipping to the fourth place among the Western stations. In urban areas it now takes a considerable effort to listen to the Munich station.

To sum up, it is reckoned on the basis of this admittedly somewhat shaky evidence that Western broadcasts are heard weekly on the average by one-third of the adult Soviet population.[24]

Listening to Western radios in the Soviet Union 1977–79

	Daily	Weekly
	In millions	
Voice of America	7.2	23.9
BBC	3.3	10.2
Deutsche Welle	2.4	8.7
Radio Liberty	2.4	7.6

Confidential Soviet opinion surveys are not available. But it was reported by dissident sources to a Western correspondent that in the early 1970s 16,000 Muscovites were asked to state their most important source of information. 'Foreign broadcasts' were named by six percent of those questioned. However seventeen percent of those questioned, who were not simultaneously asked for their names, gave the same answer. The real percentage figure is probably even higher, the correspondent added.[25]

But figures, statistics and estimates do not show the real importance of these broadcasts to educated and committed individuals in the East. Vladimir Bukovsky, who spent almost one-third of his life in camps and hospitals, described to the US Congressional Commission on Security and Co-operation how he was able to listen to Radio Liberty broadcasts in 1968–69 on a makeshift radio built secretly by prisoners in a remote camp. The Romanian dissident writer Paul Goma told a Western correspondent in 1977 that he, and others who joined him in his appeal to the Helsinki signatories, 'learned about each other via Free Europe: we learned each other's problems and thus we found each other.' RFE was also the 'only source of information' from which his fellow citizens learned of his activities.[26]

There is no question that publicity given on the air by Western media to dissidents, especially in the USSR, is for them the only means of influencing domestic affairs. As a senior Polish Communist party official once said to a BBC visitor: 'What Cardinal Wyszynski says in a sermon will only be known to a few thousand people in Poland, but if the BBC chooses to report it in its Polish service, the whole country will know'.[27]

The same is true of the 'Charter 77' movement in Czechoslovakia, of the Polish human rights activists led by Adam Michnik and Jacek Kuron and of the appeal sent to party leader Kádár by several hundred Hungarian intellectuals and artists on behalf of Vaclav Havel and other 'Chartists' sentenced to prison by a Prague Court in the autumn of 1979. To take an example in lighter vein: in a Budapest political cabaret a couple of years ago a comic routine was based on the fact that though hardly anyone in the audience knew the call-signals of the other East European radios, almost everyone instantly recognised the RFE theme.

Nothing could underline the enormous influence of Western television more convincingly than the fact that some

people in East Germany do not accept promising jobs in
Dresden because Western telecasts cannot be received there.
In Czechoslovakia a confidential poll revealed that 1.5 million
people – more at weekends – watch Austrian TV regularly.
Many cottages are built in areas where Austrian (or West
German) telecasts can be received. Even President and party
chief Dr Gustav Husak told Austrian visitors that he was
watching the Vienna programme whenever he spent a
weekend in his home in Bratislava.[28]

But what does this all mean in basic political terms? All
régimes – even if in varying degrees – have to take a better
informed public into account, and have to be somewhat more
responsive to indirect pressures engendered by Western
broadcasts. Furthermore, the régimes may have abstained
from carrying out repressive measures that would have
provoked a public reaction. This could well be true of Poland
in the stormy days in June 1976 and even of the Hungarian
official reaction to the declarations of sympathy for the
defendants at the Prague trials. As a senior Hungarian official
is said to have remarked at a closed party meeting: 'We don't
want to produce martyrs for the RFE . . .'[29]

It is reasonable to suppose that Western broadcasts and
television programmes encourage diversity, restraint and the
assertion of national identity and interests, particularly in
Eastern Europe and also among the non-Russian ethnic
groups in the Soviet Union. Furthermore, the cross-reporting
of events within the bloc by RFE–RL, and to a lesser extent by
the other broadcasters, have a secondary impact on the Soviet
citizens, still much more isolated and sealed off from the West
than the rest of the bloc. President Carter described international broadcasting as a 'key element of US foreign policy'. He
added: 'Our most crucial audiences for international broadcasting are in the Soviet Union and Eastern Europe, where
censorship and controlled media give the peoples of the area
distorted or inadequate views of the US as well as of crucial
events within their own countries and in the world at large.'[30]

Nevertheless, RFE–RL, let alone the BBC and VOA, have to
walk a delicate tightrope between what the Communist
governments regard as 'disinformation under the guise of
objectivity' and what the dissidents or even average educated

listeners in Eastern Europe label as 'appeasement of the prison warders instead of helping the prisoners'. Thus a BBC publication has revealed that Solzhenitsyn, Amalrik and Bukovsky and other dissidents complained that 'broadcasts from London did not contain criticism of the Soviet régime in general and its abuses of human rights in particular.' The author heard the same sort of complaints from internationally known Polish scholars and writers about the Polish broadcasts of RFE.[31]

All surveys confirm that the highest proportion of listeners to Western broadcasts are among university students, and the technical, scientific and literary intelligentsia. It is estimated that among the CPSU members one out of three occasionally switches on a Western programme. The audience in Eastern Europe even includes the First Secretary of a ruling Communist Party. Meeting a foreign ambassador one morning in 1977, he promptly took detailed issue with a commentary broadcast on the RFE the night before![32]

Judging by my conversations with highly-placed party officials and by reports from Moscow correspondents, this First Secretary is not an exceptional case. Even Khrushchev, according to his memoirs, regularly listened to Western broadcasts. In Budapest, Warsaw and Bucharest many radios in the homes of intellectuals and artists and even of Central Committee members are permanently set to the BBC or RFE. A prominent Polish party journalist told me, for example, that one of his best Russian friends, an alternate member of the Central Committee, has his portable set at home in Moscow tuned to the BBC all the time. They even listened together to a BBC newscast in Russian.

Nevertheless it is difficult to assess, or even illustrate, the long-range influence of Western broadcasts in general, and sustained coverage of sensitive developments in the Soviet Union and Eastern Europe in particular. In terms of domestic politics, the mere fact of the dissemination of news reduces the régimes' scope for manipulation and represents a permanent challenge to their credibility, undermining much effort at political indoctrination.

In theory, the impact of the Western broadcasts should force domestic media in the bloc to respond by becoming

more professional, more sophisticated and providing more
real news. In practice, however, as we have seen in our
analysis of Communist media, this is not generally the case.
Significant exceptions are Hungary and, to a lesser extent,
Poland. Yet the experience gained during the 1968 Prague
Spring showed that neither jamming, nor a propaganda
barrage, but only a more informative press, radio and TV can
really compete with Western broadcasts. In Czechoslovakia
during those exhilarating days of a switch from a journalism
of advocacy to one of investigation, the audience of RFE fell
from sixty percent to thirty-seven percent of the population.[33]

In terms of East-West relations, however, the definition
given by that veteran diplomatic operator and Grand Old
Man of US-Soviet relations, Averell Harriman, is more meaningful. He regards 'the flow of information to the peoples of
the Communist countries as one of the most important
protections to our national security. An ignorant people will
be easily led by the Kremlin and other politbureaus. An
informed opinion is far more difficult to dominate.'[34] There is
no doubt that the process of modernisation, the changes in
socio-economic structure, the growth of urban population
and the steadily rising number of graduates from institutions
of higher education will further increase the potential audience for international broadcasting.

5 *The Soviet Response – Jamming and Intimidation*

THE COMMUNIST RÉGIMES react to the breaching of their monopoly of information by foreign broadcasts which beam uncensored information, through a variety of public and covert methods. These range from electronic jamming of Western broadcasts to the exertion of massive political pressures on Western governments, from world-wide propaganda campaigns to cloak and dagger activities, partly by agents planted in the editorial offices of radios, all aimed in one way or another at discrediting the radios, the content of their programmes and the personalities of the commentators.

Jamming is the oldest, most direct and best-known weapon to block or to disturb the access to international information channels. Apparently the first recorded case dates back to World War I when the Germans used a five-kilowatt transmitter to try to black out telegramme traffic between Paris and St Petersburg. In 1926 the Bucharest Government jammed inflammatory propaganda broadcasts by Moscow Radio to the disputed, then Romanian, province of Bessarabia (now Soviet Moldavia). In World War II the BBC rejected suggestions that it should retaliate in kind against Axis jamming: 'Jamming is an admission of a bad cause. The jammer has a bad conscience. He is afraid of the influence of the truth. In our country we have no such fears . . .'[35]

That the best and, by implication, most dangerous propaganda is a statement of facts was recognised by Stalin when, in February 1948, he ordered the jamming of the Russian-language broadcasts of Voice of America and, one year later, those of the BBC. Since then, the extent and intensity of the electronic jamming, which is, of course, contrary to international law and the Montreux International Telecommunications Convention,[36] signed by the Soviet Union, have varied according to the given state of East-West relations and, more particularly, in relation to the internal and external crises affecting the Communist world.

In December 1950, the UN General Assembly passed by forty-nine votes to five a resolution specifically directed against jamming. It noted that some countries 'are deliberately interfering with the reception by the peoples of those countries of certain radio signals originating beyond their territories' and it condemned 'measures of this nature as the denial of the rights of all persons to be fully informed.'[37] By that time the Soviets had several hundred jamming transmitters in operation. Within five years, there were already 2,000 transmitters east of the Elbe producing screeches, howls, whistles and hisses trying to make Western broadcasts, including the signals of RFE and RL, unintelligible.

What happened after Stalin's death and particularly after the progress towards East-West *détente*? At this point it may be instructive to quote an article by the Hungarian writer, Gyula Sipos, which was published over ten years ago in a widely read cultural weekly in Budapest. He noted first that although he himself did not listen to Western stations, he heard everything through the word-of-mouth network more quickly than it was (if ever) published in the paper. In Western Hungary many people can turn the knobs on their TV sets to receive Czech or Austrian, even Italian programmes. They even saw 'the events unfolding in Czechoslovakia' (ie the invasion of August 1968) through direct live transmissions. Finally Sipos concluded, 'one smiles today at the naïve and costly effort of trying to jam Western stations!'[38]

A decade later the Russians and most East Europeans can still not afford to 'smile' and their governments are still engaged in 'naïve and costly efforts' to blot out the Munich stations. It is only in Romania and Hungary, since 1964 and 1963 respectively, that no Western station whatsoever is jammed.

Poland stopped interference with RFE broadcasts after November 1956 and despite intermittent jamming did not disturb reception on a more massive scale until January 1971 after RFE had picked up the story of the Baltic workers riots and broadcast it to Polish listeners initially kept in ignorance by local media. Bulgaria and Czechoslovakia have never ceased to jam RFE nor has the Soviet Union stopped disturbing all broadcasts of RL. Nevertheless with regard to the other Western stations, there have been brief respites and between 1963 and 1968 even the Soviets stopped interfering with the VOA and BBC broadcasts. The coverage of the invasion of Czechoslovakia by international broadcasting, however, led to a resumption of jamming.

The next breakthrough came on the eve of the opening of formal negotiations about the Conference on European Security and Co-operation in Europe. Between 10 September 1973 and the summer of 1980, the Soviet Union did not interfere with Western broadcasts, except for Radio Liberty. Ironically, the Soviets also continue to jam Kol Israel, Radio Tirana and Radio Peking broadcasts. But monitoring reports indicate that, particularly since 1975, the jammers' top priority is accorded to blocking the Munich station.[39] East Germany stopped jamming RIAS in West Berlin and China stopped interfering with the VOA.

The Soviet bloc generally employs two types of jamming. One is called 'sky-wave jamming'. It involves the use of very powerful transmitters located roughly as far from the target area as the broadcaster. It is a long-range operation with the sky-waves or jamming signals reflected from the ionosphere and calculated to meet the signals of the Western transmitters over the receiving area. Most of the sky-wave stations are operating in the Soviet Union. But Western broadcasts enjoy every day what is called 'twilight immunity'. This happens when the sun goes down a few hours earlier in the East than in the West and the original broadcast signal penetrates the target area, but the sky-wave signal of the jamming station situated far to the East where all is already in darkness is not reflected back to earth and may therefore be inoperative.

However this brief immunity period does not apply to the so-called 'ground-wave' stations, local jammers in the audience area. They are much smaller transmitters, producing a high-intensity but short-range jamming signal designed to block incoming broadcasts in their own immediate vicinity.

Ground-wave stations are used around urban centres in the Soviet Union, Bulgaria, Czechoslovakia and Poland.

It is estimated that in the Soviet Union alone 3,000 transmitters are engaged in round-the-clock jamming with a total staff of some 5,000. Though estimates vary, all experts agree that jamming is an enormously costly effort, using for instance an estimated 1,000 million kWh a year in the bloc as a whole at a time of a deepening energy crisis. In 1971, it was estimated that the Soviet Union alone spent about $300 million a year on jamming – six times the cost of its international broadcasts. An official American estimate put the capital costs of jamming equipment at $250 million and that was over twenty years ago! Jiři Pelikán, the former Czechoslovak TV director general recalls in his memoirs that according to calculations made in 1968, the costs of jamming in Czechoslovakia would have sufficed to build a whole new TV centre, including broadcasts in colour and the purchase of new equipment. When the Poles temporarily stopped jamming in 1956, they put the savings at $17.5 million, which was then the equivalent of the worldwide VOA budget. Thus it is no exaggeration to say that over the last thirty years, the massive efforts to combat Western broadcasts must have cost the peoples of the Soviet bloc several billion dollars.[40]

During a heated debate on the provisions of the Helsinki Final Act concerning the free flow of ideas and information at the Belgrade Follow-Up Meeting, the US chief delegate, Ambassador Arthur Goldberg sarcastically remarked: 'It has been said that hard currency shortages prevent the purchasing of information products from my country. Yet it is hardly a lack of dollars that motivates the jamming of Western radio broadcasts.'[41]

What particularly irritates the jammers is of course the fact that, despite the high and steadily rising costs, jamming is far from completely effective. Patient and determined listeners, even in urban centres, can find a time when clearer reception is possible. Many people go to the country on weekends where Radio Liberty can be heard with little or no interference. The same is true of the jammed RFE broadcasts in Eastern Europe. By increasing the transmitting power of RFE–RL, some of the effects of jamming can be overcome.

However the Soviets are also bound to build even more powerful sky-wave stations. Thus the outlook is for more spending on restricting the flow of news into the Soviet bloc (always excepting Hungary and Romania).

In contrast to Hungary and Czechoslovakia, let alone East Germany, the Soviet Union is not seriously affected by television broadcasts from other countries. Soviet Foreign Minister Andrei Gromyko himself launched a pre-emptive action against the potential danger of TV programmes beamed by satellites directly into domestic sets. Anticipating this new area of vulnerability, on 8 August 1972 Gromyko presented a draft resolution to the UN General Assembly making relaying of TV programmes to other sovereign states illegal without the clearly expressed consent of the receiving country. After US opposition to what was nicknamed the 'jammers charter', the Soviets took the issue to the UN Committee On Peaceful Use of Outer Space. Predictably, Unesco also got involved in this sensitive field, passing a declaration the ambiguous formulations of which could be quoted later by Soviet spokesmen as indirect support for their standpoint that space technology 'should serve only the high aims of peace and friendship among the nations', that the channels and methods of mass communications should 'be of service to the mutual understanding of nations, to the mutual enrichment of national cultures and to social progress.'[42]

As correctly noted by Western observers, the Soviet draft was a coherent concept with far-reaching consequences: 'Governments from whose territories news is broadcast to foreign lands would become controllers and censors of their societies.'[43] As stated by the chief Soviet representative at the UN, the stream of information across frontiers must come, not from 'irresponsible private firms and companies,' but from 'responsible government officials'. The Soviet demand for state control refers not just to television by satellite, but by implication to every form of mass media. This would then create a happy situation in which the states have 'complete control of the fundamental factors in social life' and thus could regulate 'the influx of information in an optimal way to further friendly relations between countries, and to comply with the hopes of mankind as a whole.'[44]

We shall see later in detail how far the Soviet external broadcasts and the Eastern European propaganda comply with what *Pravda* calls 'the ideals enshrined in Helsinki'. The basic point in all the political-ideological controversies is that the Communist media are *per se* progressive, purveying only truthful information, while Western information is *per se* 'slanderous, hostile and harmful for young people' whenever it disseminates uncensored news unwelcome to the rulers, or commentaries criticising Communist foreign and domestic policies. It is up to the ruling parties and only to them to decide what is 'true' information serving peace and understanding, what is legitimate 'ideological struggle' waged by the Eastern side and what is impermissible interference or, even worse, 'ideological diversionism'. This is the logic behind the campaign against Western broadcasting and the opposition at Helsinki and at the Belgrade meeting to the free exchange of ideas and people.

It is therefore essential to give concrete examples of the absurdity of the claim that the Communist side is always right because it inherently serves genuine humanism, peace and understanding among nations, while the West is always and by definition wrong whenever it opposes those constructive and peaceloving policies. This attitude, represented in countless variations on the international stage by Soviet bloc spokesmen, is based on the ideological premise that only Marxists-Leninists are capable of objective judgments because they alone are in the possession of objective truth. This is of course, as succinctly formulated by a British scholar, 'an argument which moves in a circle and proves nothing.'[45]

Aside from jamming, the Communist régimes have sought to meet the penetration of uncensored information via the air waves with a variety of tactics. Listening to foreign broadcasts as such has never, not even under Stalin, been a criminal offence and there is no legal ban anywhere. However, the mere discussion or repetition of items from those broadcasts can be regarded as 'distribution of hostile information'. In times of rising international tensions or domestic political difficulties, the discussion of Western broadcasts even within a family can be construed as 'spreading wittingly or unwittingly hostile propaganda.' In Stalin's later years and immediately after his death, the prisons and internment camps were also filled with people denounced anonymously for 'incitement', merely because they passed on political jokes or information heard on Western radios.

Gone is the time of indiscriminate terror, yet it can still be somewhat risky to listen to and, above all, talk about, Western broadcasts. In the crisis year of 1968, on the eve of the invasion of Czechoslovakia and just before the resumption of jamming, *Pravda* launched a campaign against 'hearsay', and agitators who used foreign radio as a source of information. The paper mentioned the case of an engineer in a factory (no names were given): 'Even before the party committee intervened, his own colleagues explained to him that he had become a sort of extended communications line for a foreign radio station which with his help was disseminating false reports about events taking place in the world.'[46]

Ten years later Yevgenij Buzinnikov, a forty-one-year-old worker in Belorussia, was sentenced to three years' imprisonment in a strict régime labour camp. The indictment stated among other things, that, from March 1975 to May 1978, Buzinnikov had been regularly listening to 'foreign anti-Soviet stations' such as Radio Liberty, the Voice of America and the BBC, and that he had been 'disseminating slanderous inventions' about the Soviet system. According to the transcript of his trial which only reached the West a year later, other charges alleged that in his correspondence with Sakharov he had passed on 'information discrediting the Soviet way of life'. Thus even though the BBC and the VOA are no longer jammed, listening to Western broadcasts can still lead to criminal charges. Over the past few years, since the Helsinki conference, 315 names of Soviet prisoners of conscience have been communicated to Amnesty International. They have been imprisoned, exiled or forcibly confined to psychiatric hospitals and the charges have frequently included references to listening to foreign radio broadcasts.[47]

In trying to restrict the flow of news into their countries and also to stop information getting out, the Soviet leadership and the hard-line East Europe régimes have traditionally sought to intimidate both potential listeners and the passing on of news heard on the radio to others. With the conspiracy theory playing such a crucial role in Communist history, it was only logical that the foreign radios had to be discredited as espionage centres. A typical example was the two-piece series published by *Izvestia* at the end of 1968 linking the BBC (at that time severely jammed) with the secret service:

> The BBC, the mouthpiece of rabid anti-Communism in the British Isles, has been taking a very active part in several extremely ugly SIS (Secret Intelligence Service) operations. This is confirmed by a number of documents in our possession . . . For example, British intelligence has long been interested in the extensive mail the BBC received from its listeners, primarily, of course, from the European socialist countries and the Soviet Union . . . In connection with all this, another document has come to light: It states that an agreement exists with the BBC to turn over to the SIS all letters sent to the BBC from listeners in the socialist countries.[48]

An American student of Soviet indoctrination saw in the articles 'an obvious intent to sow the seeds of disbelief. . .'[49] Anyone familiar with the daily life under a Communist régime would rather opt for the simple, but more likely, assumption that the KGB, which inspired or possibly even prepared the articles, wanted to strike fear into the hearts of potential letter writers, particularly among young people.

This *Izvestia* warning is an almost classic example of the Soviet double-standard. Not only do the Moscow Radio broadcasts in English to North America come through unjammed, but the radio even proudly claims that about 25,000 Americans write in. Yet Soviet newspapers time and again warn against Soviet citizens writing to the BBC, the VOA or any other Western station. The same double standard is also evident with regard to jamming. Western governments have never protested against Eastern broadcasts to their countries, even when such broadcasts have levelled violent attacks at Western policies or political systems. The self-evident fact should also be mentioned that no Western country is jamming Soviet or East European external broadcasts, no matter how wildly inaccurate or outright inflammatory they are.[50]

Nothing would be more naïve than to imagine that Soviet reaction to the entry of uncensored and thus inherently 'subversive' information via the air waves is limited to the jamming of the broadcasts and to the manifold intimidation of the population. Largely ignored by the Western media and even more by professional politicians in some key Western countries, the Soviets, long before the Helsinki Final Act, started a massive, closely co-ordinated, bloc-wide campaign combining political pressures at the highest level and an incessant barrage of propaganda, combined with numerous diplomatic *démarches* and secret service activities. Though only a small number of these activities ever come to public knowledge, an astute German observer was certainly right when he noted that such attempts to influence Western governments and public opinion are given the highest priority by Soviet bloc policy-makers.[51]

This is a traditional, crucial, yet mostly forgotten or underrated dimension of Soviet diplomacy. We can cite here only a fraction of public and covert Soviet and East European actions, all serving the basic aim that Communist criteria should be tacitly accepted in deciding what is or is not 'incompatible with *détente*'.

The Number One target was and is RFE–RL in Munich. The prelude and permanent accompanying theme concentrates on discrediting the personnel of the stations. A typical example was the lengthy TASS commentary attacking President Carter's request for more funds to strengthen the capacity of the RFE–RL transmitters. Regardless of the major changes in the control, management and financing of the radio, the Soviet statement flatly asserted:

> The two radio stations continue to be entirely in the hands of the CIA, and, as it is put in the report, are an inseparable part of the US Government. As it was proved on many occasions, the two radio centres, employ staff members of the CIA as well as former agents of the Gestapo and Hitler's intelligence services, all sorts of renegades and persons who betrayed their country and are on the payroll of the American intelligence service.[52]

But can one deny that the programmes prepared by people whom *Izvestia* in 1977 called 'fascist cut-throats' and 'dregs of humanity' are sober, restrained in tone, authentic and persuasive? Instead of producing proofs to the contrary, the standard Communist answer is that the enemy, if anything, has become 'more subtle, donning the mantle of good-wishers and advisers. Instead of frontal attacks they call for modernising, democratising and liberalising the societies of the socialist countries'. After this routine introduction, the Bonn correspondent of *Sovetskaya Kultura* in a recent article, resorted to the well-known trick of Soviet propaganda. What then is the proof of the attempt to stir up trouble in the Warsaw pact? 'The Austrian *Volksstimme* newspaper has quoted excerpts from secret instructions of Radio Liberty compiled in advance for the fiftieth anniversary of the USSR. It requested the agents of the subversive radio to interpret all current events in such a way as to spread mistrust between the peoples of the Soviet Union.' The Soviet paper carefully omitted to mention that *Volksstimme* is the organ of the minuscule Austrian Communist Party with a minute circulation. More important still, the 'secret instructions' of the Munich stations as indeed scores of similar 'secret documents' published earlier 'exclusively' in the Vienna Communist daily, were provided by the Soviet comrades. Once *Volksstimme* printed the 'documents', no matter how crudely forged or invented, they could be used in a quote 'from the Austrian newspaper'. Of course there is a division of labour, *Volksstimme* is, as it were, the 'source' on the Munich stations. Obscure or crypto-Communist papers in Beirut or New Delhi or Mexico are also used as 'impeccable foreign evidence' against the ungrateful Romanian nationalists, or Yugoslav revisionists or 'Zionists in the Czech party leadership in 1968'.[53]

But let us quote the concluding part of the article from *Sovetskaya Kultura* to get the whole flavour of Soviet propaganda: 'Lies and slander pouring out of Radio Liberty daily are concocted by Nazi hirelings, whose hands are stained with blood, traitors, former Gestapo agents, characters with a criminal past'. Unfortunately the author can mention only one couple by name, alleged war criminals, who however on his own admission, have long been pensioned! But there are other 'inveterate anti-Soviet elements' in Munich. One of them is called Lev Roitman. After the paper makes it quite clear that he is a Jew, he is accused of past 'black marketeering and other odious dealings' back in Russia. But then 'the CIA, which guided Radio Liberty's work is satisfied with the old and new scum employed there. It is satisfied with the vicious slander, insinuations and misinformation, cooked up on its instructions by former Hitlerites and criminals of all kind.'[54]

This is the kind of article which, using the tired cliché of 'as is generally known', serves as documentation for the East bloc campaign against the Munich stations. The massive use of co-ordinated attacks was launched at full blast in mid-1970 coinciding with the negotiations leading to the Soviet-West German Treaty, the Basic Treaty on relationship between the two German states and, last but not least, with the preparations for the 1972 Munich Olympic Games. Seizing upon an alleged statement by the then Chancellor Willy Brandt which, according to the Hamburg illustrated weekly *Stern*, criticised broadcasting aimed at other countries from West German territory as 'senseless', the commentator in a Moscow paper demanded the closure of the Munich stations as something 'entirely logical' and 'in the interests of an improved atmosphere in Europe'. After referring to the 'positive and important changes' between Bonn and Moscow, he raised the question: 'How long is this to go on?'[55]

From then onward hardly a day passed without similar articles in East bloc media, warning the Bonn Government, whose apparatus at that very time was infiltrated, from the personal staff of Brandt to high officials of key ministries by East German agents, that the credibility of the *Ostpolitik* would suffer. The calls for putting a stop 'once and for all to those relics of the Cold War' were taken up at the highest level. Thus the Polish Foreign Minister sent a letter in May 1971, to his West German counterpart warning that the activity of RFE disturbed the process of normalisation between the two countries. Only four days later the contents of this supposedly private communication were published and commented upon in the Polish press. One year later Prime Minister Pjotr Jaroszewicz himself took up the matter. Even in January 1976, after the various treaties with and about West Germany were signed and the Olympic Games were over, the President of the Soviet Union, Alexei Shitikov, while on a visit to Bonn, raised at a press conference the question of 'certain mass media and certain well-known radio stations in the Federal Republic' which had aroused the 'righteous indignation of the Soviet people'.[56]

The objectives of the campaign were transparent. The priority target was to oust RFE–RL not only from West Germany, but also from Portugal and Spain where the most powerful transmitters are in operation. Nevertheless, no West German Government could seriously consider not renewing the licence agreements with RFE–RL, even though Soviet propagandists were extremely successful in feeding information to *Spiegel* and *Stern*, the two publications which often provide what can only be called unpaid advertising space for Kremlin policies.[57] The campaign in Portugal also met with failure. A new fifteen-year agreement for transmitter facilities was concluded in 1977 between RFE–RL and the Portuguese Government. It is open to doubt whether the public in Portugal was as 'outraged' as *Izvestia* wants us to believe because the agreement 'according to local papers' (which papers are not stated!) 'violates the national sovereignty of Portugal and is contrary to the spirit of *détente*.'[58]

However the potentially most dangerous campaign was carried on in the US and above all in the US Congress. Senator Fulbright, who became convinced that the closure of the Munich stations was the test of US readiness to pursue a policy of *détente*, spearheaded the efforts to cut off the funds for 'the relics of the past'. He was also fed various cleverly fabricated material, including forgeries of letters allegedly written by Jan Nowak, then chief of RFE's Polish service. Nothing could prove better what a thorn in the flesh these stations are than the fact that when President Nixon visited Poland in May 1972, Prime Minister Jaroszewicz bluntly asked him 'to jettison such centres of propaganda and subversion as RFE' because its activities were in flagrant contradiction 'to the tendency towards *détente* in Europe' and stood also 'in diametrical opposition to the favourable development of bilateral relations.' The then Party Secretary and former police chief, Franciszek Sxlachcic (since quietly purged), also tried to convince Henry Kissinger that RFE was 'the main stumbling bloc in the way of improving US-Polish relations.'[59]

Cloak-and-dagger actions were also undertaken by the Polish and Czechoslovak secret services to hasten the liquidation of RFE–RL, or at any rate to discredit their reputation in Eastern Europe. On 8 March 1971, a certain Andrzej Czechowicz, at that time thirty-three years old, was suddenly produced in Warsaw at an international press conference as a Polish intelligence operator, who for the past six years had been working as an RFE employee in the Polish research and evaluation section.

Czechowicz related how he had joined the Polish Ministry of Interior in 1962 and, following a 'thorough' training, he had turned up in Cologne, apparently returning from a trip to Britain, as a 'political refugee'. By June 1966, he had succeeded in penetrating RFE where he was evaluating Polish periodicals. He was praised by *Neues Deutschland* in East Berlin as 'one of those fearless scouts whose activity serves the securing of peace against imperialism's global strategy.'[60] The exploits of Captain Czechowicz received great publicity in the East, with even his 'noble origins' mentioned as good credentials in helping him to get into the lion's den in Munich. Under the influence of his tales some gullible Western correspondents even went so far as to speculate that the RFE was manipulating a campaign against the former police chief and organiser of the anti-semitic witch-hunt, M. Moczar! It is probable that the recall of the Polish agent was timed to give what his bosses hoped would be the final push to silence the Munich stations before the Olympic Games.

Polish intelligence was also suspected to be behind a burglary in 1972 in the home of the editor of the largest Polish-language newspaper in the US. Raiders stole two genuine letters he had received from Nowak of the RFE, which later served as a basis for a forged letter sent to Senator Fulbright.[61] The campaign however finally petered out after the Munich stations had been put on a completely new basis, thus puncturing the hopes of the Soviet and East European experts in 'the department of dirty tricks'.

A less flamboyant, but not uninteresting 'disinformation action' is said to have been undertaken by Hungarian intelligence in the mid-1960s. According to a former high-ranking Czechoslovak intelligence officer, who defected while serving ostensibly as press attaché in Vienna in 1968, the Hungarian disinformation department screened all mail sent by listeners to RFE and destroyed some eighty percent of the genuine letters. Instead it created a network of RFE 'listeners' posing as students, workers, engineers or housewives who wrote to the Munich station. This long-range operation was to effect 'a radical shift in programming from political broadcasts to entertainment and music'.[62] Be that as it may, in later years the Hungarian press occasionally referred to the 'more refined' tactics of RFE and complained that young people are 'infected' by a combining of pop music with 'manipulated' newscasts. There is no way to judge the assertions of the Czech defector or the real effect of the Hungarian ploy, if indeed there ever was one. But it is noteworthy that even the Soviets responded in 1964 to the undoubted appeal of Western broadcasts, particularly to young people, and initiated a new domestic programme, called *Mayak* (Beacon) which offers popular music in addition to news and commentaries.

The potentially most harmful intelligence operation, not so much against RFE but rather against the opposition movement in Czechoslovakia, was the defection of a certain Pavel Minařik, who had worked for seven years as an announcer in the Czech service of RFE in Munich. In the course of a reduction of personnel, he was given notice in 1975. However he kept coming to the offices of the Czech service and apparently succeeded in copying or stealing various documents and letters. Ostensibly on his way from New York to Los Angeles to set up a new existence, the thirty-one-year-old Minařik was presented on 29 January 1976 at a press conference in Prague as 'an intelligence officer who penetrated RFE, the instrument of subversive and espionage activities, the CIA control centre for emigré organisations.' Prague television showed a series of interviews with Minařik. The alleged Captain in the Czech secret service, even named former party chief Alexander Dubcek along with some well-known dissident figures as having prepared all their state-

ments 'at the order of the CIA', and accused Dubcek of
maintaining a Cologne bank account.

In addition to utilising Minařik to prove the alleged
continuation of the CIA connection, the operation was
intended to discredit those Czechoslovak emigrés who were
connected with RFE and above all to inflict serious damage on
Dubcek's reputation, to frighten off potential listeners' mail
to RFE and to exert further pressure on West Germany. The
entire Soviet bloc media featured the great accomplishments
of an Eastern intelligence agent.[63] Yet it was hinted by Czech
emigrés, including a most amusing piece by Ota Filip in the
Frankfurter Allgemeine Zeitung, that Minařik was very small
fry indeed, performing only speaking-announcing duties and
that he might have established contact with the Czechs only
when his contract was terminated. All this however does not
change the fact that Prague pulled off a coup, causing
temporary disarray among the human rights activists in
Prague and the emigrés abroad. But it was only an episode
and 'Captain Minařik', his duty fulfilled, appears to have
disappeared without a trace.

Surprisingly enough, even the Romanian press picked up
the Minařik story, if with a slight delay. All dailies published
an extensive report on the affair and quoted Minařik as
saying that 'the chief goal of RFE is not only the besmirching
of the socialist countries, but above all a cunning psychological warfare and a disorientation of listeners.'[64] Romania was
the first East European country to stop jamming RFE in 1963.
There is no doubt that the broadcasts about the enormous and
positive Western echo of the independent-minded foreign
policy initiatives launched by the Romanian leadership in the
1960s helped to strengthen the domestic basis of the régime.
However, the Ceauşescu régime became furious when RFE
also began to broadcast the increasingly negative Western
press comments on the domestic situation, the massive wave
of applications tabled by ethnic Germans for exit permits to
resettle in the Federal Republic and the ferment among the
disgruntled Hungarians. President Ceauşescu himself
launched sharp public attacks on the Munich station, particularly after the emergence of a human rights group around Paul
Goma in 1977. It is not as part of the bloc-wide strategy, but

rather in the independent interest of Romania to put pressure on RFE and to silence the critics, now even joined by the great playwright Eugene Ionesco. The fact that a well-known exiled Romanian critic and RFE contributor in Paris was physically threatened, and that Romanian media launched vicious personal attacks against Ionesco and others is a sign of growing concern about the impact of 'open communication' from Munich at a time of deepening domestic political and economic difficulties in Romania.

It was the mysterious death of the Bulgarian writer Georgi Markov in London in September 1978 which dramatised the East-West battle of the air waves for a wider public. Born in 1929, Markov, a well-known writer in his native country, defected in 1969 and in 1971 came to London where he began to work for the BBC. Later he also wrote and broadcast for *Deutsche Welle* and RFE. It was apparently a series of broadcasts on his personal impressions of the Bulgarian party leader Todor Zhivkov and the situation of intellectuals, broadcast to Bulgaria by RFE in the autumn and winter of 1977–78, which particularly embarrassed the Bulgarian régime. His broadcasts roughly coincided with the sensational defection of Vladimir Kostov and his wife, perhaps the best known Bulgarian TV and radio correspondent. They, too, gave a series of broadcasts in Bulgarian, transmitted by RFE.

Markov himself told his wife that he had been stabbed with an umbrella on the street near Bush House, the headquarters of the BBC External Services. He died four days later. After a thorough forensic investigation, it was established that a minute pellet found in Markov's thigh contained a deadly toxin, called ricin. On 2 January 1979 the Coroner ruled that Markov had been 'killed unlawfully'. In the meantime, it turned out that Kostov had been the victim of a similar attack a few days earlier in Paris. The experts established that a tiny metal object in his thigh was identical with Markov's pellet. Kostov's life had been saved because the major part of the toxin had not entered his blood stream.

The Bulgarian authorities were evidently stung when *The*

Times, in a leader, expressed 'a strong suspicion that Mr Markov was murdered by an agent acting for the Bulgarian authorities.' Having already issued a short denial of any Bulgarian involvement, BTA, the official news agency came out with a long statement rejecting 'most categorically the groundless campaign'. It added that the Bulgarian authorities were ready to 'give full assistance to the British authorities for joint investigations, analysis and evaluation.' The most revealing passage was undoubtedly the following: 'Only absurd and irresponsible thinking would assume that if Bulgaria had assessed Georgi Markov as politically dangerous she would wait for ten years – so that he might do everything that he was able to do – and only then take measures against him . . .'[65]

Though the murderer managed to erase all traces, the case of Georgi Markov is not yet closed. In a letter from the Home Office to his widow, it was explained that no evidence had so far emerged 'to enable charges to be brought against any individual.' Relating this in an article on the anniversary of her husband's death, Annabel Markov said:

> When a weapon is used which, for the first time in history, allows the assassin to get clear away before murder is even suspected, it is very unlikely that charges can ever be brought against 'any individual'. But hasn't the stage been reached when the amount of circumstantial evidence gathered justifies an official protest by the British Government, whether or not the assassin is ever caught?[66]

A less dramatic and less vituperative, but nevertheless practically permanent campaign, combining press attacks and diplomacy goes on against the other major Western stations. From time to time Soviet papers complain that 'instead of decently confining itself to the (generally deplorable) affairs of Britain, the BBC concentrates on happenings in the international Communist movement.'[67] The files of the Foreign Office could also give some clues to the quantity of Soviet interventions both in London and Moscow against 'unfriendly' commentaries or positively 'harmful interviews with dissidents who, after all, do not represent anybody . . .' To equip the propagandists with proper arguments, a Moscow publishing house has just brought out a whole book on the BBC, and the history, apparatus and methods of 'one of the oldest centres of imperialistic propaganda.'[68]

Similarly, the Voice of America also comes under attack for devoting far too much time to the 'internal affairs of the Soviet Union and the socialist countries'. Recently the Moscow foreign affairs weekly *Novoie Vremya* tried to kill two birds with one stone: to deal with a so-called sensitive subject and at the same time to attack Western broadcasts to the Soviet Union. Lately the weekly has begun to publish questions, purportedly written by foreign readers, about such touchy issues as grain imports from the West, Soviet policy in Africa and so on. One of these letters was allegedly written by a certain Jaime Gonzales from Guayaquil in Ecuador. He asked how was it possible, sixty years after the October Revolution, that there were still such relics of bourgeois customs as greed, violations of labour discipline and disturbances of public order in the Soviet Union?

A commentator of the weekly referred to the difficulties in changing human beings and also to the many years of war and reconstruction. However the real culprits are the Western broadcasters. This is at any rate the inference one can draw from his reply: 'Last but not least, imperialist propaganda contributes in no small degree to the existence of relics hostile to socialism. Do you know that out of 900 hours of VOA broadcasts 170 are beamed in eight Soviet languages to the Soviet Union? In many broadcasts VOA suggests ideas and ethical-moral views to listeners which are strange to socialism.'[69]

This somewhat bizarre attempt to saddle VOA and Western broadcasting in general with responsibility for the rising rate of criminal offences in the Soviet Union, provides a useful insight into the Soviet propaganda methods. However, the attacks against the BBC or the VOA are mere pinpricks compared to the incessant stream of abuse against the Russian service of the *Deutsche Welle*, the Cologne-based West German short-wave radio station.

Founded in 1953, the station has an autonomous status and is financed by public funds. As an institution of public law *Deutsche Welle* (like its sister, *Deutschlandfunk* broadcasting on medium wave and, since 1976, in charge of transmissions to Poland and Czechoslovakia) is controlled by a board composed of representatives of the political parties, employers' federations, trade unions, and the Churches on a balanced proportional basis.

It is against this background that the Soviet attempts at interfering in German domestic politics must be seen. From 1972–73 onwards the station became a permanent target of attacks, launched mainly in the German-language programmes of Radio Moscow and the so-called 'Radio Peace and Progress' also from Moscow, to a lesser extent by Radio Prague, and of course East Berlin. The main thrust of the attacks has been all along that the East European services are in the hands of the enemies both of East-West *détente* and of West German *Ostpolitik* conducted by the Social Democrat-Liberal coalition governments of Willy Brandt and Helmut Schmidt.

The methods used to discredit the editorial staff are the same as in the case of RFE–RL. *Izvestia* flatly accused the station of being 'against the spirit of Helsinki' which is no wonder since out of 2,400 employees, some 400 are 'former Goebbels propagandists and all kinds of traitors and deserters from the Soviet Union, Hungary, Czechoslovakia and other socialist countries.' If one scrutinises the texts of the countless strident attacks, the reasons for the irritation of the Kremlin soon become apparent. Thus the Russian service was attacked for 'defending the renewal of the operating permits for the US station, RFE–RL', for reporting the domestic situation in Czechoslovakia, for quoting the comments of West German newspapers about the new Soviet constitution, for 'distorting generally known historical facts about the situation at the Horn of Africa' and presenting 'inventions about Soviet and Cuban participation in the war between Somalia and Ethiopia', for 'trying to force the Bonn government to embark on a policy of colonial expansion', for 'spreading primitive lies about the threat allegedly posed by the Soviet Union and the Warsaw Pact', etc, etc.[70]

What is the reason for the 'provocation and disinformation under the mask of objectivity?' The Soviets accuse the station of 'hankering after the Third Reich' and 'revanchism', of serving 'the circles which profit from the arms race' and even of being 'financed from ultra-reactionary circles in and outside the Federal Republic.' But basically, the Russian service seeks to undermine Soviet-West German relations 'in the service of the German opposition parties CDU–CSU and the aggressive circles of NATO.' To sum up, all this seriously harms the good climate between Bonn and Moscow and, as implied by a Soviet correspondent, only the dismissal of the 'arch-enemies' of the Soviet Union at the head of the Russian service, could bring about an improvement.

When West German newspapers replied in kind and rejected such covert threats and blatant pressures exerted on the editorial policy of German domestic media, the Soviet journalist in question said that it 'was his right as a human being and journalist', and as a 'Soviet correspondent, to state his attitude towards certain persons and spell out publicly his opinion about the actions of the enemies of the Soviet Union.' This had nothing to do with 'pressures for dismissals' or 'with interference in internal affairs of the Federal Republic.'[71]

This controversy provides yet another example of the double standard applied by the Eastern side. Even character defamation, insinuations and public mixtures of blandishments and threats are projected as something perfectly normal and legitimate. But then, basically, all Western stations are said to be alike. In the words of the Moscow radio commentator Viktor Viktorov, 'the tendentious propaganda of the Western radio centres, including also the VOA, the BBC and *Deutsche Welle* [RFE–RL was attacked earlier – P.L.] is directed against the spirit of *détente*, mutual understanding and co-operation.' Worse still, they carry on a 'psychological warfare, violating the spirit and the letter of the Helsinki accords.' Viktorov tells us that this is the view of the weekly *Deutsche Volkszeitung*; omitting to mention that the paper happens to be an East German Communist publication. . . .[72]

Whenever the Western stations disseminate factual information on a crisis or on major international issues, ranging from the invasion of Cambodia by Vietnam and the war between China and Vietnam, to the question of military balance in Europe or the Soviet intervention in Afghanistan, their broadcasts spark off a stream of sweeping propagandistic generalisations accompanied by strident and pompous accusations instead of substantive counter-arguments.

But what is the character of the westwards propaganda of the Soviet side? After all, as Leonid Brezhnev said in his speech at the Helsinki conference in 1975:[73] 'the information media can serve the aims of peace and mutual trust, but can also spread the poison of discord between countries and people throughout the world.'

6   *The Soviet Model and the 'New World Order for Information'*

THE SOVIET attitude towards the two-way flow of information is profoundly paradoxical. As we have seen, the Kremlin and most of its client states are resorting to an impressive variety of methods to fight the penetration of uncensored news. Communist representatives at international meetings are in the forefront when it comes to denouncing 'information imperialism' and the mortal dangers of the unrestricted exchange of information.

Yet, at the same time, the Soviet Union is today the single largest purveyor of broadcast information to the world. Its stations broadcast 2,010 hours weekly in eighty languages to audiences on every continent. Radio Moscow's languages include, for example, the Quechua Indian tongue of Latin America, the African Foula and Lingala and the Oriya and Mathi of the Indian subcontinent. In 1964 'Radio Progress and Peace' appeared on the scene, presented as an 'independent voice of the people'. When Western media complain of the far more aggressive content of its broadcasts, the Soviets produce the ridiculous excuse that the radio is 'owned by public organisations' such as the trade unions and the *Novosti* press agency. Since Soviet ideological spokesmen have for many years told us that the media is firmly controlled as 'the sharpest weapon of the party', these explanations merely show the contempt of the Communist leadership for any kind of criticism from outside.

'Radio Peace and Progress' added other languages, among them Creole and Yiddish, as well as the Cantonese and Shanghai dialects of Chinese to the Soviet broadcasting repertoire. Apart from the two principal stations, there are of course local stations, from Tallinn and Riga in the Baltic republics, to Yerevan and Tashkent, which also broadcast special short-wave programmes for foreign audiences in an additional nine languages. In all, some three dozen languages not used by any Western radio are included in Soviet programming.[74] In the summer and autumn of 1978, the Soviets added, to an already impressive array, twenty-nine new 500-kilowatt transmitters in twenty-four cities. On the already overcrowded air waves, the Soviet broadcasts in fact reduce the space for other stations.

In the summer of 1979, Radio Moscow launched a World Service in English, broadcast for nineteen hours a day, deliberately if somewhat crudely modelled on the BBC World Service and the VOA. It is claimed to bring in a thousand letters daily. Despite a similar mixture of news, features and pop music after the Kremlin chimes on the hour, listeners with a command of English can recognise quickly enough that the programme is not coming from London or Washington DC.[75]

The combined output of external broadcasts from the other Warsaw Pact states has doubled in the last two decades and now totals almost 1,500 hours weekly in scores of languages. About 1,400 hours of broadcasting from Soviet and East European stations are beamed to North America and Western Europe; 164 hours of that total to North America. These broadcasts have an estimated audience of about a million US listeners during the course of a month; of these listeners, 284,000 tune in at least once a week. In addition, about eleven percent of the Soviet external broadcasts are directed to the Western hemisphere, including 109 hours to Latin America. Almost ten percent (171 hours in 13 languages) is beamed to India. Broadcasts to the Far East total 333 hours, to the Near East, 186 and to black Africa, 168 hours.[76]

Janus, the ancient Roman god, was pictured with faces both on the front and back of his head, and therefore credited with the faculty of looking both ways. Even a cursory review of the content of Soviet external broadcasts and policy statements made by leading ideologists, lead to the inescapable conclusion that Communist propaganda is Janus-faced. It is most instructive to compare the constant assertions made by the Soviets, even by Brezhnev himself, about their media 'serving human aims, the cause of peace, the consolidation of trust and friendship between nations,' with a few recent samples from external broadcasts.

On President Carter's energy proposals (to Asia):

> The imperialist course of monopolies is aimed at preserving oil reserves in the United States, and at plundering the countries of the Third World, the oil reserves of which are becoming exhausted. To keep and increase its riches at the expense of the plunder of others, such is the policy of imperialist monopolies. This policy no doubt aggravates the contradiction between monopolistic capitalism and the people of the countries of the Third World.

On the us Congress (in English):

> Quite some time has passed since Church has tabled and then pushed through the Senate a resolution with help from anti-Soviet and Zionist circles . . . All the so-called facts are dreamed up by Zionist propaganda. . . . It is exceedingly strange that Mr Church is allowed to spread deliberate lies with impunity and to do so at such a lofty and respected forum as the American Senate. Because of this we imagine that the us has no laws envisaging punishment for defamation.

On us foreign policy (in English to Asia):

> As is known, it is mainly the United States that, during the independent development of India, tried to enslave the country economically . . .

(In Arabic to the Middle East)

> Here we have to expose the real essence and blatant designs of the American-Zionist policy . . . the American-Zionist imperial plan . . .

(In English to Africa)

> It appears that American officials are setting various contingencies which could involve the dispatch of American troops to Rhodesia (which) could be used in Rhodesia only on the side of

the unlawful Smith régime. All the more so since the United States has already done a lot to bolster the Rhodesian racists.

The hounding of 'dissidents' by the American authorities is assuming a mass character . . . The police . . . are directing their main effort not so much against the criminals who represent a real threat to society, as against those who disagree with the policies of the ruling circles.[77]

One could go on to quote many more examples to show how Soviet and East European media take full advantage of the political freedom of the West. Thus TASS correspondents in the US could freely interview prisoners in a North Carolina jail, and send back a report claiming that 'political prisoners' in the US are 'forcibly injected with mind-twisting drugs.' Communist newsmen have open access to Western politicians. Their publications are sold on the news-stands and their acerbic comments on NATO or US policies receive broad and unfiltered coverage in Western newspapers, radio and television media.

The Soviet and East German attack against the so-called *Berufsverbot* in West Germany is another instance of the double standard. This provision (admittedly controversial in West Germany itself) means that members of the DKP, the Communist party operating in the Federal Republic (and professing total loyalty to the Soviet Union), are not accepted as members of the civil service. Communist propaganda seeks to persuade its domestic public and foreign listeners that there is rampant political repression in West Germany, and that democratic citizens in great numbers are prevented from entering or practising their profession. As a West German observer commented, 'Let us try to imagine the reaction of the Soviet Government if Western radio stations – in similar fashion to the Eastern campaign against *Berufsverbot* – called upon the Soviet public to implement the socialist right to the expression of minority opinion (constitutionally guaranteed in 1936) by admitting Solzhenitsyn and other dissidents to state functions.'[78]

The initial coverage of the drama of the take-over of the US embassy in Tehran by the 'National Voice of Iran', the powerful Soviet transmitter in Baku, some one hundred miles from Iran, provided yet another proof of just how *Pravda*'s assertion that 'the substance of the activity of the Soviet press, radio and television . . . completely accords with the high ideals enshrined in Helsinki,' is interpreted. In its Persian-language broadcasts the station called the US embassy 'a centre of corruption and anti-Iranian conspiracies'. It found the embassy take-over and the seizing of American hostages 'totally understandable and logical'. When a State Department spokesman complained about the inflammatory broadcasts, TASS dismissed as 'groundless' what it called the 'US attempt to distort the meaning of the material in the Soviet press.' In its usual way, the agency sidestepped the substance of the US complaint, which had been primarily against Soviet Persian-language broadcasts to Iran. Nevertheless, two weeks later the 'Voice of Iran', which Moscow maintains is not an official, government-sponsored station, shifted its stand and spoke out in favour of releasing the hostages.[79]

Basically, the Soviets have always insisted that the maintenance of an absolute monopoly of information in their sphere of influence is as completely natural as their endeavour to exercise as much influence as possible on the mass media in the capitalist countries. At one of the important periodical (once or twice yearly) conferences of the Central Committee secretaries in charge of ideology, the Polish representative, Jerzy Lukaszewicz, flatly stated:

> The slogan of the 'free exchange of ideas and peoples' is directed in its very essence against *détente*. It is seemingly progressive and has become therefore popular among those circles of the population in the capitalist countries which are genuinely interested in peaceful coexistence. But behind this façade there is the business of the advocates of a psychological warfare against the socialist countries. Such a completely unrestricted 'free exchange of ideas and people' would mean that one could freely propagate slanders of the socialist order, anti-humane ideas of militarism and fascism, the cult of strength and careerism. We are advocates of a free exchange of true information about all questions of national and international life, of broad cultural relations and direct contacts between people, but we will not tolerate a subversive propaganda, and will continue to fight that it should be declared illegal and banned in the whole world. No exchange of ideas should be allowed to violate the

sovereignty of a state, to undermine its law, mores and traditions.[80]

These words have been repeated time and again by Eastern spokesmen. Less is said of course about the other face of Soviet external propaganda, its offensive function as the so-called fourth pillar of foreign policy, in addition to diplomacy, the armed forces and the economy. In reality, the Soviet propaganda apparatus is a wolf in sheep's clothing. The aggressive statements, quoted earlier, are part and parcel of what the Soviets like to call the 'ideological struggle'. As the leading ideologist Boris Ponomarev, Central Committee secretary in charge of international relations, said: 'No kind of *détente* leads or should lead to the peaceful coexistence of ideologies. This is a Communist axiom. Experience has proved that political *détente* leads not to the disappearance, but on the contrary, to a reinforcement and expansion of the ideological struggle.'[81]

What this veteran functionary (who, two years after Khrushchev's secret speech in 1958, still had a large picture of Stalin hanging in his office!)[82] really meant by the term 'ideological struggle' is not difficult to define. He himself said in a speech, which was only reprinted in the Prague-based international Communist monthly, that victory in the revolution depends on the 'breaking of the class enemy's grip on the mass media and propaganda' in addition to the take-over of the army and the establishment of a new state apparatus.[83]

This is the language which senior Communist officials understand but which is, of course, not used at international gatherings with representatives of the West and the Third World. In other words, the attempt to undermine the capitalist or Western systems by seizing control over the mass media, which, according to Ponomarev 'have never had such a crucial role in the social-political battle' as now, is legitimate and justified. Countless authoritative publications in Russia and the satellites have emphasised that the 'creation of optimal conditions for social struggle in the interests of socialism, the working class and all anti-imperialistic forces' is an integral part of the ideological struggle. The Communist leadership combines defensive action aimed at protecting its closed system and its own controlled media with manifold offensives to impose its own criteria upon Western governments, media and public opinion.

Consider, for example, the vicious, arrogant and pompous attacks incessantly launched against all Western media in general, and against selected commentators and correspondents by name, if they dare to question Eastern policies or actions. When Western colleagues point out concrete cases, the Eastern propagandists assert that they merely carry out their 'journalistic duty to collect and to provide information'. The double standard was impressively illustrated by the Soviet radio commentator, Vladimir Ostrogorski, when polemicising with a West German journalist about the meaning of 'party-mindedness' in broadcasting:

> Yes we are party-minded, we take the side of socialism, of peace, of international co-operation. We report from this standpoint in radio. Does this mean that we approve or indulge in interference? On the contrary, precisely because we are for socialism, peace, international co-operation, we are against interference. We are against interference, because it endangers peace and makes international co-operation more difficult. The interference is incompatible with the policy of peaceful coexistence . . .[84]

This is the kind of sophism Communist propagandists can present behind the protective cover of a total information control, unexposed to any meaningful debate. When, for example, a Soviet press representative on a popular television discussion programme in Cologne sharply attacks *Deutsche Welle*, or when he and other Soviet emissaries publicly rebuke well-known German journalists for their opinions, they are purported to discharge their journalistic duties in the service of peace and understanding.[85] But when US Ambassador Malcolm Toon was prevented from delivering the usual 4 July message on TV and radio to the Soviet citizens in 1977 because he refused to delete certain oblique references to human rights, the action was obviously legitimate. Radio Liberty and the Voice of America were, by the same token, guilty of 'impermissible interference' when they dared to broadcast in Russian the message Toon was not allowed to read in Moscow.

Access to Western media, public and political establishments is taken for granted by Communist propagandists, starting from the premise that unlimited propaganda for 'real socialism' and against capitalism is fully legitimate under the conditions of peaceful coexistence. Yet as we have just seen, not even a US Ambassador, let alone a Western journalist, can avail himself of similar facilities to project the Western standpoint or political views in the Soviet sphere of influence.

Let us take a typical statement, made by the veteran Soviet media spokesman and functionary in charge of Unesco affairs, Yuri Kashlev: a statement repeated by him and other Soviet propagandists on every possible occasion with minimal stylistic variations:

> It is understandable that no ruling class could possibly consent to share information media with anyone else when relations between states with different social structures are involved. . . . No country will permit the mass information media to be used among its citizens for the propagation of hostile views and ideas which run counter to its political ideals and its morals, laws and traditions.[86]

His own colleagues have produced the most convincing evidence against Kashlev's high-sounding, but in essence senseless allegations. Thus, for example Spartak Beglov, the well-known chief *Novosti* commentator received a high government order for his fiftieth birthday and, perhaps in a somewhat elated mood, told the publication of the Soviet Journalists Federation 'how he succeeded in influencing political events and discussion in other countries.' He gave two examples: 'He alerted through his commentaries the Australian public to the consequences of setting up US military bases. When in Scandinavia, people were discussing joining the Common Market, he drew attention to the danger to peace which such a step would cause.' He was asked just how he carried out 'counter-propaganda'? 'One has to act according to a blueprint for direct counter-propaganda to offset the slanders of 'Sovietologists' with arguments. One often has to avail oneself of letters. Many papers, for example

The Times (of London) are not willing to print articles, but give space for a letter,' Beglov said and also explained how he contributed to the debate about the Vietnam war in the US in this way.[87]

In contact with editorial offices, publishers and institutions in 110 countries, *Novosti* journalists fight against 'the advocates of Cold War and aggression and tear off the masks of ideological diversionists, be they common bourgeois enemies of the Soviet Union or newly fangled slanderers, such as helpers of Solzhenitsyn, Zionist racists or the forgers in Peking.' With its enormous apparatus, *Novosti* supplies well over 100,000 articles, often free of charge, in addition to a steady stream of 'Letters to the Editor', to thousands of newspapers and periodicals. The agency is an important weapon in the world-wide Soviet campaign aimed at projecting the peace-loving image of the Soviet camp and isolating the US as an imperialistic, racist and aggressive power. In particular, the thrust of the global propaganda network is directed against any increase of military spending and weapons development by the US and NATO. The massive and well-organised campaigns have always used all channels of public communication: mass media, petitions, public letter writing and demonstrations.

The Soviet Union has applied basically the same methods in all campaigns, from those against the atom and hydrogen bombs (until Moscow became capable of producing them), to the propaganda against the neutron bomb in 1977 and the recent barrage of warnings against the deployment of medium range US nuclear missiles in Western Europe. In June 1980 a sudden spate of letters to *Die Welt* in Bonn and *The Times* in London, allegedly from irate Soviet citizens protesting about 'Slanders' against Soviet action in Afghanistan, followed the same pattern. In fact, the basic methods were already employed in the 1930s as Arthur Koestler and Babette Gross, among others, have described.[88]

According to a CIA report prepared for the House Permanent Select Committee on Intelligence, the Soviets spend 'at least $2 billion a year to spread pro-Communist and anti-US propaganda through a worldwide network that includes international front organisations controlled by the Kremlin'.

The Report added that dozens of international 'Communist fronts' pose as independent organisations, but are actually 'funded and controlled by the Soviets'. It also stressed that with 'a worldwide network of assets,' including not only media, but also seventy-five Communist parties outside the bloc, nearly 500 Soviet newsmen working abroad ('many of them intelligence officers') and, last but not least, the KGB, the state security service, plus the intelligence and propaganda resources of Cuba and Communist Eastern Europe, 'the Soviets are able to orchestrate propaganda campaigns on a worldwide basis with relative ease.'[89]

While some of the alarming assertions in the report are probably exaggerated and motivated by the vested interests of the CIA itself, no one can deny that the Soviets are indeed able to launch massive worldwide campaigns with 'relative ease'. It is enough to recall, for example, that one of the most influential publications in Europe, *Der Spiegel*, recently devoted almost twenty-five pages to an interview with two top Soviet propagandists touring Western Europe and the NATO capitals, in a bid to win public support for the Soviet side in its campaign against NATO's latest efforts to offset at least some of the overwhelming Soviet nuclear and conventional superiority on the European continent.[90] There is no doubt that such *Spiegel* interviews, or *Novosti* articles and letters carried in serious journals which feel an urge to carry both sides of the arguments, are major propaganda successes for the Kremlin.

Here again, one is confronted with the ubiquitous double standard. Which Soviet newspaper has ever carried such a *Spiegel*-type interview, unfiltered and uncensored, or given a Western commentator or politician the opportunity to publish an uncensored, uncut article which opposed basic Soviet policies? Could anyone imagine a Western correspondent in Moscow or Prague appearing on television or in a radio discussion, and sharply criticising Soviet policies, singling out by name certain commentators as being particularly anti-Western? But then, of course, in Soviet external propaganda and domestic information policies, as *Pravda* claims: 'a clear ideological direction, genuine humanism, national characteristics and internationalism are organically inherent.' Both external and internal propaganda are 'weapons of the party' serving and faithfully reflecting any shift in the 'general line'.

It is a stunning paradox that at a time when, throughout the Communist world, pressures for more truthful and more comprehensive coverage of the international and domestic scene are growing, when even the Soviet Politbureau acknowledges the persistent failures of the State-controlled media, the export of the Soviet model appears to be making headway in parts of the Third World and is sympathetically viewed by some Unesco officials. In the non-aligned movement, Yugoslavia has staunchly and successfully defended the principles of genuine independence from *all* blocs; not just NATO, but also the Warsaw Pact. At and after the Havana summit meeting in 1979, President Tito, one of the founding fathers of the non-aligned movement, spearheaded the opposition to the Soviet-Cuban-Vietnamese line which regards the Third World countries as 'natural allies' and as a kind of reserve to the Soviet camp.

Yet in the vital field of communication, the Soviets and their allies appear to have succeeded in presenting the old Soviet model in a new packaging as an acceptable basis for the Unesco-sponsored 'New World Order for Information'. In any event, whatever their real feelings, Soviet spokesmen no longer dismiss the 'New Order' as 'meaningless and irrelevant',[91] but enthusiastically embrace it as yet another lever to weaken Western influence. The Soviets provide – 'as part of the general policy of the socialist community' – help for the 'national information media of the developing countries' and seek 'to strengthen co-operation with Asian, African and Latin American countries with no political strings attached.' This is how an authoritative article in *Pravda* by Yuri Kashlev, the executive secretary of the USSR Unesco Commission spelled out the Soviet position on the eve of the important Tashkent meeting. He added meaningfully that it was due to the 'joint action of the socialist and developing countries that international organisations have been able to adopt a number of important documents, dealing a blow at colonialism in the field of information.' The Soviet Unesco

Commission and the Soviet Journalists' Federation responded 'to the desire expressed by many developing countries to get a better idea of the Soviet Union's experience in building up and developing a socialist system of mass information media' and organised an international seminar of journalists to 'exchange experiences in the development of the mass information media and the training of journalists.'[92]

On the basis of the coverage, particularly in the local press, the Tashkent meeting (2–8 September 1979) must be regarded as a significant step towards uniting the Third World countries and the Soviet bloc, with the apparent blessing of the Unesco officialdom, against the information media of the West. In his opening speech, the party chief of Uzbekistan and alternate member of the Soviet Politbureau, S. R. Rashidov, heaped lavish praise on Unesco and enthusiastically supported the idea of a 'New World Order for Information' seen as the 'struggle for national sovereignty in the sphere of information and culture against the imperialistic domination of the spiritual life of the people of Asia, Africa and Latin America.' Immediately afterwards, the Director-General of Unesco, the Senegalese Amadou Mahtar M'Bow, spoke out against colonialism in information media and praised the Tashkent seminar as a 'useful contribution' to the development of the national infrastructure. Perhaps to underline the ever closer links with Unesco, M'Bow even received a honorary degree of the Tashkent University.

It is of some symbolic significance, too, that no fewer than eleven members of the Executive Bureau of the Uzbek Communist Party, and two 'responsible functionaries' from the Central Committee apparatus of the CPSU (all mentioned before Kashlev and the secretary of the Journalists Organisation in the protocol list), participated at the opening meeting of the seminar which was attended by media representatives from fifty-two European, African, Asian and American countries. Inspired by a personal message from Leonid Brezhnev, expressing sympathy for the Third World efforts to seek protection against 'the ideological expansion of imperialism and spiritual colonialism', the participants went beyond just endorsing Unesco's efforts in favour of a 'New World Information Order.' They also proposed the setting up of a world press institute which should draw up an 'international code of ethics and conduct' for journalists. Scrutiny of the detailed reports of *Pravda Vostoka*, the local paper, revealed the usual spokesmen of the pro-Soviet propaganda line, from the Finnish President of the IOJ (the Prague-based International Organisation of Journalists) Kaarle Nordenstreng, to the Dean of Moscow's University Faculty of Journalism, J. N. Zassurski, and the extreme leftist, controversial American communication researcher, Professor Herbert Schiller. A Unesco official, the Venezuelan A. Paskuali, was quoted as criticising the insistence of the capitalist press on the 'free flow of information', to which he replied with the profound observation that 'we do not want free foxes in a free hen run . . .' In the plethora of Third World editors and officials there was apparently only one French journalist (himself closely co-operating with Unesco) as a token representative of the West. Needless to say, the Western media were the chief target of all statements.[93]

The main and tested instrument for selling the Soviet model and for assisting Soviet bloc strategic expansion plans in the field of communications is the International Organisation of Journalists. Founded in 1946 and claiming 150,000 members in 109 countries, it is undoubtedly one of the most important Soviet front organisations. While the World Federation of Trade Unions and the International Union of Students – both in Prague – have never recovered from the Cold War and become completely discredited in the West, IOJ (together with the much smaller OIRT, the International Radio and Television Organisation, also Prague-based) was quick to profit from the communication conflict between the West and the Third World.

An analysis of the 1978 issues of its glossy monthly magazine, *The Democratic Journalist*, founded in 1953, provides some interesting and revealing clues not only to the main emphasis in its propaganda, but also to the indoctrination programme in the training centres for journalists from the developing countries. The impression of a close liaison with Unesco not only dominated the deliberations in Tashkent, but also the pages of the ioj magazine. Out of fifty-two longer articles, Hifzi Topus, of the Unesco division of 'free flow of information and communication policies', alone contributed four essays. Soviet bloc and Cuban propagandists accounted for thirty-one major articles with the rest produced by Western Communists and 'progressive' Third World media experts.

But the content of the articles is even more revealing than such statistics. In the twenty-fifth anniversary issue, the lead editorial proudly claims that in the seventh number of the magazine in 1954, the ioj had raised 'the question of a code of ethics for journalists'. Thus the directors of what claims to be the 'largest democratic organisation of journalists in the world', themselves inadvertently admit that their basic line has not changed since 1953–54, the year when the Soviet Union and Eastern Europe were slowly recovering from the ice age of Stalinism, when Khrushchev and his associates were still waging a deadly struggle against the Stalinist Old Guard, and when in Czechoslovakia itself, the present head of state and party leader, Dr Gustáv Huśak was still in jail.

A perusal of the mainly Soviet, East German and Czech contributions confirms that the claim of continuity is well founded. The articles radiate a spirit and reflect a general approach which indeed could have been published even thirty years ago. For example S. Haskovec, director of a Prague journalists school, at an international journalists meeting in Bagdad in November 1977, attacked the us and West European news agencies, which 'boast of their so-called disinterested, objective reporting of pure facts'. He went on to explain:

> Even news which can be basically factual in detail cannot present a true picture of the developing countries if it is presented from the viewpoint of a stranger, without proper understanding of the problems and aspirations of these countries. Truthful reporting is not the simple accumulation of particular partial facts. . . . Only a proper evaluation of the complexity of social and economic events can result in a true journalistic picture of reality. The proportional representation of facts is also of supreme importance for objective reporting. I should like to stress once more the word proportional, because even news that

seems to be factual in singularities may be completely false in its overall context and impact unless set in correct relationship to other events. I therefore suggest that proportionality should be regarded as one of the new qualities of information.'[94]

What he calls a 'new quality' is in fact the good old Stalinist justification for deliberately misleading the public. This is the logic behind the censorship and filtering. A Stalinist would argue: 'There are thousands of flights, why report the occasional crash which is not *typical* of aviation in the socialist countries. . . . ?' It is also part of the 'true journalistic picture of reality' when the IOJ proudly lists its protests and concern for the fate of journalists persecuted by 'the reactionary régimes', but remains silent about the hundreds of outstanding Czech journalists who were sacked, and even jailed like Jiři Lederer.

However, if one reads the articles by Professor Zassurski or his colleague Berezhnoi, the reader immediately understands that what is needed is 'a party spirit and a class approach in the practice of mass communications media'. This is why the Soviet press remains 'the sharpest weapon' and rejects bourgeois theories that the press has only an informative character. The theories about 'the free flow of information', 'the right to communication', the 'right of access to information media' must also be combatted.

The pages of *The Democratic Journalist* are in fact the best evidence of what the 'new concept of newsworthiness' and a 'truly democratic press' means in practice. In addition to the heavy ideological material, the reader is informed of 'neo-fascist publications in West Germany', of the 'massive sacking of progressive journalists in West Germany' (though only one example of a disciplinary case against a broadcast editor is mentioned), of the sinister aims of the newly-named USIA in Washington DC, of the disgusting images of the Third World in West German children's books, of the fight against the neutron bomb, of the imperialistic propaganda and racist theories spread in Latin America and many other depressing events in the capitalist world. Yet what a contrast in the East where 'communist media works in the service of peace, progress and humanism', where the Bulgarian press is developing creatively, children's films and international photo exhibitions are shown in Moscow, a new Romanian weekly is published and another course for journalists begins in Budapest. What particularly strikes the observer is the fact that this magazine purportedly produced for journalists and media people, nevertheless presents the same type of diet as any Soviet or Romanian newspaper: a picture of unmitigated gloom, depression and plunder in the West – and a happy, constructive and forward looking life in the Communist world with the media selflessly helping the journalists both in the already independent countries and in the revolutionary movements in Africa and Latin America.

Western readers would be tempted to dismiss such publications as third rate, old style propaganda sheets in striking contrast to the journalistic approach of the Italian and Spanish, or even of the French Communist newspapers. But *The Democratic Journalist* and the other magazines, books and pamphlets produced in Prague are intended primarily as vehicles for ideological indoctrination. Great care is taken to curry favour with Unesco officialdom and hail the close co-operation, as reflected in the organisation's involvement in the much-publicised exercises at Bagdad and Tashkent.[95]

The Soviet bloc is now reaping the fruits of fifteen years of training and continues to indoctrinate carefully selected journalists and information officials from Third World countries. The main training centres are in East Berlin and Budapest, but following the call of the last IOJ congress in 1976 for even greater efforts to train journalistic cadres from the developing countries, a new international school, specialising in graduate courses for journalists, has been set up in Bulgaria. Romania even offers a three-year university level course for such students.

East Germany not only provides between 5,000 and 10,000 military advisers for front-line states in Africa and spends an estimated $200 million on development and military aid. It also plays a key role in what may be called 'journalistic development aid' in Africa. Since 1963 the 'School of Solidarity' now also called 'International Institute for Journalism-Werner Lamberz' (after a former East German Politbureau member who died in a helicopter crash in Libya in 1978) has trained 432 journalists from thirty-nine countries in Africa and Asia. At first glance, the figure is not very high. But the East German media experts emphasise quality and not quantity. As explained by the director, Sonja Brie, the programmes for the relatively brief courses, which last only a few months, start from the assumption that the participants have already had two to three years' experience. The students have to work very hard indeed before they are sent for a stay of several weeks with newspapers, radio or the ADN, the central news agency. News editing, precise formulation, lay-out, photography, operating a telex machine, learning the difference between electronic and print media and participation at press conferences are part of the practical knowledge offered by the school. However the director stressed that 'great attention is paid to the basic theoretical issues of social information and journalism. Participants are stimulated to reflect about the essence of the freedom of press, of relations between objectivism and partisanship of information, the psychological aspects of journalistic work.' She certainly hit the nail on the head with her statement that the participants win 'experiences which can only be collected in the countries of the real socialism . . .'

She also reveals that the school remains in touch with the graduates and has so far organised three meetings. In their own countries the graduates often become chief editors, foreign correspondents or functionaries of journalists' organisations or information ministries. The twenty-second course, completed in July 1979, was attended by eighteen students, primarily from southern Africa as well as representatives from journalists' organisations and ministries. 'As in the past, there have been also Unesco grantees among the participants,' the director added.[96]

The chairman of the GDR Journalists Federation, Harri Czepuck, described the real motives behind the training of future journalists from the Third World. They study at the 'School of Solidarity' in order 'to convince their countrymen of the necessity to develop independently from the old colonial power and in friendship with the socialist countries.'[97] The publications of ANC, the guerilla movement in South Africa are printed in East Germany, and members of ZAPU, ANC and SWAPO also attended the latest course.

At the graduate meeting celebrating the fifteenth anniversary of the Berlin school in the autumn of 1978, the chief of the ZAPU mission in East Berlin, Albert Ndindah, himself a graduate of the institute, sharply condemned 'the poisonous weapon of Anti-Communism used by the reactionary forces to separate the new states from their natural allies, the socialist community.' This is of course the spirit which the comrades from East Berlin to Budapest and Moscow would like to instill into the participants at the various training courses. The graduates, joined by the secretaries of the IOJ and the directors of the sister institutions from Hungary and Bulgaria also 'dealt with the still existing imperialistic influence on mass media, which they regard as a danger both for the socio-economic progress of the developing countries and the spreading of objective information.'[98]

What this 'objective information' means and what kind of journalists are reared in the 'School of Solidarity' was impressively shown in an article by an Ethiopian student in the newspaper put together by the participants at the course: 'Really, the GDR is on its way to becoming a paradise, because you find no one hungering, no beggars, no unemployed, only peaceful, well-nourished and well dressed people . . .' Or a participant from Nepal learned – of all places behind the Wall in East Berlin – 'how much the man, each single human being is worth . . .'[99]

The Budapest-based international institute of the IOJ has in the past sixteen years trained over 400 journalists from thirty-eight developing countries from Asia, Africa and Latin America. So far the courses have been given mainly in English, once in French and once in Spanish. Henceforth however the number of French language courses will be increased. A six months' course in the first half of 1978 was attended by fifteen participants from Algeria, Benin and Mali. There are also special seminars or conferences. One at the end of 1977 was attended by women journalists from Ghana, Angola, India, Ethiopia, Iraq and Syria. The institute is maintained and directed by the Association of Hungarian Journalists which has recently purchased a new modern building for the school; while the air fares are paid by the IOJ, the Hungarians provide full board and lodging, and even grants, for the participants.[100]

The East Germans have begun to prepare a major recruiting drive in Latin America too. President Czepuck hinted that the East German Federation is already discussing with the Cuban comrades how the aid for Nicaragua and other countries could help to 'promote the triumph of anti-imperialist and anti-colonialist forces.' Every year the East German journalists collect about half a million marks solidarity aid, but Czepuck warned that the GDR journalists will face more material demands in connection with the future tasks in Latin America. He announced that the 'School of Solidarity' will be enlarged in order to cope with the growing demand for participation at the courses, and 'to enable developing countries to make their own contribution to the elimination of the still existing positions of imperialism, neocolonialism and racism in the most efficient way.'[101]

In addition to the normal activity of the special school, there are also special courses. Thus leading editors of eight African and Arab news agencies attended a two-month course organised by ADN and the East German Journalists Federation in East Berlin in the autumn of 1979. The seminar provided an exchange of experiences about managing, planning and organising agency work.

East Germany has also, during the last ten years, organised courses for some thousand journalists in twelve countries. The seminars in Kongo Brazzaville, Ethiopia, Mozambique and Guinea-Bisseau were attended by 243 participants.[102] They were taught by Communist communication functionaries from East Berlin, for example by Wolfgang Kleinwächter, that 'the main question is not how much information flows from where whither, but rather which information should be exchanged and distributed worldwide and for what purpose.'[103] An example of the kind of information fed by their masters to the journalistic cadres in some Third World countries was witnessed on the spot in the city of Arusha by West German journalists covering a conference about the perspectives of German-African relations. On the last day of the conference the Tanzanian government paper, *Daily News*, carried a front page report about an alleged 'nuclear conspiracy between Bonn and Pretoria.' When asked by the journalists, the Tanzanian Minister of Information Sepetu, a frequent visitor to East Berlin and married to an East German citizen, claimed complete ignorance of the background and referred to the freedom of press prevailing in his country.[104] Similar propaganda is detected by West German observers in newspapers in Guinea, Mozambique and Ethiopia. However, clumsy attempts to whitewash the Soviet intervention in Afghanistan in an East German magazine, *Nachrichten*, mailed to the officials and editors in Nairobi from neighbouring Tanzania, backfired. The Nairobi paper, *Daily Nation* attacked the East German pamphlet as propagandist trash: 'Instead of offering nonsense to the people of Kenya, it should explain what the 100,000 Soviet soldiers are doing in Afghanistan,' the paper's editorial suggested.

East Germany's propaganda penetration in Africa may have an even more lasting and deeper impact than its massive military aid. Most Western media experts are not aware of the clever division of labour between the Soviets and the smaller client states. There are two main reasons for the growing engagement of East Germany, Czechoslovakia, Hungary and Bulgaria in extending development aid to the Third World countries. They are not suspected of superpower ambitions and many local personalities (even in more developed Asian states such as Japan) are not always aware of the real relationship between the smaller countries and Moscow. The second reason, particularly in such sensitive fields as communication, is straightforward: the East Germans are, technically, the most highly developed mass media experts and have a great international reputation. At the same time, they can also neutralise the West German influence or even isolate the Federal Republic despite its greater economic potential. A network of co-operation agreements, concluded with journalists' organisations, ministries and the radio and television centres in the Third World facilitates the penetration. A combined Cuban-East German effort could also produce tangible short-term results in Latin America.

This, then, is the broader background to the evolving community of real or perceived interests between the Soviet bloc, an increasing number of Third World countries (particularly those with a degree of press freedom similar to that in East Germany) and the Unesco bureaucracy. More quickly than expected, the Soviet camp has succeeded in projecting itself as 'a natural ally' and in offsetting any attempts to equate 'Western imperialism' and 'Soviet hegemonism'. The Tashkent international conference may also have marked the beginning of a full-scale Soviet subversion of the pool of fifty-seven non-aligned news agencies. Yuri Kashlev dropped a meaningful hint in his *Pravda* piece, when he not only belittled the pool as being 'very modest with inadequate material and technical facilities, and short of well-trained personnel' but also complained: 'Their collective efforts are not helped by the fact that the group of developing countries which belongs to the pool consists of different régimes the interests of which do not coincide.'[106] In short, the projected 'world press institute', or a new pool dominated by Moscow's 'natural allies', should replace the non-aligned unit still headed by the independent-minded and outspoken Yugoslavs. The Yugoslavs, in contrast to some Unesco officials, have no illusions as to the long-range aims of the Soviets and their Cuban and Vietnamese 'non-aligned' allies.

The Soviet-controlled information, cultural, scientific, legal and religious front organisations such as the IOJ, have been traditionally successful in creating support for Soviet policies among the unsuspecting. How else could one explain that an authoritative spokesman of the same superpower which occupies Eastern Europe, which has suppressed uprisings and reform movements in East Berlin, Budapest and Prague, which has spread its influence deep into Africa and virtually seized Afghanistan, can assert that the USSR does not seek to gain any political, financial and ideological influence over the Third World? Or that it is the international news agencies, radio stations and publishing houses which pose the real danger to the information media and independence of the developing countries?

It is therefore vital that the debate is broadened and that the Communist model is not hidden behind a smokescreen of tired clichés and shopworn phrases, but seen and grasped in its daily practice, in the way it affects the lives of tens of millions of people. When Karl Marx was asked by his daughters in 1865 for his favourite motto, he replied: *De omnibus dubitandum* (to doubt everything).[107] With the

Western media dissected, analysed, threatened and attacked from all sides, is it not high time to remember Marx's words and to contrast the sombre facts of Communist media with the lofty rhetoric of Soviet and East European spokesmen? This is why we have to look at the record of compliance with the oft-quoted Helsinki Final Act.

PART III
From Helsinki to Madrid: Prospects for a Freer Exchange of Information

The XX Soviet Party Congress has proved how the alleged lies of today become the truths of tommorow.

*A German diplomat at the
Belgrade conference*

7   A Test of Will in Belgrade

THE FINAL ACT of the Conference on Security and Co-operation in Europe (henceforth CSCE), signed in August 1975 in Helsinki by the leaders of thirty-three European countries, the United States and Canada is a very long, extremely complex and profoundly ambiguous document. The fate of the 40,000-word-long agreement resembles that of some literary classics: they are often mentioned – but rarely read.

Though neither a treaty nor a legally binding document, the Final Act set in motion a chain of events with unexpected, far-reaching and at times dramatic consequences. What initially appeared to be a major and unilateral concession legitimising Soviet control over Eastern Europe, turned out to be the beginning of a dynamic process which has established the human rights issue as both a legitimate and a key element in East-West diplomacy. The emergence of numerous vocal and daring human rights groups in the Soviet Union, Czechoslovakia, Poland and Romania was an impressive example of the hopes and expectations engendered by the Final Act. The formation of various groups to promote and to monitor the observance of the human rights provisions of the Helsinki accord and the response of the West, which held the Soviet and East European governments accountable for not fulfilling their commitments, produced a completely new situation on the eve of the first formal review of Final Act compliance in 1977–78.

Before making an assessment of the great implementation debate, we have to summarise, however briefly, the Final Act itself and the rules of procedures. Its three main sections came to be known as 'baskets' during the three years of negotiations which led to the Helsinki summit meeting. In addition to the ten introductory principles guiding relations between the participants, Basket One deals with enhancing military security. Basket Two contains provisions for improving trade, economic and scientific co-operation. Basket Three deals with humanitarian issues such as human contacts and reunification of divided families, and measures to ease the flow of people, ideas and information between East and West.

Under the rule of consensus, each of the thirty-five participating states, regardless of size and population, had and has an effective veto power over all decisions. This means that decisions, even about procedural or seemingly secondary issues, can only be passed unanimously. Each state can reject any proposal or document by merely denying consensus. The last part of the Final Act spelled out that in 1977 a Follow-Up Meeting should be held in Belgrade which would carry out a 'thorough exchange of views' on the implementation of the Final Act provisions and other matters, including 'appropriate modalities' for holding further similar meetings.

The preparatory meeting began on 15 June 1977 in the Yugoslav capital and lasted for eight weeks. The haggling over procedural points was in fact a highly political exercise. The Soviet bloc sought to restrict the agenda to a 'positive and forward-looking' discussion and to block a real debate about the record of implementation. A coalition of the Western states and neutral and non-aligned participants managed to isolate the Soviets and, after difficult bargaining, to force them to accept a timetable, agenda and rules for the main conference which would allow a thorough review of whether the signatories had complied with the Final Act provisions.

The substantive Follow-Up Meeting lasted, with a three-week Christmas recess, for some five months from 4 October 1977 to 9 March 1978. Apart from two weeks of formal public speeches at the beginning and end of the conference, the sessions of the plenary and the subsidiary working groups were closed to the public and there was no transcribed protocol of the speeches and debates. After sharp and even acrimonious exchanges and the tabling of no fewer than 109 diverse proposals, the review conference finally agreed to accept a brief concluding document which merely stressed the importance of the CSCE process and 'reaffirmed the resolve of their government to implement fully, unilaterally, bilaterally and multilaterally all the provisions of the Final Act.' Without going into any details, the document noted that the participating states disagreed in important respects, but agreed to hold a further conference: a preparatory meeting in September 1980 followed two months later on 11 November 1980 by the main conference, both in Madrid.

In view of the growing discrepancy between public and media expectations and the actual results produced by the 420 diplomats, aided by a large number of back-up clerical staff, the Belgrade meeting ended on a note of deep and barely disguised cynicism among most journalists and diplomats. Yet Congressman Dante B. Fascell, the Chairman of the US Congressional commission monitoring the implementation of the Helsinki agreement since June 1976, was certainly right in stating that the Belgrade meeting was a more significant event than the Helsinki summit itself.[1]

The CSCE process cannot be judged in simplistic terms of who won and who lost. On the face of it there were only winners – or reversing the argument, only losers. The East managed to block any attempts to formulate a substantive document and also vetoed a paper produced by the neutrals and non-aligned (the so-called N+N) group. On the other hand, it was subjected to almost ten weeks of criticism for violating the letter and the spirit of the Helsinki Final Act particularly with regard to Basket Three. More important still, by the end of the meeting, the Soviet bloc became completely isolated, with even Romania publicly taking an independent line both on military security and procedural matters. The West succeeded in reviewing actual implementation and providing widespread publicity for its condemnation of Communist practices, but it resoundingly failed to improve and to make more specific some important Final Act provisions, particularly in the field of human contacts and information, which had been differently interpreted. The lack of co-ordination, both within

NATO and between NATO and the N+N group, combined with different priorities and tactical approaches chosen by the individual delegations, contributed to the flood of formal proposals. This indirectly helped the Soviets to block any progress towards a concluding document containing substantive statements. Last but not least, differing priorities and diplomatic vanity also caused strains and irritations within the Western camp.

Public opinion and opinion-makers have, ever since Helsinki, tended to swing from one extreme to another; from Cold War rhetoric to *détente* euphoria and then again back to unmitigated gloom. There is evidently a need for a dose of realism and a sense of proportion. The continuation of the CSCE process itself must be regarded as an important accomplishment, particularly in view of future opportunities. Having looked at the general issues, it is time to return to our special preoccupation, the provisions in Basket Three concerning the dissemination of, and access to, information, the exchange of news and working conditions for journalists.

The debates, both at the plenary meetings and in the committee charged with the review of the Basket Three, were often bogged down in seemingly irrelevant or legalistic arguments about Principles VI and VII in the introductory part.

The first principle is the non-intervention pledge, which forbids any 'direct or indirect, individual or collective' interference in the internal affairs of the signatory states. The text goes on to list examples of acts constituting such intervention: armed intervention, military or economic coercion, assistance to terrorist or violent activities. Throughout the whole conference, as indeed before and after the Belgrade meeting, the East consistently interpreted this principle as a lever to block any discussion of human rights violations, and to justify violations of the provisions about information such as jamming RFE–RL or harassing foreign reporters visiting Soviet bloc countries. However the overwhelming majority of the signatories pointed out that Principle VII reaffirms 'respect for human rights and fundamental freedoms, including the freedom of thought, conscience, religion and belief.' A series of Western and neutral spokesmen stated that the Warsaw Pact interpretation of the non-intervention principle was inconsistent with established international legal practices as well as with the substance and negotiating history of the Final Act text. It is an interpretation, which, if accepted, would render meaningless the review of implementation which the Final Act mandates.

The examples of acts constituting intervention are of a totally different nature than the dissemination of news and ideas. Western speakers also stressed that any state had the right to inquire into the fulfillment by another state of commitments which both have undertaken. Us Ambassador Goldberg repeatedly emphasised that the raising of such questions in normal diplomatic discourse – as at Belgrade – could not be considered as a threat of intervention or coercion as described in the non-intervention principle. Moreover, Soviet interpretation of the non-interference principle is inconsistent. The Soviet Union itself, for example, has discussed and voted on numerous occasions for UN resolutions condemning the human rights practices of specific states.[2]

Under the concerted pressure of so many of the participating states, the Soviets and their Czech, Polish and East German allies tacitly shelved their earlier position which stated that no one had the right to raise questions about the manner in which another country was implementing the Final Act. When the US delegates and other Western diplomats raised sharp questions about the fate of persons who had been exiled or imprisoned merely for asserting their basic rights guaranteed in Principle VII, the Soviets and some of their allies responded with attacks on the US and Western record, singling out crime, racism, unemployment, Vietnam and Chile, even going back to events which took place five decades ago. However the shift in Soviet tactics was welcomed by Western diplomats because it meant that the Eastern side implicitly accepted that such questions did not constitute illegal interference in the internal affairs of a country and that an inquiry into the observance of the Final Act provisions was a matter of international concern.[3]

The preceding chapters contain ample evidence that the Communist states regard information as a state monopoly, and that the ruling parties view any flow of information not subjected to control by them as inherently subversive. In view of the crucial importance of mass media, propaganda and indoctrination for the Soviet bloc, it was inevitable that (aside from the humanitarian issues of family reunification, freedom of movement and dissident trials) the conflicting interpretation of the Basket Three provisions for information emerged as the most controversial area in the confrontation at the Belgrade review conference.

What then do the provisions about information actually contain? To start with, the participating states express the desire to develop 'mutual understanding' and 'make it their aim to facilitate the freer and wider dissemination of information of all kinds, to encourage co-operation in the field of information and the exchange of information with other countries, and to improve the conditions under which journalists from one participating state exercise their profession in another participating state.'[4] Three main fields are specifically dealt with:

(a) Improvement of the circulation of, access to, and exchange of information: The most important subheadings refer to 'the improvement of the dissemination . . . of newspapers and printed publications, periodical and non-periodical, from the other participating state;' improved access for the public to printed information, in particular through the 'increase in the number of places where these publications are on sale;' to better 'possibilities for taking out subscriptions;' to improved 'opportunities for reading and borrowing these publications in large public libraries and their reading rooms as well as in university libraries.' In connection with film and broadcast information 'the participating states note the expansion in the dissemination of information broadcast by radio, and express the hope for the continuation of this process, so as to meet the interest of mutual understanding among peoples and the aims set forth by this Conference.'

(b) Co-operation in the field of information: the Communist régimes prefer this provision because of easy control and scope for manipulation: co-operation between mass media organisations, including press agencies, exchange and joint production of radio and TV programmes, contacts between journalists' organisations and journalists, exchange of articles and 'experience and views between experts in the field of the press, radio and television.'

(c) Improvement of working conditions for journalists: The participants desire to improve the conditions under which journalists exercise their profession and intend to examine visa applications 'within a suitable and reasonable time scale'; to grant permanently accredited journalists 'on the basis of arrangements, multiple entry and exit visas for specified periods'; to facilitate the issue of temporary residence permits to permanently accredited correspondents; to 'ease, on a basis of reciprocity, procedures for arranging travel by journalists . . . in the country where they are exercising their profession, and to provide progressively greater opportunities for such travel, subject to the observance of regulations relating to the existence of areas closed for security reasons;' to give 'an expeditious response' to requests for such travel; 'to increase the opportunities for journalists . . . to communicate personally with their sources, including organisations and official institutions;' to give journalists 'the right to import, subject only to its being taken out again, the technical equipment necessary for the exercise of their profession;' to enable journalists to transmit 'completely, normally and rapidly' their reports, including 'tape recording and undeveloped film' for publication, or broadcasting on radio or television.

The last paragraph in the chapter on information is one of the most important: 'The participating States reaffirm that the legitimate pursuit of their professional activity will neither render journalists liable to expulsion nor otherwise penalise them. If an accredited journalist is expelled, he will be informed of the reasons for this act and may submit an application for re-examination of his case.'

The review of the compliance with these provisions and the debate on the proposals tabled by the participants overlapped, although basically the arguments about the various proposals amounted to a continuation of the review phase because the diplomats often cited past examples as justification for new proposals. The basic difference between the US delegation and the European Community delegates was one of priorities. While the US chief delegate, Ambassador Goldberg concentrated on public condemnation of the Soviet and Eastern European violations of the human rights provisions, and even in the later phases engaged in rhetorical duels with his Soviet bloc counterparts, Western and neutral delegates advanced specific ideas, seeking concrete if limited progress in the field of human contacts and information. Following most of the proceedings in Belgrade on the spot, I gained the impression (since then further strengthened) that the US negotiating tactics were, even within the delegation, not unanimously approved. Ambassador Goldberg, sarcastically called 'an unguided missile' by a Western diplomat, contributed through his negotiating style to a sense of malaise. But co-ordination among the other NATO members was also less than satisfactory. What indeed should one say about the French who, in the final hectic phase of the conference, searching for a generally acceptable concluding document, put a draft on the table without the approval of the other Community members (it was, of course, rejected by the East)?[5]

The controversies at the closed sessions of the plenary and the subsidiary working body dealing with Basket Three continuously revolved around the different interpretation of interference in the internal affairs and the inherent differences between the two systems. Every Eastern statement about access to Western newspapers, jamming or journalistic freedom boiled down to the claim that the information media should serve understanding between peoples, peace and progress, and, simultaneously, observe certain standards of good behaviour. Governments, the Warsaw Pact speakers argued, had to take responsibility to ensure that both the print and broadcast media met these criteria in their work.

Both before and at the Belgrade meeting a flood of statistics was produced to give the impression of a high level of CSCE implementation. Thus the Soviet Union published the full text of the Final Act in twenty million copies, the GDR in two million and Czechoslovakia in 1.5 million copies, while the comparative figures for West Germany were only 40,000, for the US 7,000 and for Britain 7,500. Eastern speakers also kept repeating that they import a greater number of books, film and other cultural and information material from the West than vice versa.

Western and neutral diplomats rejected this kind of statistical smokescreen as irrelevant and misleading. The Final Act did not call for any government-guaranteed statistical reciprocity in the dissemination of such material. Dissemination of information was generally described as the Basket Three area in which the Eastern countries had made the least implementation progress since signature of the Final Act. As the Austrian representative Franz Ceska put it in his speech: 'The quantitative balance is not relevant. Decisive is the availability of and access to information and newspapers for the individual. Every adult citizen should have the possibility to buy or to subscribe to a paper he wants. We do not regard as desirable to allow the state to select what he can and what he cannot read.' The Austrian arguments and examples were in some ways more devastating for the East than Goldberg's rhetoric. For example, after a heated exchange between the Soviets and the Americans, the Austrian delegate quietly remarked that it cannot be concern about war propaganda and pornography which blocks the sale of Austrian papers in some participating states. He showed an issue of the illustrated cultural monthly *Das Fenster* (The Window) from the Tyrol which is regularly confiscated on the border of a participating state (East Germany) and not even sent back to the publisher, although, measured even by the strictest standards, it contains no anti-Soviet, pornographic or subversive material. Another concrete example was the sale of one hundred copies of the Austrian Communist daily, *Volksstimme*, as against only three copies of all other Austrian papers in a participating country, although there are 'no language barriers' (yet again a reference to the East German régime).[6]

Speaking as a member of the US delegation, Professor Joyce Hughes singled out mail censorship. 'When an American friend is unable to obtain delivery of a subscription to the *National Geographic* magazine for a Soviet schoolboy, or a copy of the *World Almanac* for a teacher in Czechoslovakia, the flow of information is choked, not widened,' she said. Such specific cases violate the 'freedom of transit' guaranteed in the Universal Postal Declaration, dating back to 1875 and renewed in 1974, which the Soviet Union has signed. Professor Hughes' complaint evoked the words of Zhores Medvedev, the Soviet dissident scientist, who calculated that the Soviet mail censors work so poorly that letters from Western

Europe took twice as long to reach him as the letters Lenin sent from Western Europe to his relatives in Siberia, which went through the Tsarist mail censorship![7]

The most acrimonious exchanges naturally took place over the harassment of US and Western journalists which coincided with the meetings in Belgrade. There were also episodes which reflected the profound changes both in the US perception of the Communist world and the actual relationships among Communist parties. In connection with a trial of four Charter 77 human rights activists in Prague, Ambassador Goldberg condemned the fact that Czechoslovak authorities refused to grant a visa to the correspondent of *L'Humanité*, the French Communist daily, therefore preventing him from covering the trial. A curious spectacle: an American 'imperialist' defending the French Communists . . .

The basic point about access to information is that the West virtually guarantees distribution of newspapers and publications for which there is sufficient interest, while the Warsaw Pact governments import and distribute only those materials to which they themselves tolerate public access. What an American scholar noted about East-West trade is also valid for the two-way flow of information: 'For the West, the underlying rule is that any trade can take place unless a government prevents it, while for the Communist countries . . . the rule would be that no trade takes place unless the state initiates it.'[8] Or, put another way, the Soviet side can simply deny entry and sale of Western publications by failing to act, while in the Western democratic countries any restriction of the import and distribution of goods, including printed matter from the East, is imaginable and possible only if the government actually takes overt action. The difference in the very substance of the systems therefore underlies the startlingly different approaches of the two sides to Basket Three (and also Basket Two on trade).

The flavour of some of the confrontations about the sensitive issues of 'free flow of ideas and information' may be conveyed by the details of the debate about electronic jamming. The Soviets sent their deputy chief delegate, a certain Sergei

Kondrashev, to the Basket Three front to hold the ground against the Western attacks and to lead the counter-offensives. Kondrashev is not only a veteran of the CSCE verbal battles, but was also said to have worked in the past as a key KGB officer and, in the mid-1960s, as deputy head of the Disinformation Department of the secret service.[9] In Belgrade he launched vicious attacks against Radio Liberty, operated by 'traitors whose hands were dripping with blood'. The Soviets banned only the entry of racist, warmongering and pornographic publications. But in the West the sale of Soviet publications was suppressed for ideological reasons, he claimed. Rejecting Western complaints, Kondrashev reiterated that Radio Liberty, alone among forty radio broadcasts beamed to the Soviet Union, would continue to be jammed because states had the right to take measures against information which endangers their security and moral health.

The West German, American, Italian and Canadian delegates not only pointed out that jamming violates the provisions of the Final Act, but also remarked that Western broadcasts are the chief source of objective news for Eastern Europe. What really disturbs the Eastern authorities is that people are getting information which the local media does not carry. The West German representative, Wilfried Hofmann, warned against arrogating the right to decide what is 'true' and what is 'objective' reporting. Was it forgotten that under Stalin many things were claimed to be true which subsequently turned out to have been lies? 'Communist history, in particular the twentieth Soviet Party Congress has proved how the alleged lies of today become the truths of tomorrow.'

The Eastern speakers echoed the familiar line of Soviet propaganda that – in the words of Kondrashev – 'a stop to psychological warfare was the indispensable condition for a broadening of the exchange of information.' The East Germans hastened to stress that the Final Act 'did not give a licence for foreign correspondents to spread misleading reports and slanders;' while the Czechoslovak representative pointed out that many obstacles stood in the way of a broader exchange of news. Thus the information media in 'certain capitalist countries concentrated on ideological subversion against the socialist countries, rather than on developing friendship and mutual understanding.'

Once again, the West countered with facts rather than phrases. The French delegate quoted all the news and commentaries about France which were published by Soviet papers in the previous three days. These were all correct, or at least close to the truth, but nevertheless conveyed a completely unobjective, negative picture of France. He added sarcastically, 'if the Soviet papers print photos of queues before the labour exchange, then I can only say that at least there are no queues in front of the food shops in Paris . . .'

We may quote some statistical evidence to support the observations of the French diplomat. The Hamburg-based Institute for Peace Research analysed the reporting of *Neues Deutschland*, the East Berlin Communist organ, about the Federal Republic: fifty percent of the reports and commentaries were critical of West German constitutional bodies and institutions, often sharply so and with a polemic tone; thirty percent dealt exclusively with such crisis symptoms as unemployment and inflation; only twenty percent could have met the standards of more or less objective reporting, but it should be added, half of these items referred to the DKP, the West German Communist Party and other Communist organisations. The study concluded that, measured by Eastern criteria, eighty to ninety percent of the coverage of West Germany in the SED central organ was interference in the internal affairs of the Federal Republic![10]

A strictly personal, but nevertheless highly revealing examination of the Soviet coverage of the US was carried out by the Moscow Correspondent of the Swiss daily, *Neue Zürcher Zeitung*.[11] Taking the period from 1 July 1968 to 30 June 1969, and comparing the reporting of six central Soviet daily newspapers, he took into account only the coverage of the domestic political scene in the US. Of 188 photos, seventy-nine depicted policemen in action, mainly using sticks or brandishing a weapon, often with a police dog attacking demonstrators; fifty-seven showed demonstrations (including twenty-seven against the Vietnam War); forty-one photos were devoted to racial tensions, followed by twenty-one photos about poverty, hunger and unemployment. Of

564 articles and reports (not short news items), ninety-six dealt with the presidential campaign, partly in a business-like way reporting on the programmes of the candidates, partly, however, suggesting to the reader that the electoral process was undemocratic; ninety-three articles were devoted to crime, drugs and other phenomena under the term 'sick society'; seventy-four described poverty, hunger, misery and unemployment; forty-three attacked police brutality; thirty-four wrote about militarism and fascism in the US; twenty-two about student demonstrations. It is true that twenty reports dealt with the Apollo space flights, but this figure must be compared to the thirty-one reports dealing with the activities of the totally insignificant American Communist Party. The correspondent concluded that the Soviet press in the period under review gave a picture of the US as a brutal, fascist-type police state where, under the rule of reckless exploiters, there is nothing but misery, poverty, crime and depression.

These few examples suffice to show the hollowness of Communist verbal acrobatics about what is 'psychological warfare' and what is 'ideological competition'. And this is the background against which the Communist proposals tabled in Belgrade must be judged. Thus Czechoslovakia presented what could be called a 'code of good behaviour' for journalists who should serve 'the lofty goals of peace and mutual confidence' as spelled out in the Final Act. After listing in detail these 'lofty goals', the proposal also called on the participating states 'not to allow the abuse of the mass information media for the purposes of propaganda in favour of war, violence and hatred among peoples' nor 'the dissemination of false information and the deliberate misinformation of the public'. Journalists should 'respect the law, customs and morality of the participating states' and not allow the use of media for interference in the internal affairs of the participating states.

On the same day, 11 November, the conference was flooded with similar propagandistic and generalised proposals by the East. The Bulgarians, famous for their very slow production of statistical yearbooks, suggested that 'business circles should be provided with already existing information', and that agreements should be concluded about the exchange of encyclopedias; also 'all forms of co-operation in the field of sport' should be encouraged (a third Bulgarian document!). Then, on the very same day, the Czechs came out with yet another proposal. This time that the signatories should not permit their information media at home and abroad to make propaganda for war, the use or threat of force, etc. This suggestion, like the previous Czechoslovak idea, was immediately and firmly rejected by Western speakers as an unwarranted step to exert government influence on the mass media for which there was absolutely no basis in the Final Act.[12]

The flood of totally irrelevant Eastern proposals was completed by the East German suggestion that the participating states should 'make the Final Act as widely known as possible!' All these moves were merely a transparent ploy to counter the previous much more concrete but somewhat uncoordinated proposals tabled on 7–8 November 1977 by the European Community, and supported by all participants outside the Soviet bloc.

The Western moves concentrated on access to information and the working conditions of foreign correspondents. One proposal stressed the role of demand for newspapers and printed publications, the improvement of possibilities for the taking out of subscriptions and also sought indirectly to convince the Communist régimes to dismantle the frontier censorship of printed matter from the West. This proposal, the Eastern speakers rejected outright, because 'demand in the socialist states plays a significantly less important role than in the West'. Furthermore, they 'will continue to ban entry of printed material containing subversive, pornographic and war propaganda'.

Other Western moves sought to make some seemingly minor – but in practice extremely important – provisions about the working conditions of foreign journalists more specific. One European Community proposal suggested that journalists should have the right to import and take out not only technical equipment as specified in the Helsinki document, but also 'personal reference material necessary for the exercise of their profession.' A number of British, German, American, French and Austrian journalists on leaving the country, at various times, had had their notes and even books confiscated at the border by the authorities in Czechoslovakia, Poland and the Soviet Union. Another proposal intended to add a clarifying sentence to the paragraph about the expulsion of journalists: 'The participating states confirm that journalists will not be expelled, or otherwise acted against, as a result of news or opinions, published or broadcast in the media they represent, whether or not they are the authors.' Subsequent events in East Germany showed how topical and important the proposals concerning expulsion and easier access to sources were.[13]

The most comprehensive, if somewhat controversial, package of proposals was put forward by Switzerland and involved both working conditions for foreign journalists and the dissemination of information.[14] The Swiss document suggested a meeting of experts to draw up a draft convention to facilitate both the work of foreign correspondents and their access to information, including the opening of generally accessible reading rooms. The Swiss chief delegate explained that 'it is in the working conditions for journalists that the greatest inequality exists in application of the Final Act.' A minimum of security should be provided for journalists since 'responsibility can only be exercised in freedom, ie in the absence of all constraints.'

The Swiss draft encompassed all the points raised in the various separate proposals submitted by other Western states; from facilitating travel to guarantees against expulsion and permission to take out notes and reference material. The idea was welcomed officially, but several Western diplomats were privately sceptical as to whether the idea of a convention was not too ambitious. The East immediately referred to a code of ethics which should be included in such a convention. This was firmly refuted by several Western diplomats. The Austrian representative said that the journalist is permanently confronted with the question of journalistic ethics and that therefore professional ethical standards should be best drawn up by the journalists themselves, while the state should restrict itself to creating the necessary conditions for the smooth activity of the journalists.

In informal talks, the Soviets remarked that first one had to agree on a precise mandate for such a group of experts, a condition which was clearly impossible to fulfil in view of the short time at the disposal of the delegates already engaged in the battle over the concluding document. Finally, the Soviets made it completely clear that the Western proposals for easier dissemination of information and improvement of working conditions for journalists were out of the question. Three months before the official termination of the meeting, the Soviets already went on record in informal talks, as stating that the maximum concession would be a sentence in the concluding paper that the next follow-up meeting should again examine the question whether further improvement of the working conditions for journalists would be possible.

It is important to underline the fact that on the crucial issues of the free flow of information, of improving the dissemination of information and the working conditions of foreign journalists, the Soviet bloc was totally and publicly isolated. Both the neutral and non-aligned states, including Yugoslavia and Finland (in an informal document circulated in December and again in early February) and NATO (in a formal proposal tabled on 21 February 1978) came out in favour of a series of concrete steps in the field of information. But the Soviet Union and its client states vetoed all the initiatives. It may be true that the tide of proposals, which in Basket Three alone involved thirty-six documents, ten of which directly related to the field of information, harmed the chances of progress. However, in retrospect, it is evident that the Soviets regarded the entire Belgrade meeting, in the words of a German diplomat, as 'a damage-limiting exercise'.[15]

Under these circumstances, the appeal made by Ambassador Goldberg that the conference should 'give the process of *détente* a human measure and a humanitarian face' was a pathetic gesture but nothing more. There is much more material available now almost five years after Helsinki and two years after Belgrade, for judging Eastern compliance with the Final act provisions. Instead of the pathos of the former Supreme Court Justice Arthur Goldberg, the cynicism of Alexander Zinoviev may be a better prelude to what we can expect in the next chapter: To talk about 'Communism with a human or democratic face, would be tantamount to imagining capital without money or profit'.[16]

8 Eastern Compliance with the Final Act

THE REAL TEST of a genuine improvement of East-West relations is not the frequency of summit and high-level meetings nor the number of contracts signed and debts incurred. The true yardstick to measure the depth and durability of normalised relations is the degree to which there is a two-way flow of ideas and information, coupled with freedom of movement in both directions. This is the reason why the Basket Three provisions about humanitarian questions and information go to the heart of the closed Soviet-type system. Sensitivity to the freer flow of information does not stem from the personal characteristics of the men in the Kremlin, as is sometimes thought by naïve Western commentators. The total control over political communication is rooted in the very essence of the Communist régimes.

We need not agree with all of Solzhenitsyn's political statements or his vision of history to accept what he proclaimed in his Nobel Prize lecture: 'Blocking of information makes international signatures and treaties unreal; within the zone of stunned silence any treaty can easily be reinterpreted at will.' The Western position has always been that genuine security and co-operation cannot be attained without lowering the artificial barriers which prevent reunification of divided families, hinder personal travel, restrict the free interchange of cultural and informational material or serve to impede contact and communication between the people of East and West.[17]

It would be untrue to assert that the Western countries completely complied with the provisions of the Final Act. For example, American denial of the application of the most-favoured-nation clause in trade with some Communist countries, which penalises their exports to the US is certainly not in accord with the spirit and letter of the Helsinki document. There is also a traditional imbalance in cultural exchanges, with the East European countries showing many more films and translating many more books from the US, Britain, France and the German-speaking states than vice versa. But such statistics could be produced with equal ease by Finland, Denmark, Norway or Holland. The one legitimate complaint with regard to the Western compliance with the Final Act provisions about information is the visa policy in some Western countries, including the US. However, the visa practice is a matter of public debate in the US and West Germany, while a similarly open debate in the Eastern press about this or similar issues, emigration, for example, would be impossible.[18]

Nevertheless, as far as the stereotyped Communist arguments about the statistical imbalance in cultural exchange are concerned, no international agreement can provide newspapers, books or films from the East with guaranteed readerships or audiences. What it can do is to promote the removal of artificial obstacles to free choice. The Final Act does not call for any government-assured statistical reciprocity in the dissemination of cultural or information material.

Reciprocity in the freedom of choice and access and not reciprocity in – often manipulated and uncontrollable – statistics is what the entire CSCE exercise is about. The single most important factor in the implementation of the Basket Three provisions about information is that Western, unlike Eastern citizens, have free access to what they wish to read, hear or see. Democratic governments in West European countries have neither the ability nor the desire to control the dissemination of information.

Some years ago, the Czechoslovak authorities complained officially and privately about the reporting of the Austrian press. During an official visit in 1976 to Prague, Chancellor Bruno Kreisky was asked at a press conference whether such anti-Czechoslovak articles did not harm good-neighbourly relations. The Austrian statesman smilingly assured his questioner that the criticism of the Prague government was nothing compared to the flood of attacks he himself and his government are constantly subjected to in the Austrian press. It goes without saying that the Chancellor's remark was ignored by the entire Czech press the next day! This episode confirms once again that it is the free flow of information (and not meaningless, polite phrases) which could lead to the furthering of understanding.[19]

Before going into a point by point review of the Eastern record of compliance with the Final Act, we should briefly deal with the double standard with regard to access to media. A couple of examples will show how nonsensical the Communist charges are. A Soviet author, writing in an authoritative monthly in the pre-Helsinki phase, accused the capitalist countries of 'doing everything to hamper the access of the masses to Soviet books and printed matter, even subjecting those who buy such material to police interrogation. And the progressive products of literature, theatre, cinema? The books are published in ridiculously small editions, revolutionary plays are not allowed to be shown in large theatres, and films which unmask bourgeois reality are boycotted by producers and distributors.'[20] At the Belgrade conference, Kondrashev complained that two unnamed British distributors allegedly refused to sell Soviet newspapers for economic reasons. Even when offered compensation for possible losses, they were said to have remained adamant. According to the Soviet diplomat, this made it clear that Soviet publications are suppressed in the West for ideological reasons.[21]

There is not much point in replying to such accusations since every inhabitant of New York, Washington, Cambridge, Mass., London, Cologne, Paris or Vienna can quote off the cuff examples for 'revolutionary' films, plays, etc, regularly shown in 'large' theatres and cinemas. More interesting is a recent report from the *New York Times* that 'Soviet trade officials have begun a direct-mail campaign in the US to sell subscriptions to *Moscow News*, a weekly paper; *Sputnik*, a monthly feature magazine and *Soviet Union* magazine. So far nearly half a million letters have been sent to potential subscribers.' A Soviet commercial representative said that there 'has been a moderate success with a return of fifteen orders for every thousand letters sent out'. He also revealed that during the last several years 200,000 letters promoting *Moscow News* had been printed and mailed from the Soviet Union to lists of potential subscribers purchased from commercial list brokers in New York. As a result subscriptions rose from virtually nothing to 3,000. The latest advertising brochures offered prizes ranging from 'an exciting, all-expense-paid trip to Moscow' to 'Soviet-made radios, watches and cameras.'[22]

This report sheds a characteristic light on the total lack of reciprocity and the built-in advantages for the Soviet side in the 'ideological battle'. It is enough to recall how the Soviet or Czech papers consistently warn against letters written to Western radio stations. Who could imagine *Foreign Affairs*, *The Economist* or *L'Express* launching advertising, let alone direct-mail, campaigns with letters sent to hundreds of thousands of potential subscribers? Even books and magazines already paid for by Western relatives and friends disappear from international mail and never reach the people to whom they are addressed.

To illustrate the vigilance of border control, the chief of the political department of the customs at Moscow Airport has proudly claimed that on the average 1,500 publications are confiscated every week from travellers coming from abroad. The Soviet custom guards are thus 'waging an incessant battle against the infiltration of the ideological poison through the emissaries of foreign secret services.'[23]

Yet, at the same time, the opportunities open to *Novosti* and the Soviet-type East European press agencies in the West are practically unlimited. They can place an order to publish a book in the US, Germany or Austria. None of the US or Western press and feature services can do the same in the Soviet Union. As illustrated in the preceding chapters, *Novosti* can carry on political campaigns of prime importance through placing letters-to-the-Editor in Western newspapers. But Americans or other Westerners cannot do the same in Moscow, East Berlin, Prague or any other Communist capital. It is not even possible to correct obvious mistakes or deliberate distortions in material published in the local media.[24] As an American participant said at an international journalists conference at the Aspen Institute, Berlin: 'The us would consider it a small step forward if *Izvestia* would allow twenty inches of space to an American spokesman to comment on Arbatov's twenty inches worth of opinion which *Novosti* had been able to put in the American press. This would be real reciprocity.'[25]

Consider the interesting experience of Leonard Marks, former Director of the us Information Agency, and subsequently Chairman of the us Advisory Commission on International Educational and Cultural Affairs. In this capacity he visited the Soviet Union and four East European countries in 1975 and has since then talked to a great number of us and Soviet bloc representatives. Marks has long been advocating the opening of American book stores in the capitals of Eastern Europe, where local citizens could come in, look at books in English, buy them, listen to tape recordings and see educational films. When he suggested this to P. Demichev, the Soviet Minister of Culture, the reply was: 'All right, but we will tell you what books to put in there.' Marks added that Demichev had a 'pretty good sense of humour' and that the us could nevertheless not tolerate his suggestion.[26]

Another typical case is the exchange of official publications. Thus the us and the Soviet Union each have the right to distribute 62,000 copies of *America* magazine and of *Soviet Life* respectively in each other's country. In the Soviet Union the copies of *America* are usually sold out within an hour, most traded on the black market at astronomical prices. Yet the Soviet authorities regularly returned a certain number of copies. The Americans later found out that the returns roughly equalled the number of unsold copies of *Soviet Life* in the us. The reason for the low sales in the us is of course that the people are not interested in buying the magazine.[27]

The basic point is, however, that the Soviet bloc countries can have outlets to disseminate their publications anywhere in the Western world. Take the case of neutral Austria, which for many years now has had excellent relations with the Soviet Union and most Communist-ruled countries. There is a study library of the Austro-Soviet Friendship Society in Vienna, with a large catalogue accessible to all, where any

Austrian can read Soviet and East German publications; if not available they can be ordered from Moscow. As pointed out by the Austrian representative in the Basket Three commission in Belgrade, Austria 'would also like to have the Soviet-Austrian Society in Moscow possess its own office with a similar library for printed matters from Austria and corresponding access to the library for local citizens.'

In Austria, with a population of some 7.5 million, forty-nine newsstands sell papers from Eastern Europe. In Vienna alone, Globus & Co, the Communist-controlled publishing and printing firm, operates three shops where a wide range of newspapers, periodicals, books and records from the Warsaw Pact states are available.

In an effort to increase the sale of Austrian papers in Eastern Europe, the Austrians suggested in Geneva, and repeated in Belgrade, that the problem of foreign exchange (the perennial excuse of the East), is not unsurmountable. With good will it could be resolved through clearing arrangements.[28]

Hopes were raised when, in the spring of 1977 and at the Belgrade conference in February 1978, in informal talks with Western delegates, the Soviets claimed that they had increased the import of Western printed matter. News agencies reported that on the eve of the Belgrade meeting even in the capitals of hard-line régimes, in Prague and Sofia, Western newspapers were put on sale.

What then is the experience of Austria, a country which no one can accuse of subversive and imperialist designs against the 'socialist community'? The Communist-controlled Globus & Co has a monopoly for selling Austrian newspapers to East European countries and the figures supplied by the company to the Austrian Foreign Ministry cannot possibly be suspected of manipulation to the detriment of the Soviet bloc!

According to information from Globus, there has been 'no reduction' and 'no change' in the sales figures in 1978 and 1979![29] One must add that the figures refer primarily to subscriptions by institutions in the various countries. Only in Hungary are papers offered for sale to the general public – but even there exclusively in a handful of selected first-class tourist hotels, frequented by Western guests. The local

| | SALES | |
	of Austrian non-Communist newspapers May 1977	of Communist newspapers in Austria
Soviet Union	67	120
Czechoslovakia	109	47
Hungary	342	61
Poland	26	17
Romania	28	46
Bulgaria	30	9
East Germany	3	96

population can buy or subscribe only to the *Volksstimme*, the Austrian Communist daily which sells in Hungary twice, in Czechoslovakia five times and in East Germany fifty times (!) as many copies as all other Austrian newspapers together. The reason is threefold: first, many Czechoslovaks and Hungarians genuinely buy the paper because of the Austrian television programmes; second, by displaying *Volksstimme* along with an occasional issue of the *Morning Star*, *L'Humanité* or *L'Unità*, the Soviet bloc régimes can lend 'an international air' to their dreary newspaper stands; thirdly, the *Volksstimme* is, since the purge of the 'revisionist' wing in the Austrian party in 1969, basically a copy of the Soviet press except for domestic political comments irrelevant to the foreign reader. This means that, in contrast to the French and Italian Communist organs, *Volksstimme* is never confiscated in Eastern Europe.

In sum, the Austrian press is, as before, not really available even in neighbouring countries with a relatively large proportion of German-speaking inhabitants. Nowhere, not even in Hungary, are non-Communist Austrian newspapers displayed or sold at newsstands generally accessible to the public.

Personal impressions, the experiences of other colleagues and resident diplomats and, last but not least, the figures released by the circulation departments of major Western newspapers confirm that there has been no improvement whatsoever with regard to circulation of and access to information. Let us look first at the figures. According to a survey by *The Financial Times*, the combined sales figures of two British papers (*The Times* and *The Financial Times*), of *Le Monde*, *Frankfurter Allgemeine Zeitung* and *Corriere della Sera* within the Soviet bloc fell from 7,152 in 1975 to 6,993 in 1977. Thus Helsinki did not produce any increase, but, on the contrary, a slight drop in sales. Has the Belgrade meeting changed the situation, particularly in view of Soviet allegations about 'doubling' the purchase of Western papers? A spot check on two respected Western papers may be instructive.[30]

	Le Monde			*Frankfurter Allgemeine*		
	1975	1977	1979	1975	1977	1978
Bulgaria	128	206	181	23	28	29
Czechoslovakia	339	339	331	126	116	108
East Germany*	–	–	1	–	–	–
Hungary	313	341	312	209	210	241
Poland	1,072	877	856	238	267	258
Romania	608	664	504	219	160	135
Soviet Union	228	275	145	109	131	145

*It is assumed that copies of Western newspapers are purchased by the East German authorities through a West Berlin wholesale distributor and not directly from the newspapers themselves.

It is also important to remember that most of the copies are bought by foreign tourists and the rest by the government authorities, newspapers and the few libraries with 'restricted departments'. Even in this respect there are differences between the various Communist regimes. In Budapest, for example, tourists can at least buy the newspapers in the few luxury hotels. But in Prague, Sofia or Moscow they are available only in very small numbers, serving mainly as a proof that Western press is 'on sale'. In reality, it is extremely difficult even for Westerners to obtain recent newspapers. In Moscow, Prague or Sofia the newspapers are generally at least a week old. I once found in a Sofia hotel two copies of *Le*

Monde, each eleven days old; in contrast, *Pravda* and *Izvestia* were always available the next day. In Prague the favourite ploy is to offer Turkish or Swedish papers, incomprehensible not only to most foreigners, but – what is more important – to most Czechs. One finds both in Moscow and Prague occasionally eight- to fifteen-day-old copies of the *Toronto Globe and Mail*.

The Western newspapers are not only generally out of date, but also horrendously expensive. In Hungary for example – at any rate until the latest steep increase of food prices and restaurant charges in the summer of 1979 – one could have a modest meal for the equivalent of what a copy of *Time* magazine or the West German glossy illustrated weekly, *Quick* cost in local currency. Nevertheless despite the prices, which are twenty to thirty times higher than those of local equivalent publications, there is brisk demand for Western newspapers. Thus a Hungarian journalist, working for the Budapest weekly *Élet és Irodalom*, related how he was searching for the latest issue of *Time*. In one hotel he was offered a three-week-old copy, in another a two-week-old issue and it was only in the third hotel that he managed to buy the latest *Time* – and then only because the salesman happened to be an old schoolmate!

An important cosmetic measure applied by the Soviet bloc propagandists is to offer Western newspapers for sale during large international conferences or party congresses attended by many Western delegates and foreign correspondents. But the papers are withdrawn from public view once the meeting is over and the foreign visitors have departed. I could observe repeatedly, for example, during the last Czechoslovak party congress in 1976, and during the visit of Hua Kuo-feng to Bucharest in 1978, that a great variety of Western newspapers were available and that the authorities were perfectly capable of offering copies from the previous day. During the Czechoslovak party congress, the delegates in the Hotel Intercontinental in Prague could choose between the *Neue Zürcher Zeitung*, *Figaro* or the *International Herald Tribune*. In the same hotel lobby a couple of months later in 1976 and several times in 1977–79, I could only see a handful of Communist dailies from East and West. The same tricks are of course also applied in the Soviet Union. An American reporter stationed in Moscow was able to buy the *Herald Tribune* on a newsstand in an Intourist hotel only once in two years and that was when an official US delegation visited Leningrad.[31]

The Communist authorities present the usual arguments, either selectively or in a package: hard currency shortage (which however does not prevent them from engaging in costly jamming or massive military aid for African states); the subversive or pornographic character of Western papers (fear suspended during international conferences or when convenient articles are quoted from or special supplements and advertisements placed in the same papers); and finally the tired cliché of there being 'no demand' or 'insufficient interest' on the part of the local population. But the repeated offers of concluding clearing arrangements or trying a pilot project to ascertain real local demand as suggested, for example, by Austrian, Swiss and US speakers on several occasions, have never been taken up.

How can one explain the curious phenomenon that tiny Austria, with a German-speaking population, had in April 1979 a market for 627 copies a day of *Le Monde*, more than the paper's combined sales in the same month in the Soviet Union and Poland with a combined population almost forty-two times greater than that of Austria? In view of this incredible discrepancy, the routine explanations of Soviet bloc diplomats need not be further commented upon.

However it is interesting to show how the régimes try to 'sell' the absence of Western press to their own public. Thus the weekly, *Literaturnaya Gazeta* in Moscow, published under the title 'Nothing but the truth' an article about discussions with members of a tourist group from Western Germany. Two propagandist lecturers of the *Znanie* ('Knowledge') society met the overwhelmingly elderly people for a freewheeling question and answer session in German. Someone inquired as to why no Western newspapers and periodicals are sold on the newsstands. The answer was:

First, there is a great quantity of progressive periodicals from the West. Second, papers such as the *Frankfurter Allgemeine*, *Le*

Monde, *The Times* and the *International Tribune* are sold in the hotels and at Moscow Airport. Third, we have a weekly periodical *Za rubeshom* ('Abroad') which carries translations from *The Times*, *New York Times*, *Le Monde*, *Stern* and *Spiegel*. Thanks to the magazine *Innostrannaya Literatura* ('Foreign Literature') the works of many Western authors are better known in the Soviet Union than in their own countries.

In order to block off any further questions, the second lecturer added: 'Such hostile anti-Soviet radio stations as Radio Liberty and Radio Free Europe, which incidentally broadcast from the territory of your country, are of the opinion that all this is not enough and try to enlighten the Soviet people.' The conversation quickly shifted to the two stations, with the tourists surprised to hear about them at all, until one of them remarked angrily: 'You see our country was alienated from us by the Americans. One hides from us Germans what is going on . . .'[32]

The article reflected above all the feeling that its target was not so much the German tourist group, but Soviet public opinion. The readership of the weekly (with a circulation of over 1.5 million) has a high proportion of university graduates and intellectuals, potential readers of the Western press.[33] Yet the report, which included other questions about human rights, strikes, etc, showed a lack of sophistication and did not really answer the questions allegedly raised. Instead it hinted that the questioner himself was rather suspicious because he had already asked about the drop in Jewish emigration to Israel, and, last but not least, implied that anyone who raises the question of the lack of access to Western press reflects or repeats the 'slanders' of the Munich stations.

Are there improved 'opportunities for reading and borrowing these publications in large public libraries and their reading rooms as well as in university libraries', as spelled out in the Final Act? As before, access to Western publications is still limited to those having a special permit. US libraries and reading rooms, except in Hungary and Poland, are visited by relatively few students or interested adults. This is due partly to the presence of uniformed police guards outside and even more to the spot or regular checks on visitors. The treatment of visitors also reflects the ups and downs in the internal situation in a given country and also in relations with the West. In Czechoslovakia, those visiting the American reading room (situated in an annex of the US Embassy) in Prague were harassed in different ways in 1978, particularly before the tenth anniversary of the invasion of Czechoslovakia, when the situation was tense in the entire country. By 1979, US diplomats noted no deliberate interference with people visiting the reading room. However there is no guarantee of free access in any Communist country because the situation might change overnight.

The attitude towards Western Communist publications and the Yugoslav press also varies from country to country and from period to period. Copies of the French and Italian Communist papers are generally unavailable when the parties or the papers criticise Soviet policies vis-à-vis the Jews, the dissidents or the restrictions on cultural freedom. Yugoslav papers are generally difficult to get in Moscow, Sofia and Prague, but not in Bucharest or Budapest. During an eighteen-month stay in 1978–79 in Moscow, a correspondent was not able to buy one single copy of the Spanish Communist newspaper. Romanian papers are freely available in Moscow where there are few potential readers, but cannot be found in Kishinev, the capital of erstwhile Bessarabia, today Soviet Moldavia, where 'Moldavians', that is ethnic Romanians, constitute the majority of the population.

Hungarian-Romanian relations are of course something very special. Nevertheless, it is of some interest to recall that possibilities for ethnic Hungarians to subscribe to Budapest papers are very limited and that on more than a dozen trips to Romania, including extended tours of Transylvania, I have never been able to find one single copy of a newspaper from Hungary proper, as distinct from the Hungarian-language Romanian-controlled publications. Thus, as a Hungarian Communist writer once bitterly remarked, the Helsinki Final Act should also be applied to the protection of the ethnic minorities in Eastern Europe.

Finally, the single most powerful argument against the orthodox Communist explanation of why Western papers are not available for the general public, is the everyday practice in

Yugoslavia. Though the country is ruled by a Communist single-party system, the newsstands in Belgrade, Zagreb and on the Dalmatian coast are indistinguishable from those in neighbouring Austria or Italy. Virtually every major Western newspaper is available and copies are on sale the next day. It happens from time to time that a copy of a certain newspaper is not available, the buyer being told that 'it has not arrived yet'. Should the salesman know the buyer personally, he or she is told that the issue has been held back. Somewhat later *Sluzbeni List*, the official gazette publishes a brief decree usually signed by Deputy Minister of Interior, Draško Jurišić, announcing the confiscation of a newspaper. Between January and June 1979, he signed decrees to confiscate copies of four Austrian, fourteen West German, six Italian, one US, one French and two British papers, which included anything from *Punch* to *Spiegel*, from the German illustrated *Praline* to the Austrian popular tabloid, *Kronen Zeitung*. In November––December 1978, nine West German and two Italian papers were banned.[34] What were the reasons? Evidently, such politically 'sensitive' stories as the speculation about the fate of Madame Tito who had mysteriously disappeared from the public eye since mid-1977 and only reappeared three years later at the Marshal's funeral, commentaries about the growing role of the army, or the sudden resignation of Stane Dolanc as executive secretary of the ruling party. Such practices remind us, as did the confiscation of the domestic journals and the purge of 'too liberal' journalists in the previous chapters, that Yugoslavia cannot be judged by the standards one associates with democratic systems. Nevertheless, compared to all other Communist régimes, Yugoslavia is still a virtual paradise as far as circulation of and access to information is concerned.

Thus we can sum up the Eastern record in this respect as dismal, with no substantive improvement anywhere compared to the pre-Helsinki situation. The example of Yugoslavia shows that there are no valid reasons to block the entry of Western newspapers and publications or access to them for the local public. The fear of uncensored information, even if it is provided in a foreign language and at an excessively high price in local currency, has proved stronger than the wish to respond to the Western challenge and to fulfil the provisions of the Final Act. The Hungarians or Poles could most easily afford to facilitate newsstand sales of Western press, but such moves would place the Soviets and the hard-line régimes in a painfully embarrassing position, which in turn would backfire on the more liberal régimes. At the time of writing, the prospects for a Yugoslav-type development – free import with prior supervision of the copies – are virtually nil.

The second major issue concerns the working conditions for foreign journalists. A cursory review of the practices on a country-by-country basis shows no improvement. In the Soviet Union and East Germany the position of the resident foreign correspondents has definitely become worse since the Belgrade meeting. The proposals put forward at that conference are therefore more topical and necessary than ever.

Before turning to concrete cases, we have to take into account the general setting. The Communist régimes which control their own media so tightly, regard all foreign journalists as carriers of subversive ideas posing a potential threat to national security. The vast apparatus dealing with external contacts, ranging from the press departments of the foreign ministries and the central committees to the respective state security services, seeks to gain for the régimes the best possible image abroad and to stop unpleasant and politically sensitive news getting out. The propaganda functionaries as a rule prefer groups or delegations of journalists with a fixed schedule of programmes and minimal possibilities for causing mischief. A variety of institutions, from the foreign ministries to the tourist organisations and the chambers of commerce, regularly invite Western journalists. In contrast to the West, such invitations extended by dictatorships can be potentially dangerous as a basis for self-imposed censorship. But regardless of who covers the costs, the institutionalised exchange of delegations helps to provide a kind of cover-up for continuous blocking of person-to-person contacts and access to non-official sources of information.

Journalists considered 'unfriendly', 'prejudiced' or 'hostile', are the targets of special attention. Selective issuing of entry visas is one of the main traditional weapons against 'trouble-makers'. Thus for example the correspondents of the *Frankfurter Allgemeine* and *Le Monde* covering Eastern Europe and based in Vienna were, between 1976–78, refused a visa for respectively three and two years by the Czechoslovak authorities. Not exactly the 'suitable and reasonable time scale' promised in the Final Act! They were 'punished' for the factual information and background knowledge they provided to their readers about political, economic and social developments in Czechoslovakia.

Articles or speculations about personnel changes or power struggles in the top leadership are particularly disliked by the Agit-Prop officials east of the Elbe. The personality and politics of the supreme leader are sacred subjects which can be discussed only in a manner which is respectful and inspired by the wish to 'promote mutual understanding'. This means, for example, that in Romania, where everything is dominated by the Ceauşescu family, the coverage of politics and economics must be restricted to statistics without value judgments.

Secrecy continues to be one of the most powerful barriers to meaningful coverage of the Soviet bloc countries. In this respect most Communist states fail to provide full economic and commercial information as envisaged in the Basket Two of the Final Act. The provision of useful commercial information by the Soviet Union and the GDR has, if anything, worsened and has remained poor in Bulgaria, Romania and Czechoslovakia. Not only business and financial circles, but also commentators and reporters are affected by the lack of meaningful economic information. Thus oil reserves and other relevant data have been regarded since 1947 as a state secret in the Soviet Union – the world's largest producer of oil. The latest foreign trade book did not even contain data on coal and non-ferrous metals, nor detailed figures about oil exports but merely a total value of oil and oil products combined.[35] Needless to say figures on gold and foreign exchange reserves and debts, let alone maturity and interest rate structure are regarded as 'supersecret'.

A Polish example shows, however, that things can change. In a confidential memorandum submitted to a Western bank consortium, the Polish state bank revealed that the borrowings in the spring of 1979 totalled just over $15 billion and that the debt service ratio reached fifty-four percent in terms of export earnings in convertible currencies. Alas, this veritable breakthrough was not due to the fact that the Minister of Finance remembered the relevant provisions of the Helsinki document, but simply to the realisation of the need to inform some sceptical creditors, just about to float yet another $500 million loan on behalf of Poland![36] Yet it would be obviously better for everybody concerned if Comecon countries furnished their partners, and thus also the press, with reliable and up-to-date information about their foreign trade, balance of payments and five-year plan targets.

The clumsy and strictly hierarchical structure of Communist government apparatus excludes personal or easy access to high-ranking officials with real decision-making powers. President Ceauşescu gives, for example, lengthy interviews to all and sundry, at least once, often two to three times a week. But these are monotonous exercises in questions and answers prepared weeks in advance and hardly ever provide additional information beyond that already spelled out in the leader's frequent speeches to domestic audiences. In general, top Communist officials are accessible only to groups and, there again, chances for a real conversation or follow-up questions are virtually nil.

Editors-in-chief of major newspapers, preferably on the eve of a high-level visit from their countries, can also from time to time be honoured by an interview with the leaders in Prague, Sofia or Warsaw. However, as they are generally ignorant of the special problems and difficulties of the country in question, such interviews rarely enlighten the readers – apart from some personal impressions gained of Dr Husák or Edward Gierek. But basically senior officials are rarely, and high party functionaries virtually never, accessible for Western reporters.

At the same times, 'unfriendly' or 'hostile' Western journalists can also be 'punished' by denying them access even to middle- or low-level officials, enterprise managers and departmental chiefs in ministries. As the 'well-meaning' or 'objective' correspondents are given more assistance, their less accommodating colleagues can be put at a competitive disadvantage. Old-timers in Moscow in the past, or national stringers (part-time correspondents) recommended to Western agencies or newspapers by the local Communist authorities, are occasionally 'tipped off' in advance. The example of a Moscow correspondent getting information about Soviet space shots earlier than his colleagues being a case in point.

The denial of access for journalists put on a black list for their 'unfriendly' comments is a favourite method applied by officials even in Yugoslavia. Although the Yugoslavs do not harass or expel foreign journalists, they are more sophisticated than most other régimes in Eastern Europe in playing off one correspondent against another by providing top-level access for the more friendly ones. As Yugoslav politicians are much more forthcoming than their counterparts in the bloc, such practices can be irritating, although in the final analysis they harm only the Yugoslavs themselves. However, despite such occasional tricks, Yugoslavia cannot be coupled with the other Communist countries and its record of compliance with the Final Act's provisions concerning information and working conditions for foreign journalists is good.

Aside from various forms of official harassment, such as police interrogation or expulsion, visiting and accredited foreign journalists are subject to permanent supervision with the degree varying from country to country. This involves not only the tapping of telephones and the provision of specially 'prepared' hotel rooms, but also (often unnoticed by the persons concerned) a round-the-clock shadowing by the secret police.

I discovered years ago in a certain Communist country that I was being followed permanently. After having jotted down the number plates of the various cars 'escorting' me on my tour of the country, I confronted a high official with my observations:'You want to catch up with the West and yet five or six strong young men and several cars waste time and fuel only to report in which pub I had a bite on my way to an interview arranged by your government?' In contrast to most other functionaries in the same country, the senior official, cultured as he was cynical, did not even try to deny the evidence, but answered me with a smile: 'You see, what is done in a Western country by one person, has to be done in our country by many. This too shows how underdeveloped we are!'

In general, the East European authorities prefer casual visitors or journalists without a knowledge of the language spoken in the country or of the political background and national history, and dislike specialists or permanent correspondents staying on 'too long'. This is one of the main reasons for the harassment or expulsion of certain Western newsmen from Moscow. The ability of a correspondent to do his or her job depends not only on the character and resilience of the journalist concerned, but also on the support provided by the home office. Sometimes the régimes inform a newspaper that their Soviet or East European correspondent cannot get a visa, but someone else from the same paper would be welcome. Experience shows that newspapers resisting this kind of pressure fare better in the end and enforce access for their blacklisted correspondent, while those caving in to pressures often lay themselves open to future blackmail.

The threat of expulsion hangs like Damocles' sword over the heads of the 300 permanently accredited Western newsmen in Moscow. Sooner or later most of them are faced with the dilemma of holding back on a story in order to protect lines of communication, future opportunities or simply professional survival, or telling the full story even if it provokes harassment and possibly expulsion. As a Western observer aptly remarked, governments that do not allow freedom for their own journalists to criticise are not willing to make exceptions for foreigners to do so.[37] This is the reason why the best journalists after their tour of duty in Moscow write either a series of articles, or more often a whole book 'to really tell it like it is'.

It is well known that Western correspondents in Moscow are obliged to live in special quarters for foreigners, 'protected' by police around the clock, that hiring of Soviet personnel must be done through a government agency, that large areas are either inaccessible or can be visited only with special permission, that contact with Soviet officials is sharply restricted. However, following the Helsinki conference, some progress was made in working conditions which have made life easier for foreign correspondents. Accredited newsmen and their families now get multiple entry and exit visas for a period of one year and if they leave the country by train or plane no prior notification is necessary. However, if one leaves by car the press department of the Foreign Ministry must be notified forty-eight hours in advance, as is the case when leaving the capital for a trip within the Soviet Union. The exact route must also be announced. Travelling within the Soviet Union has become somewhat easier, but large areas and important cities (for example Sverdlovsk) are still 'off limits' to foreign newsmen or diplomats. As there is no complete list of forbidden zones, journalists too have to rely on the provisional maps compiled at some of the bigger embassies, keeping a track of the permissible zones and routes. Another much publicised concession was the possibility of direct access to government authorities without going through the Foreign Ministry press department or *Novosti* press agency. However in practice it is still quicker and easier to do it through *Novosti*, even if it is a matter only of contacting the Moscow City Council for a story about restoring old buildings.

However, these initial improvements have been completely overshadowed since 1978 by a spate of ominous incidents, ranging from harassment to expulsions. It is no longer just the continuing jamming of Radio Liberty broadcasts, or the denial of an occasional visa to a Western reporter. It is a concerted campaign, seeking to intimidate the Soviet public, to frustrate contacts with dissidents and to warn Western correspondents off sensitive subjects such as dissident trials, racial discrimination and ethnic tensions.

The methods vary from minor harassments, such as allegations of traffic offences and 'disorderly behaviour' in hotel rooms, to physical assaults, character assassination via television and outright expulsion. The campaign began with the expulsion of George Krimsky, an AP correspondent, in February 1977, followed by the detainment and interrogation of Robert C. Toth, the *Los Angeles Times* correspondent in June, 1977. Krimsky, accused both of espionage and violation of foreign exchange regulations, was the first US correspondent expelled from the Soviet Union since 1970. Both newsmen and their papers denied the Soviet charges.

In some ways, the most sensational development was the trial of two American journalists, Craig Whitney of the *New York Times* and Harold Piper, of the *Baltimore Sun* in July 1978 for allegedly slandering Soviet radio and television. They had quoted dissident sources that the filmed confession of a leading Georgian human rights activist had been fabricated. The court found the two correspondents guilty, fined them and demanded a retraction of their report in their newspapers. The two journalists did not appear before the court and refused to print retractions. But they were not deprived of their accreditation. The implications were ominous because, as a *New York Times* spokesman noted, 'the action implied that American reporters can be hauled into court at any time and penalised for reporting in a full and fair manner on events in the Soviet Union.'[38] Threats of American retaliation may have contributed to the Soviets stopping short of an expulsion. But it remains to be seen whether the new tactic will be applied again to restrict the flow of information out of the Soviet Union.

A couple of months before the Whitney-Piper trial, Soviet television presented a film showing five American newsmen allegedly carrying on espionage activities. Under the title 'The Free Press at Work for the Central Intelligence Agency', it included secretly taken shots of the reporters and warned the audience that anyone who listened to Western broadcasts or was approached by newsmen should think first whether the CIA might be behind it. The US embassy protested against this clear violation of the Helsinki accords, and accused the Soviets of deliberately distorting the function of foreign correspondents.[39]

Piper of the *Baltimore Sun* was not only sharply and repeatedly attacked for his reporting, but, together with another American correspondent, castigated by a Turkmen newspaper for wearing 'exceedingly brief shorts' while jogging in a public park in Ashkhabad. This upset Turkmen women who were said to be unaccustomed to such sights.[40] The attack against Robin Knight, a correspondent of *US News and World Report*, and his wife in Tashkent was in a much more serious vein. While entertained in a tea house by his Intourist 'guide', Knight must have been given a drug which knocked him out for several hours. His wife was also threatened. The journalist had been previously criticised in the Soviet press for reporting on discrimination against Jews and African students, as well as on strong anti-Russian feeling in Lithuania.[41]

Such articles are embarrassing for the Soviets not just for reasons of their international prestige but above all because they are broadcast back in Russian by the Voice of America and Radio Liberty. In addition to press attacks against the content of such pieces, the authors will be 'unmasked' as either spies, or at the very least inconsiderate rowdies, black marketeers or morally 'unstable elements'. Thus while the correspondents of *The Financial Times* and *Business Week* were accused of rowdy behaviour on trips they had made in the country,[42] the only Austrian correspondent, Erhard Hutter of Austrian radio and television, was expelled in October 1978 for allegedly engaging in illegal business activities, dealing in icons and other objects of art. Previously the Soviets had been pressing both in Moscow and Vienna for Hutter's recall. Married to a Russian, Hutter, after a seven-year stay in Moscow, knew many dissidents and had had an interview with Andrei Sakharov. The combination of all these factors proved more important than the wish to maintain good relations with the Austrian Government.[43]

A West German TV correspondent and his cameraman were expelled in May 1979, after an alleged row in a restaurant two and a half months earlier, involving the German cameraman and the official escort. The Federal Republic retaliated and expelled two Soviet newsmen. Observers however were convinced that the completely unmotivated expulsion was a move to provide political and moral support for the East German leadership, at that moment involved in a running quarrel with West German media.[44] The fact that the AFP correspondents were also reprimanded underlined the impression that the Soviets had embarked upon a concerted campaign of intimidation. During the same period, the Soviet authorities denied an entry visa to an Italian journalist who had been assigned to Moscow by *Corriere della Sera*.[45]

The provision of the Final Act concerning the 'complete, normal and rapid' transmission of information is occasionally interpreted in an unusual way. In 1978–79 Klaus Bednarz, Moscow correspondent of the ARD West German television network was three times denied the right to transmit films: on a dissident trial, on the investiture of the new archbishop of Tallinn and, in May 1979, on the working conditions of foreign journalists in the Soviet Union.[46]

Two further cases of interference with normal journalistic work received world-wide publicity. In June 1978, the Soviets did not allow transmission of photos and TV coverage when Irina McClellan attempted to chain herself to a gate at the US Embassy in Moscow to protest denial of permission to join her husband in America. On the eve of the Soviet-American summit in Vienna, Antonina Agapova wanted to demonstrate in front of the US Embassy in Moscow asking permission to join her son, a sailor who fled to Sweden in 1974. TASS refused to transmit the photo taken by AP because 'the trade union organisation' at the Soviet news agency regarded it as a 'deliberate provocation on the opening day of the Vienna summit'. Furthermore the 'members of the local TASS union want to protect their rights claiming that they did not want their work used for sordid aims such as a deliberate provocation aimed at disturbing the atmosphere at the Vienna conference.' Such action violated both the Final Act and its agreement with TASS, the Associated Press complained.[47]

When quick action is needed the gathering of news and the filming of an event is not blocked by 'union members', but with force – on the spot! Thus in May 1978 when a Soviet gunman occupied the office of Finnair a cameraman of CBS, the American television network, was struck from behind and forced to submit the film to a policeman. A Reuters correspondent was also detained for trying to cover the story.[48]

The proposals put forward in Belgrade to allow journalists to take their documentation and personal notes out of the country are very topical. The recent experience of American correspondents has been particularly instructive. A *New York Times* correspondent, David Shipler, had wanted to send a carton of notes and papers back to the US. Impounded by customs officials on 5 June 1979, the notes were returned the next day, but 321 pages of other material he had gathered during his tour of duty have never been returned. A month later seven books were seized from the household goods shipment of another *New York Times* man.[49] The us Commission on CSCE has noted that in 1978 twenty-five percent of requests for travel by American correspondents in the Soviet Union were either denied or modified, that the government has harassed Soviet employees of American news agencies and that travel by correspondents has been lately restricted.[50]

Group tours organised by the Foreign Ministry to Soviet republics, including protocol-ridden visits to factories and collective farms are no substitute for access to sources and freedom of movement in covering a vast and exciting country. As a correspondent who has been twice stationed in Moscow (in the late 1960s and 1970s) put it, apart from granting multiple exit and entry visas, 'nothing essential has changed in the way the régime treats the foreign press. The changes are tokenism and cosmetics.' But it is still something of a mystery why the Soviet leadership has decided to engage in actions which can only have an adverse impact on Soviet standing abroad.

East Germany, as noted earlier, is a 'front-line state' as far as the East-West flow of information is concerned. It is a sign of inherent weakness that the leadership, faced with growing internal ferment in the wake of economic difficulties, has decided to make a series of symbolic retreats, violating both the Helsinki accords and the so-called Basic Treaty of 1972 between the two German states.

Reprisals against the West German press began in December 1975, when the East Berlin correspondent of *Der Spiegel* was expelled on account of an article published in his paper, although he had not written or researched the piece. This case lent a special significance to the proposal submitted at the Belgrade conference that the paragraph in the Final Act about expulsions should be made even more specific to protect journalists from expulsions for opinions published in their media 'whether or not they are the authors'. It was followed by the expulsion of Lothar Loewe, the ARD correspondent in December 1976, the closure of the *Spiegel* bureau in East Berlin in January 1978, and, in May 1979, the expulsion of the correspondent of ZDF, the other West German TV network.[51]

This latter move was preceded in April 1979 by the imposition of tight, new restrictions on foreign journalists. They had to obtain from the Foreign Ministry prior approval for all interviews and give twenty-four hours' notice if travelling outside East Berlin, stating the goal and purpose of the trip. Infringement of the regulations involved warnings, withdrawal of accreditation and finally closure of the bureau. The Soviet press immediately supported the measures which contradicted the exchange of letters before the Basic Treaty about journalists having the 'right to exercise their professional activity' as well as about free information and reporting. A few weeks after this decree was issued, the ZDF correspondent in East Berlin was expelled, although Stefan Heym, the prominent dissident writer, had only made a statement before the ZDF cameras and did not give a formal interview.[52]

Be that as it may, the blow was the direct consequence of interviews with disgruntled East German citizens and broadcast the same evening by the West German media, and of course seen at the same time in the GDR. Yet as stressed by Professor Wolfgang Seiffert, until his defection in 1976 an authority on international law in East Germany, the retaliation against the West German reporters was sheer nonsense because, even according to East German law, what journalists write or broadcast in the Federal Republic can only be subject to West German legislation! In any case, the East German retreat from previous liberalisation measures show just how reliable and how credible the Communist declarations about peaceful coexistence and the durability of treaties and declarations are. A new criminal law adopted in June 1979 now threatens prison terms of up to five years for citizens who spread, directly or indirectly, news abroad or who illegally send scripts, manuscripts or other materials abroad which are liable to cause harm to the interests of the GDR.[53]

Czechoslovakia has also consistently violated the relevant provisions of the Final Act. During the tense period of the massive campaign against the Charter 77 human rights movement in early 1977, two Western journalists were taken off a train and had their notes and documentation confiscated; two accredited agency correspondents in Prague were even attacked with tear gas when attempting to interview a prominent dissident figure. The West German TV correspondent Helmut Clemens was expelled in July 1978. It is reckoned that between August 1975 and August 1978, at least sixteen foreign correspondents (three American, three West German, two French, two Dutch, two Norwegian, one Finnish, one Belgian, one Austrian and one Swedish) were harassed and/or had their notes confiscated at the conclusion of a visit.

In November 1978 a prominent Western scholar and authority on Czechoslovakia, Professor H. Gordon Skilling of the University of Toronto, was detained for twelve hours and his personal papers confiscated. Furthermore, eight Italian journalists working for the foreign broadcasting department of Radio Prague were fired in March 1976 for their 'Euro-communist' sympathies. As mentioned earlier, several Western correspondents have had to wait for years for an entry visa. Currently there are only two news agencies represented by foreign nationals in Prague. All Western press agencies have been told that their local employees can no longer interview anyone or attend press functions except as translators.

Yet at the same time there were also some signs in 1978–79 that the authorities intended to improve their relations with the foreign press. Five Austrian journalists, as well as several Swiss, British and other foreign correspondents stationed in Vienna were given accreditation in Prague. This meant that they automatically received an entry visa, generally within twenty-four hours. The accreditation, however, has to be renewed every six months, a condition which most of the Austrian newsmen, by reason of the demands of their work, could not always fulfil. It was simply not possible to appear every half year in a Prague office merely to renew their accreditation. But the spate of trials of human rights activists in the autumn of 1979 put an abrupt stop to the almost imperceptible improvement of the situation.

Romania has the perhaps strictest and tightest regulations about state secrets in Eastern Europe. Contacts between ordinary citizens and foreign journalists are allowed only if the ministry in charge of the given person or the chairman of the municipal or county People's Committee gives him or her permission.[54] Conversations with foreigners have to be reported immediately to the police or the employer. Journalists have no access to sources, and interviews generally take place in the presence of at least two other persons – one of them taking notes. Not even in the Soviet Union or in Czechoslovakia are journalists who know the country or speak the language so closely followed as in Romania. This is, however, equally true of East bloc correspondents stationed in Bucharest.

The first known cases of the harassment of foreign journalists were reported in connection with the emergence of the civil rights movement around Paul Goma in the spring of 1977. At that time the Belgrade correspondent of the *New York Times* was denied entry, but the decision was reversed within forty-eight hours. Later the Romanian authorities said that it had been a mistake and invited him to visit the country whenever he wanted to.[55] In December 1977 Romanian police searched a Swedish and an Austrian journalist who covered a party conference and were booked on a flight to Belgrade. Unpublished manuscripts of satires and poems, and letters to Amnesty International and the UN alleging human rights violations, were confiscated before the two newsmen were allowed to fly to Belgrade.[56] The Belgrade correspondent of *The Times*, Desa Trevisan, was denied a Romanian visa in May 1978 because of her previous coverage of ferment among the Hungarian minority and the miners' strike in the Jiu valley. She eventually received a visa to cover the Hua Kuo-feng visit to Bucharest. In March 1979, three Dutch journalists accompanying the Dutch Foreign Minister to Bucharest were detained for a couple of hours after they interviewed relatives of Romanian dissidents who founded a Free Trade Union and a Committee in Defence of Religious Freedom. The Romanians complained to the Dutch ambassador that the

newsmen were 'stupid' and did not contribute to 'the excellent relations between Holland and Romania.'[57] In summer of
1980 the Belgrade correspondents of *The Sunday Times* and
the *Observer* publicly protested against being shadowed and
harassed by the secret police.

In the early 1970s, Bulgaria committed several blunders in
the treatment of visiting foreign journalists. A West German
commentator was denied accreditation at a party congress on
account of his previous 'unfriendly' articles. An Austrian
editor, accompanying his Foreign Minister, was detained by
two militiamen and could be released only through a last-
minute intervention after he had manged to alert the Foreign
Ministry. It turned out that he had been on a black list for a
book and articles written six years earlier. His case showed
that even the abolition of visas, as is the case between Austria
and Bulgaria, does not help, indeed implies dangers, if one of
the two has a secret blacklist unknown to the other government, let alone the journalist concerned. However during the
last two to three years the government appears to have drawn
some conclusions and shown more skill in contacts with the
foreign press. In Bulgaria, the most closely watched visitors
are journalists from neighbouring Yugoslavia and particularly
from Skopje, the capital of the Macedonian Republic within
the Yugoslav Federation.

Poland has a relatively good record of compliance with the
Helsinki accords. The exceptions were two French left-wing
journalists held for nine hours by Polish police in October
1978 after they had talked to rebellious peasants; a journalist
from a Paris Trotskyite weekly who was released only after a
démarche by the French Foreign Minister and by the French
Journalists' Union, and a special correspondent of the British
Catholic *Herald* who was refused a visa to cover the Pope's
visit. One must also mention the fact that in 1978–79 six well-
known Polish Catholic journalists were several times refused
exit permits to travel to the West.[58]

It must be taken into account that these are only the known
cases. Thus minor incidents are very often not reported to the
embassies concerned. Nevertheless the following story also
reflects the atmosphere, even in a relatively easy-going country such as Poland. A young French journalist paid a short

visit to the country in 1978. On his departure from Warsaw Airport the customs officials confiscated his notes and documentary material. He protested and drove back to the city. The Foreign Ministry said that they had nothing to do with the incident and that he should wait until he got the notes back. The reporter however got tired of waiting and left the next day. Two weeks later he was rung by the Polish Embassy in Paris and informed that he could pick up his notes. Evidently the Poles are technically not so well equipped as the Romanians who in the same year confiscated the notes, documentation and books of a French and Swedish journalist, after their tour of Transylvania – but only for three hours.

Hungary has by far the best record among the Warsaw Pact states as far as the compliance with the provisions of the Final Act in the humanitarian and information field is concerned. The abolition of visas between Hungary and Austria also means that Austrian journalists, or correspondents travelling with an Austrian passport, can enter the country at any time. Access to official sources is possible only through the Foreign Ministry's press department, but on the whole foreign journalists are relatively satisfied with their treatment compared to the experiences they have had in other East European countries.

To sum up, the improvement or deterioration in the working conditions of foreign journalists reflects the political conditions, the general climate and the degree of sophistication of each Communist country. In those countries where the attitude has all along been more outward looking, as in Hungary or Poland, the Helsinki accords have helped to give a further impulse to the trend, but they have not created a new situation. In the Soviet Union, East Germany, Czechoslovakia and Romania the same domestic factors operate in favour of a hardening of the line and therefore the treatment of foreign journalists has also deteriorated. Nevertheless, the provisions of the Final Act, the debates at the Belgrade review conference and the preparations for Madrid, have provided potent ammunition with which the journalists can fight for their rights and protest maltreatment, and, in some countries at least, they have strengthened the hand of the opponents of hard-line policies within the ruling parties themselves.

Basically, one can conclude that régimes which allow more leeway for their own domestic media are also less afraid of the foreign press, realising that in the final analysis candour is a better propaganda method than repression tinged with fear. However, it should be remembered that the work of foreign correspondents, not only in the Communist world, but also in other dictatorial environments, is also threatened by the publishing and business bureaucracies, which worry that stories bringing out unpleasant realities could endanger advertising revenue or orders from the countries concerned. Last but not least some diplomats tend to forget that the primary duty of the journalist is to inform the public and not to sacrifice truth for the sake of what is perceived as higher interests of the state. The combination of all these factors can be a powerful restraint to investigative journalism. Greater compliance with the provisions of the Helsinki Final Act would therefore make not only the life of journalists easier, but, perhaps, also the world safer.

Conclusions

A DISPASSIONATE ANALYSIS of Soviet-type Communist communication policies reveals a yawning gap between rhetoric and realities, claims and facts. If one accepts the view, expressed so often by the Communist propagandists, that 'in the field of ideology there is not and cannot be any peaceful coexistence,' then the West should show a much greater willingness to pick up and return the ideological challenge than it is currently doing. Judging the Soviet model in terms of its record, we can draw some basic conclusions:

For all the changes in the political climate, standard of living and style of leadership, the Stalinist model of news rationing, filtering and censoring according to the given political priorities, has been upheld. The main function of the media is not to inform the public, but to serve the ruling party, which in turn maintains its claim to being infallible. Information is regarded as a state monopoly and any flow of information not subjected to control from above is seen as inherently subversive.

The West has little reason for self-congratulation. The attacks on investigative journalism in the US, Britain, France and West Germany are as well known as the challenges to the traditional right of the journalist to protect his or her sources. From time to time, reporting on Soviet and East European affairs by the 'instant experts' detailed to cover a major event, produces superficial, or sometimes even false, accounts of the situation in a country. Yet such mistakes (hardly ever due to deliberately malicious reporting as charged by the East) or occasional examples of Western non-compliance with the provisions of the Helsinki accords pale into insignificance in comparison with the record of the Soviet bloc countries. The elaborate structure of control, manipulation and censorship of the mass media, as well as the Communist concept of newsworthiness, are based on the premise that it is up to the governments of the individual states to decide what their inhabitants may or may not receive in the way of information. They should not only be able to exercise total control over their own media, but also have the right to decide what news from foreign sources may or may not be broadcast to their citizens.

As illustrated in the preceding chapters with a wealth of documentation, the Soviet bloc press consists – with a few exceptions in Hungary and Poland – of newspapers without news, official gazettes in disguise. Information is regarded as a privilege and access to uncensored news depends on rank and connections. The propaganda for domestic achievements and the denigration of the West are so overdone that even ordinary people notice the exaggeration. Most intellectuals and an increasing number of young people with higher education tend to agree with Talleyrand: *'Tout ce qui est exagéré est insignifiant.'*

The most isolated hard-line régimes are also the most vulnerable to the entry of uncensored information via the air waves. The electronic jamming of Western broadcasts through more than 3,000 transmitters must have cost the Soviet camp billions of badly needed dollars during the past three decades. Total control over incoming and outgoing information is still seen by most Soviet and East European rulers as one of the main means of maintaining their legitimacy.

It is high time to pay more attention to Soviet external propaganda and its offensive function as the so-called fourth dimension of foreign policy. The Communist leadership combines the defensive action aimed at protecting its closed system with manifold offensives to impose its own criteria upon foreign governments, media and public opinion. The starting point in all the controversies is that Soviet bloc media are *per se* progressive, purveying only truthful information, while Western information is *per se* 'slanderous, hostile and subversive' whenever it contradicts or criticises Communist policies or disseminates uncensored news about international and domestic events. It is up to the ruling Communist parties, and only to them, to decide what is 'truthful' information, serving 'peace and understanding', and what is impermissible 'subversive interference'. The line between legitimate 'ideological battle' and 'subversive propaganda' can be drawn only by the Eastern side.

This double standard is the basis for the claim that Communist media can legitimately wage unlimited propaganda for 'real socialism' under the conditions of peaceful coexistence. This means that Soviet and East European propagandists have full access to Western media and public. They can start a direct mail-order subscription campaign, place an order to publish a book, write letters to the editor and criticise Western policies or media personalities on television talk shows. But no Western journalist or newspaper has similar facilities to project the Western standpoint or other political view within the Soviet sphere of influence. Nowhere in the West are Soviet bloc broadcasts jammed, nor are there any institutional or legal barriers to the sale and distribution of domestic or foreign Communist newspapers.

The fact that Soviet propagandists have begun to express support for the 'New World Order for Information' should be cause for concern rather than for satisfaction in the Third World. The experiences of non-aligned Yugoslavia are telling proof of the dangers involved in Soviet bloc propaganda penetration. From the time of the Stalin-Tito break, up to to our days, Yugoslavia has waged a constant fight against the Moscow-sponsored thesis of the non-aligned being 'natural allies' of the Soviet camp.

No country, however, can call itself genuinely non-aligned without remaining fully independent of the world's largest and most tightly controlled propaganda centre in Moscow.

Though Yugoslavia is by no means a Western democracy, but a single-party regime, it has fully complied with the provisions of the Helsinki Final Act concerning the circulation of and access to information as well as the working conditions of foreign journalists. But the Soviets and most other East European countries have resoundingly failed to respect and to carry out the solemn undertakings signed by their own governments in August 1975. This is the reason why the Yugoslav example should be used as the key argument in the ongoing battle for compliance with the Helsinki accords.

It is startling that at a time of continuous international debate about communications and the long-term aims of Soviet foreign policy, so little is known about the character, structure and role of Communist mass media as carriers of political indoctrination at home and the means of expansion abroad. Both the Western and the Third World countries will have to stop refusing to read the evidence. The historical and current facts, the case histories and the quotations from authoritative Communist spokesmen and publications should convince us that there is no reason whatsoever for the balance in the vital field of communications and political-psychological confrontation to be tilted in favour of Soviet interests.

Throughout the Communist world, pressures for a more truthful and more comprehensive coverage of the international and domestic scene are growing. The disenchantment of the cultural, technocratic and administrative élites and the youth with the dreary diet of filtered, manipulated and censored information is a fact the regimes themselves indirectly, if sporadically, have to admit. With the freedom and control of the press moving to the centre of the North-South confrontation, it is important not only for the media, but also for an informed and alert public to know more about how the old and often forgotten Soviet-type 'information order' works in practice. Whatever the real or perceived dangers posed by transnational news agencies and media producers, the past and present of the Communist information systems can only reaffirm the timeliness of Camus' words: 'None of the evils which totalitarianism . . . claims to remedy is worse than totalitarianism itself.'

Bibliographical Notes

The material in this book for the most recent period is based on primary sources: Soviet and East European publications or information collected during the author's trips to the area, as well as interviews with Western and Communist newsmen. All references to the diplomatic negotiations in Belgrade and afterwards, if not otherwise specified, were gathered from the participating diplomats and their documents. Books used in the preparation of this study, are cited directly in the footnotes.

PART I

1. See, for a detailed examination of the issues involved, the excellent study by Rosemary Righter, *Whose News? Politics, the Press and the Third World* (London, 1978). The MacBride report was sharply criticised by Mort Rosenblum in the *International Herald Tribune*, 25 February 1980; in *Neue Zurcher Zeitung*, 23 May 1980; and by Gerald Long, managing director of Reuters, in IPI *Report*, March/April 1980. In contrast, Communist media was positive in its assessment. See, for a typical comment, *Népszabadság*, Budapest, 24 February 1980.
2. J. L. Talmon, *The Origins of Totalitarian Democracy* (New York, 1960), pp. 2–8.
3. Frederick J. Fleron *Soviet Studies*, XIX, No. 3 (1968).
4. Maurice Cranston, 'Should we Cease to Speak of Totalitarianism?', *Survey*, London, Summer (1977–78) Vol. 23 No. 3.
5. Richard Lowenthal, *The Model of the Totalitarian State* in *The Impact of the Russian Revolution 1917–67* (New York, 1968).
6. The term used by Patrick O'Brien, in 'Constitutional Totalitianism', *Survey*, Ibid.
7. *Pravda*, Moscow, Editorial 27 July 1965.
8. *Pravda*, 6 May 1979.
9. See his preface to Alain Besançon's book, *Court traité de soviétologie à l'usage des autorités civiles, militaires et religieuses* (Paris 1976), and his essay in *Marxism in the Modern World* (Stanford, 1966).

10. For good descriptions of work and atmosphere in the editorial office at *Pravda* see Robert Kaiser, *Russia, The People and the Power* (London, 1976) and Hedrick Smith, *The Russians*, (New York, 1976).

11. For the figures and a somewhat optimistic study of the Yugoslav press see Gertrude Joch Robinson, *Tito's Maverick Media* (Chicago, 1977). The broader political setting to the Yugoslav media situation is given in Dennison Rusinow, *The Yugoslav Exeriment 1948–1974* (London, 1977)

12. *Spotkania*, No. 5, opposition publication of young Polish Catholics, quoted after RAD Background Report/201, RFE Research, 21 September 1979.

13. Paul Roth, 'Die sowjetische Agentur Novosti', *Osteuropa* Stuttgart, 3/79.

14. *Ifju Kommunista*, Budapest, July 1979.

15. NIN, Belgrade, 18 December 1977.

16. Veljko Mičunović, *Moskovske godine*, 1956/58 (Zagreb 1977), p. N399.

17. Yuri Kashlev, 'Against 'Information Imperialism',' *Pravda*, 3 September 1979.

18. See the brilliant analysis by Alexandre Zinoviev, 'Le jeu à l'histoire,' *Le Monde*, Paris, 18 May 1979.

19. Mičunović, Ibid., p. 409. For the Jakubovsky article see *Rudé právo*, Prague, 25 March 1975, for Ljubičić piece *Pravda* 13 April 1975, for Dolanc article and Yugoslav complaint because of Czech paper's changing 'the victory of the Yugoslav partisans together with anti-Hitler coalition' to 'in co-operation with the Soviet Army' see Olaf Ihlau's Belgrade dispatch, *Süddeutsche Zeitung*, Munich, 18 April 1975.

20. *Magyar Hirlap*, Budapest, 13 August 1971.

21. See Paul Lendvai, *Anti-Semitism in Eastern Europe*, pp. 282–84 (London, 1971).

22. Mihailo Marković, 'Widersprüche in Staaten mit sozialistischer Verfassung', *Europäische Rundschau*, Vienna 75/4.

23. Michel Tatu, *Power in the Kremlin* (London, 1969) pp. 176–77.

24. Jiři Pelikán, *Ein Frühling der nie zu Ende geht, Erinnerungen eines Prager Kommunisten* (Frankfurt 1976), pp. 244–45.

25. Antony Buzek, *How the Communist Press Works* (London, 1964) p. 136.

26. For figures for outside contributors see *Der Spiegel*, Hamburg, 6 May 1974; also Kaiser and Hedrick Smith, *New York Times* 9 October 1975, *Reuter* from Moscow 8 January 1976 for over-staffing.

27. See for details H. Gordon Skilling, *Czechoslovakia's interrupted revolution* (Princeton, 1976), pp. 828 and 887. See for

treatment of sacked journalists with personal case histories *White Paper On Czechoslovakia*, published by the International Committee for the Support of Charter 77 in Czechoslovakia (Paris, 1977). pp. 114–16. for the text of the original Press Law of 1966, pp. 154–57, for the 1968 June Law on the abolishment of censorship, pp. 158–59 and for the Law of September 1968, reintroducing censorship, pp. 160–61. The authors estimate that 'about 2,000 journalists are not allowed to work in their profession'.

28. Svetozar Stojanović, *Kritik und Zukunft des Sozialismus*, (Munich, 1970).

29. James Reston, *The Artillery of the Press, Its Influence on American Foreign Policy (New York, 1967)*.

30. Gayle Durham Hollander, *Soviet Political Indoctrination* (New York, 1972), pp. 37–40.

31. Gerald Huebner, 'Brunnenvergifter', *Horizont*, East Berlin, 39/79.

32. *Pravda*, 16 September 1968.

33. *Zhurnalist*, Moscow, No. 11 1970, quoted by Hollander.

34. For the most recent experiences see in particular Kaiser, Hedrick Smith and Hollander. Perceptive observations also by Nils Morten Udgaard, *Der ratlose Riese, Alltag in der Sowjetunion*, (Hamburg, 1979).

35. *Frankfurter Allgemeine Zeitung*, 21 August 1979. Another airliner crash was reported by Western agencies from Moscow in June 1980, but it was denied by a Soviet official.

36. Udgaard, p. 198.

37. *New Statesman*, London, 13 April 1979. Both Klebanov's group, founded on 25 November 1977 and another underground workers' union, called SMOT, formed on 28 October 1978 were subsequently liquidated by the KGB through harassment, arrest and detention in psychiatric hospitals of workers associated with the two movements. See for details and a chronology of events relating to the independent trade unionists, Radio Liberty Research, RL 304/79, 11 October 1979.

38. Interview with Pešić, NIN, 20 June 1979. For criticism of NIN see *Politika*, 30 January 1979 and FAZ, Frankfurt, 2 February 1979.

39. John Newhouse, *Cold Dawn* (New York, 1973), pp. 55–57.

40. Henry A. Kissinger, *A World Restored*, (New York, 1964) p. 29.

41. Zhores Medvedev, *Bericht und Analyse der bisher geheim gehaltenen Atomkatastrophe in der Udssr*, (Hamburg 1979). See for earthquake and summing up particularly pp. 231–38. Also, by Medvedev, 'Facts behind the Soviet nuclear disaster', *New Scientist*, London 1977, No. 1058, pp. 761–64; and for the original disclosure, 'Two decades of dissidence', Ibid., 1976, No 1025,

pp. 264–67. See also, in the spring of 1980, Western reports and Soviet denials about the causes of the outbreak of anthrax in Sverdlovsk in 1978. There were also heated disputes over reports of strikes in the large car and truck factories in the cities of Togliatti and Gorky; *Financial Times*, 13 and 23 June 1980; denials by TASS on 15 and 25 June.

42. Gerhard Simon, 'Massenmedien in der Sowjetunion', *Osteuropa*, 3/74.

43. For details of the *Kommunist* article see the *New York Times* 15 October 1979, Reuter and AP from Moscow on the previous day. The two Soviet scientists, however, covered the same ground in *Pravda* 14 July 1976. For details of previous warnings see Radio Liberty Research RL307/79.

44. Paul Goma, a noted Romanian writer launched a civil rights movement in the spring of 1977 and sent a public letter of protest, signed by scores of other Romanian intellectuals, to the Belgrade preparatory meeting on European security. They were protesting against the violations of human rights and the refusal of their applications for exit permits. After a long period of harrassment, most of the protesters, including Goma, were allowed to emigrate. Károly Király, a former alternate member of the Political Executive Committee has written several petitions to the Bucharest leadership, asking for concrete measures to improve the political and educational situation of the Hungarian minority. Other important figures also sent similar letters to President Ceauşescu. But only Király dared to puncture publicly the carefully fostered fiction of a national question 'fully resolved in Marxist-Leninist spirit.'

45. BTA, Sofia, IV/13, 1977.

46. Roger Tatarian, quoted in Leonard R. Sussman, 1977, *Mass News Media and The Third World Challenge*, The Washington Papers, No. 46, Beverly Hills and London.

47. For details concerning readership surveys of *Izvestia* see Zhurnalist, 2/68, 8/68 and 6/70, quoted in Hollander.

48. *Frankfurter Allgemeine Zeitung*, 19 April 1979.

49. See specifically Reuter on 23 March 1979 from Moscow about the tv commentary, *Novoe Vremya*, 20 April, *Pravda* 29 April, *Izvestia* 18 May and 10 June 1979.

50. *Literaturnaya Gazeta*, 25 October 1978, *Pravda* 3 November and 19 November, *Izvestia* 15 December 1978; For the shift see particularly *Pravda* 6 January, also Radio Moscow's broadcasts in Persian on 18, 30 and 31 December 1978. On the day the Shah departed from Iran, TASS attacked him and on 17 January 1979 *Pravda* printed the dispatch, while on 25 January *Izvestia* wrote

that the Shah 'left the country accompanied by the curses of his people and the lamentations of his parasites'.

51. Radio Prague 12 February 1979. In contrast to all other East bloc countries and Yugoslavia, the Ceauşescu régime in Romania published only the barest minimum on the changes in Iran. The Romanian President visited Iran five times, while the Shah travelled three times to Romania. He was scheduled to go to Romania again on 11 September 1978, but the visit 'was postponed through mutual agreement', *Scînteia*, 6 and 11 September 1978.

52. See Reuter 14 September 1979.

53. Figures from *Deutsch-deutsche Pressefreiheit*, Hrsg. Erich Böhme, Hamburg 1978.

54. *Die Zeit*, Hamburg, 14 September 1979.

55. *Der Spiegel* 29 August 1979.

56. For refugees see *Die Flucht aus der Sowjetzone und die Sperrmassnahmen des kommunistischen Regimes vom 13. August in Berlin*, Bonn 1961. For the current situation see *Der Spiegel*, Ibid.

57. Since late 1978–early 1979 there has been a subtle, but significant shift in the reporting on Elena Ceauşescu. While previously she was always listed as Number Two on ceremonial occasions, lately she has been treated more and more as an equal to her husband with the headlines now spelling out the name of both in the same type.

58. Márványi György, 'Rejtett Uzenetek', *Elet és Irodalom*, Budapest, 28 April 1979.

59. The account of the coverage is based primarily on *The Pope in Poland*, a mimeographed 128-page publication by Radio Free Europe research, Munich 1979. The report about the Bialystok station from *Die Welt*, Hamburg, 5 June 1979.

60. A brief version was printed by *Time* 2 July 1979. For the complete text see rfe Background Report, 15 July 1979.

61. For a crackdown on Catholic activists in Czechoslovakia see *Frankfurter Allgemeine Zeitung*, 8 November 1979. There is also some opposition in Hungary against what younger priests and some bishops regard as a far too lenient attitude taken by Cardinal Lèkai towards the régime.

62. *Polityka*, Warsaw, 11 February 1978.

63. *Trybuna Ludu*, Warsaw, 24–25 February 1978.

64. Quoted after *One Sentence On Tyranny, Hungarian Literary Gazette Anthology*, 1957, London.

65. Buzek, op. cit.

66. *La Repubblica*, Rome, 22 June 1978, *The Times*, London, 23

June 1978, Radio Liberty Research RL 179/78. See also Tatu p. 245 and p. 314

67. See *L'URSS Et Nous*, Paris, 1978, especially *Introduction*, by Francis Cohen, p. 20. *Le Monde*, 6 September 1978 and 29 November 1978 (quoting *l'Humanité* of the previous day).

68. Borsányi György, *Kun Béla, Politikai Életrajz*, Kossuth Könyvkiadó (Budapest, 1979). The book was previously announced as the main attraction of the so-called annual Book Week, interviews were already carried with the author and a first review written by the cultural editor of *Népszabadság* was also broadcast by Radio Budapest.

69. For details see Paul Lendvai, *Die Grenzen des Wandels* (Vienna, 1977), p. 95.

70. See Hollander. Also Alex Inkeles, *Public Opinion in Soviet Russia*, (Cambridge, Mass. 1950); Lev Vladimirov, *The Russians*, (New York, 1968).

71. Quoted from the 600 pages of original documents, published in Polish in two volumes by *Aneks*, 1977–78, London.

72. A good summary of how the Soviet articles carefully avoided the taboo subjects in *Le Monde*, 23 August 1978.

73. See for details Wolfgang Höpken, 'Ein Stück unbewältigte Vergangenheit. Anmerkungen zur Publikation von Tito-Reden in der udssr und der ddr', *Osteuropa*, 3/78.

74. Udgaard. pp. 123–24.

75. Information from Polish journalists who were present at the meeting in Warsaw.

76. See fn. 71.

77. For a summing up of the situation see Anneli Ute Gabanyi, 'Die Zensur in Rumänien – nicht abgeschafft, sondern verstärkt', *Osteuropa*, 4/79.

78. *Viaţa Românească*, Nr. 7–8 1978; Bucharest. In the 1970s the circulation of this monthly was 2,888 copies, a ridiculously low figure for a Communist country. Figure from *Südosteuropa–Handbuch, Rumänien*, (Göttingen, 1977), p. 551. But in May 1974 the Political Executive Committee of the Romanian Communist Party ordered a drastic cut, on the average up to 50 percent, of the circulation of cultural periodicals.

79. Ibid.

80. Definition by Louis Blom-Cooper in a discussion with Stuart Hampshire on 'What is censorship?' in *Index on Censorship*, July-August 1977, London.

81. From his speech held before Budapest party activists on 6 June 1979 and published in *Pártélet*, Budapest, 9/79.

82. A selection of some interesting pieces was published in Hungarian in *Magyar Füzetek 2*, Paris, 1978.

83. See comments by Zsolt Krokovay in *Magyar Füzetek*; an English translation is available in RFE–RAD Background Report/173, 3 August 1978. See also Cranston, *Survey* Ibid. For harassment of underground authors, see Balázs, R. and B. in *Index*, April 1980.

84. For details see *Vjesnik*, Zagreb, 22 September 1979.

85. UPI, 13 October 1979, AP and DPA 15 October 1979. See also *International Herald Tribune, Die Presse*, Vienna, *Frankfurter Allgemeine Zeitung*, 16 October and *Le Monde*, 17 October 1979.

86. Robert Tucker, *The Soviet Political Mind*, (London 1972). p. xii. Also for the following Yevtushenko quote.

87. See François Fejtö, 'Objektivität und ideologischer Kampf', *Europäische Rundschau* 2/74.

88. Merwyn Matthews, *Privilege in the Soviet Union. A Study of Élite Life-Styles under Communism* (London, 1978). pp. 34–35.

89. See Hedrick Smith, Chapter XIV. on 'Information'.

90. For Soviet agents posing as TASS or *Novosti* staffers see John Barron, *KGB, The Secret Work of Soviet Secret Agents* (New York, 1974), pp. 11, 20, 149, 180, 255.

91. For 'white' and 'red Tass', see Smith, Kaiser and Udgaard; all rather vague on details. The most detailed, though also incomplete, description is in Vladimirov, pp. 91–93.

92. Mičunović, p. 453, diary entry from 24 May 1958, referring to TASS special bulletin on 22 May.

93. Author's estimate based on information from East European colleagues.

94. Information from Hungarian and Romanian sources; see also same assessment in Buzek, pp. 204–5, Kostov in RFE broadcast of 13 October 1977. For the various bulletins and intrigues also Pelikán, pp. 188–92.

95. Kostov Ibid.

96. Gierek story based on highly reliable Polish source. Quote on Kiss from secret Hungarian party archives, cited by János Berecz, *Ellenforradalom Tollal és Fegyverrel* (Counterrevolution with Pen and Weapon) 1956. (Budapest, 1969), p. 80.

PART II

1. Quoted in *The Financial Times*, London 9 October 1978.

2. For a perceptive analysis see Gerhard Wettig, *Broadcasting and détente* (London, 1977), p. 88, also pp. 81–96.

3. David M. Abshire, *International Broadcasting: A New Dimension of Western Diplomacy*, The Washington Papers No. 35 (Beverly Hills and London, 1976).

4. Sir Michael Swann, *The BBC's External Services Under*

Threat?, Address to the Royal Society of Arts, 11 January 1978 (London, 1978), p. 7.

5. *BBC Handbook* (London 1980). For Albanian figures and detailed statistics see also *Unesco Statistics on Radio and Television 1960–76* (Paris, p. 1978).

6. Abshire, p. 18.

7. All figures quoted for East European audiences from East Europe Area Guidance and Opinion Research mimeographed release by RFE August 1979. Results based on interviews with 6,808 East Europeans above the age of fourteen, field work carried out between March–May by seven institutes in Austria, Denmark, Sweden, France, Germany, and the United Kingdom. It was pointed out that the Romanian results were partly based on unrepresentative samples because the farmers' subsample was too small and that figures for Bulgarian listeners were also based on a relatively small sample. See also Wetting, pp. 77–8.

8. *Neues Deutschland*, 29 May 1973. For detailed audience figures of West German tv broadcasts in East Germany see *Deutsch-Deutsche Pressefreiheit* pp. 30–31.

9. See *Die Zeit*, 23 May 1979, Abshire p. 29, Wettig p. 78.

10. *BBC Handbook* 1980.

11. Radio Moscow in German, 17 March 1976 quoting extracts from a new book by Vachnadze, *The Aerials are Directed Against the East.*

12. *The Board for International Broadcasting* (BIB) Fifth Annual Report 1980, covering the period from October 1979 to September 1980 (Washington DC 1979), p. 7. All further details for RFE and RL operations from this and the previous Reports.

13. BIB Fifth Annual Report, pp. 43–44.

14. Ibid., pp. 45–50.

15. *Recollections*, (New York, 1970), p. 188.

16. Abshire, p. 32.

17. Sean Kelly, *Access Denied, The Politics of Press Censorship*, The Washington Papers No. 55 (Beverly Hills and London, 1978), p. 72.

18. Quoted in Hollander, p. 40.

19. See for the multiplication effect of Moscow correspondents' reports particularly Udgaard, p. 193.

20. BIB Fifth Annual Report, pp. 14–15.

21. Details about coverage of Pope's visit from RFE–RL Public Information and Research.

22. BIB Fifth Report, p. 3; and Sixth Report, p. 58.

23. See fn. 7 and BIB Fourth and Fifth Annual Report for audience figures. The estimates vary from year to year.

24. BIB Fifth Report, pp. 22–26. As there are fewer Soviet visitors,

particularly from the Baltic and the Central Asian republics than from Eastern Europe, and as all opinion research is said to be carried out exclusively in the West, the estimates for Soviet audiences are generally regarded as less reliable than those for the smaller East European states. Even the estimates for Bulgaria and Romania must be treated with some caution since the samples are bound to be always less representative than those for the other countries simply because westward tourism from Bulgaria and Romania is still rather small.

25. Udgaard, p. 193.
26. For these and other details see statement of Sig Mickelson, President of RFE–RL on 19 May 1977 before the Congress Commission on Security and Co-operation in Europe, *Hearings*, Ninety-Fifth Congress, Volume III (Washington DC 1977), p. 41.
27. Gerard Mansell, *Why External Broadcasting?*, BBC lecture, 11 March 1976 (London, 1976), p. 15.
28. For example to Chancellor Kreisky. See also *Kronen Zeitung*, Vienna, 20 November 1979.
29. Statement is said to have been made by Mihály Kornidesz, departmental chief of the Central Committee in charge of science, education and culture on a visit to the Music Academy in Budapest.
30. Report to the Congress on 22 March 1977. Quoted in BIB Fifth Annual Report, p. 5.
31. See *BBC Handbook*, p. 62. Criticism of RFE Polish-language broadcast was also voiced in *Kultura*, the emigré Polish monthly, published in Paris. There is no way for an observer to assess the relevance of these complaints or, alternatively, the counter-arguments of the Western stations with regard to the dangers of 'destabilising' an already volatile situation in certain countries. The Board for International Broadcasting holds for example that 'informative international broadcasting contributes to a sense of realism and moderation among rulers and ruled alike'. See Fourth Annual Report.
32. Story related in the BIB Fourth Report (covering the period between October 1976–September 1977). One could only speculate that the First Secretary might have been Gierek or Kádár.
33. Abshire, p. 70. The figure of sixty percent is much higher than the estimates of RFE listeners in the 1970s (oscillating between thirty-seven and thirty-four percent). It may have originally referred to the proportion of the population listening to Western broadcasts in general. But the rapid fall in audience, particularly in the summer months of 1968 was noted by most observers.
34. Report of the Presidential Study Commission on International Radio Broadcasting, *The Right To Know* (Washington DC 1973).

35. Quoted in RFE paper on 'Jamming'.
36. Article 35 of the Convention states: 'All stations, whatever their purpose, must be established and operated in such a manner as not to cause harmful interference to the radio services or communications of other Members or Associate Members.'
37. G. A. Codding, *Broadcasting Without Barriers* (New York, 1959), p. 75.
38. *Élet és Irodalom*, Budapest, 22 February 1969.
39. For details see BIB Fourth and Fifth Annual Reports.
40. For details see RFE on 'jamming', Report of Presidential Study Commission; J. Hale, *Radio Power* (London, 1975), pp. 132–33; Pelikán, pp. 188–92.
41. Speech by Ambassador Goldberg, Belgrade, 13 October 1977.
42. For details see R. D. Heffner, 'Offener Himmel oder Vorzensur?' in *Osteuropa*, 7/1974.
43. Wettig, p. 60. See also pp. 58–62.
44. Soviet Ambassador Malik at the UN General Assembly 25 October 1972, quoted by Heffner. For the second quote see V. Korobeinkov, *Mezhdunarodnaya Zhizn*, Moscow, 1/1976.
45. Carew Hunt, p. 100.
46. *Pravda*, 31 July 1968, quoted by Hollander, p. 114.
47. See BBC Caris Report No. 11/79.
48. *Izvestia*, 17 and 22 December 1968, quoted by Hollander, p. 115.
49. Ibid, p. 115.
50. See Mickelson, *Hearings*, p. 44, also Wettig, p. VIII.
51. Wettig.
52. Quoted after Mickelson, p. 41–2.
53. See Lendvai, *Anti-Semitism*, pp. 289–91, for the use of the 'feedback' and 'cross references' technique against Czech reformers, using some Beirut papers.
54. *Sovetskaya Kultura*, Moscow, 14 September 1979; the author is Alexander Urban, now in Bonn; he was previously in Vienna, correspondent for TASS.
55. *Komsomolskaya Pravda*, Moscow, 21 November 1970, quoted in Wettig, p. 17.
56. *Süddeutsche Zeitung*, 1 June 1971; *Nowe Drogi*, Warsaw 7/1972; *Die Welt*, 19 January 1976.
57. For the role of *Stern* in connection with the campaign against Solzhenitsyn see the writer's interview with the Moscow correspondents of the *New York Times* and *Washington Post*, 30 March 1972. For *Spiegel's* insinuation that Andrei Amalrik had close contacts with the KGB, the Soviet secret service and that his famous study *Will the Soviet Union Survive 1984?* had been in some way written in collaboration with the KGB, see an unsigned article in

Spiegel 12/1970 and three weeks later Amalrik's rejoinder that the German weekly was highly irresponsible in printing rumours 'spread by the KGB itself in order to discredit me, to harm the success of my book and to make propaganda for the KGB as an organisation which knows everything.'

58. *Izvestia*, 15 March 1977.
59. Wettig, pp. 36–39. See also Bernard Levin in *The Times*, 17 April 1975.
60. See *Der Spiegel*, 15 March 1971 and *Die Weltwoche*, Zurich, 19 March 1971 for some colourful details.
61. Wettig, p. 37.
62. For details see Ladislav Bittman, *The Deception Game*, *Czechoslovak Intelligence in Soviet Political Warfare*, (Syracuse, New York, 1972), pp. 148–49. The author claims that he visited Budapest as deputy chief of the disinformation department of Czechoslovak intelligence together with his boss in 1965. A certain János Fürjes, previously Hungarian press attaché in Vienna, was, according to Bittman, heading the Hungarian disinformation department at that time and was also in charge of the operation against the RFE. See also pp. 171 and 189 for case histories of spreading rumours and seeking to personally discredit Czech emigré journalists in 1965–67. Bittman added: 'When it is difficult to disprove all or part of an author's contentions, the intelligence service assembles basic facts about him, fills them out with unfavourable particulars, and presents this package to the public as proof of the author's immorality, thus indirectly refuting his allegations' (p. 189). This observation is true of course not only of the Czechoslovak intelligence service!
63. On 21 January 1976 Radio Prague began to broadcast quotes from letters sent by Czechoslovak emigrants to RFE; announced on 27 January the return of an unnamed Czechoslovak intelligence officer, and presented Minařik on the 29th at a press conference attended by two hundred journalists.
64. *Scînteia*, 7 February 1976.
65. The best and most up-to-date account is Kyrill Panoff, 'Murder on Waterloo Bridge, The case of Georgi Markov', in *Encounter*, London, November 1979.
66. *The Observer*, London, 16 September 1979.
67. *BBC Handbook* 1978, p. 62, quoting *Zhurnalist*, Moscow.
68. Vladimir Artyomov and Vladimir Semyonov, *The BBC: History, Apparatus*, Methods of *Propaganda*, Moscow, Iskusstvo, 1979. The 256-page book was produced in an edition of 50,000 copies.
69. *Novoie Vremya*, 32/1979.
70. Quotes in order of listing, *Izvestia*, 26 November 1975; TASS

commentary 24 February 1977; 'Radio Peace and Progress' 13 February 1976 in German; Radio Prague, 18 October 1976; 'Radio Peace and Progress', 14 September 1977 in German; Ibid., 22 February 1978; Ibid., 5 May 1979.

71. For allegations about financing, NATO, CDU, etc, see among others, TASS 24 February 1977; 'Radio Peace and Progress' 5 May 1979; Radio Moscow 14 May 1979 in German; *Izvestia* 10 August 1979. For the personal attacks against Botho Kirsch, head of the Russian service, see N. Portugalov, Soviet correspondent in Bonn in interview with *Literaturnaya Gazeta*, 14 March 1977; *Novoie Vremya* 4 July 1979; *Krasnaya Zvezda*, 4 October 1979. The article also attacks a chief news editor who retired three years earlier. Since 1978, Portugalov has been a 'consultant' to the International Information Department of the CC of the CPSU in Moscow. See, for his hard-line attitude to Germany, an interview in *Der Spiegel*, 9 June 1980.

72. Moscow Radio in German, 27 February 1979.

73. *Pravda*, 1 August 1975.

74. See for details *BBC Handbook* 1978; *BIB* Fourth Annual Report.

75. AP, 1 August 1979, in *International Herald Tribune*, Paris. 2 August 1979; *Daily Telegraph*, London, 7 August 1979.

76. *BIB* Fourth Annual Report, Abshire, p. 22.

77. The quotes in order as listed from 'Radio Peace and Progress' Moscow, 26 April 1977; TASS International Service 10 March 1977; 'Radio Peace and Progress', 31 January 1977; Ibid., 27 April 1977; Radio Moscow, 10 March 1977; TASS International Service, 24 February 1977. Quoted from Mickelson, *Hearings*, pp. 43–44.

78. Wettig, pp. 40–1.

79. Radio Moscow in Persian, 6 November, 9 November 1979; *Washington Post*, 12 November 1979; for Soviet denial see TASS 12 November 1979, *International Herald Tribune*, 22 November 1979.

80. For text see *Nowe Drogi*, Warsaw, No. 2/1974, pp. 27–38.

81. *Pravda*, 29 June 1975. See also Suslov's speech about an 'historic victory' due to the recognition of the 'Leninist principles of peaceful co-existence' throughout the West, delivered at an ideological conference in Moscow, *Pravda*, 17 October 1979.

82. Mičunović, pp. 449–50. The Yugoslav Ambassador noted this in his diary on 14 May 1958 in the midst of the Soviet campaign against Yugoslavia because of the 'Revisionist' Yugoslav Party programme. He added sarcastically: 'I don't believe that in other societies and systems there is a profession similar to that exercised by Suslov, Ponomarev and the army of their subordinate party and state officials. They are the judges of theoretical and ideologi-

cal questions related to socialism. That's why their current campaign against our programme and our Seventh Congress is natural and unavoidable.'

83. Quoted after the German text in *Problems des Friedens und des Sozialismus*, Prague 6/1974. The article was written for the fifth anniversary of the World Communist Conference held in Moscow in 1969.

84. Radio Moscow in German, 17 September 1975; see also commentary by Rudi Singer, Radio DDR, 25 April 1976.

85. See Wettig pp. 23–4; also fn. 71.

86. His article in a collection of articles, published in Moscow in 1974 and quoted in Wettig p. 47, fn. 3. See also Kashlev's similar articles written jointly with Zassursky in *Unesco Courier*, April 1977.

87. Interview in *Zhurnalist* 6/75 quoted in Paul Roth, 'Die sowjetische Agentur Novosti (APN)' in *Osteuropa* 3/79.

88. See Arthur Koestler, *The Invisible Writing* (London, 1954), pp. 188–213; Babette Gross, *Willi Münzenberg* (Stuttgart, 1967), pp. 157–311.

89. Quoted after *US News & World Report*, New York, 7 August 1978.

90. *Spiegel–Gespräch* with Vadim Zagladin and Valentin Falin, deputy heads of the International respectively of the Information Department of the Central Committee of CPSU, 45/1979.

91. See, for Soviet reservations in December 1977, expressed in a closed session, Righter, p. 174.

92. Kashlev, *Pravda*, 3 September 1979.

93. Jean Schwoebel of *Le Monde*, quoted in *Pravda Vostoka*, 5 September 1979, said at the Tashkent meeting that 'the Helsinki Final Act calls for co-operation not only between diplomats, but also among journalists'. He initiated, with Unesco support, the periodical publication of a joint newspaper, compiled in theory by sixteen different newspapers, including a Hungarian and a Polish daily. See also for coverage *Pravda Vostoka*, Tashkent, 4, 5, 6, 8 and 9 September 1979; also AP from Moscow, 8 September 1979.

94. For twenty-fifth anniversary see 'Twenty-five Years of *The Democratic Journalist*, and 'Twenty-five Years of the IOJ Activities on the Pages of *The Democratic Journalist*, in *The Democratic Journalist*, Prague 11–12/78. Haskovec quoted from the 5/78 issue, which published details of his speech given in November 1977 at the Bagdad conference.

95. All topics quoted from the twelve issues in 1978, including also the sections 'From the World of the Press' and 'For Information'. In his anniversary article, the Editor of the magazine,

Oldřich Bureš, specifically praised the 'close co-operation with Unesco'.

96. See for a detailed account, Sonja Brie's article in *Deutsche Aussenpolitik*, East Berlin, 2/79. Figure for military engagement in Africa from *International Herald Tribune*, 22 November 1979.

97. *Neue Deutsche Presse 31*, 1977.

98. See Sonja Brie, Ibid. See, for East German propaganda, Anita M. Mallinckrodt's essay in *Drei Jahrzehnte Aussenpolitik der DDR*, pp. 260–73 (Munich-Vienna 1979).

99. Quoted in *BZ am Abend*, East Berlin, 26 August 1978.

100. *The Democratic Journalist*, 7–8/1978. See MTI report of the school, 14 April 1980

101. *Horizont*, East Berlin, 36/7 1979.

102. *Jugend*, East Berlin, 12/1978.

103. By the same author 'Massenmedien und internationale Beziehungen' in *Deutsche Aussenpolitik*, 10/1977.

104. For further details see 'SED-Journalismus als Exportartikel' in *Deutschland Archiv*, Cologne, 10/1979, pp. 1016–18.

105. See, for a detailed account, *Frankfurter Allgemeine Zeitung*, 31 January 1980.

106. 3 September 1979.

107. Karl Marx, Friedrich Engels, *Über Kunst und Literatur* (Frankfurt-Vienna, 1968), p. 48.

PART III

1. See his article 'Did Human Rights Survive Belgrade?' in *Foreign Policy*, New York, Summer, 1978.

2. *The Belgrade Follow-Up Meeting to the Conference on Security and Co-operation in Europe: A Report and Appraisal*, Commission on Security and Co-operation in Europe, 17 May 1978, Washington DC.

3. Ibid. See also Per Fischer, 'Das Ergebnis von Belgrad' in *Das Belgrader KSZE Folgetreffen* (Bonn, 1978), pp. 23–32. Ambassador Fischer was the West German delegation chief at the Belgrade meeting.

4. All direct citations from the official English text of the Final Act.

5. For a detailed account see *Das Belgrader KSZE Folgetreffen*, pp. 79–192; for the list of all proposals particularly pp. 187–92. See also *A Report and Appraisal*.

6. All quotes from speeches and debates at closed meetings are based on my notes made at briefings or informations from diplomatic sources.

7. Medvedev quote from Hedrick Smith.
8. Raymond Vernon, 'The Fragile Foundations of East-West Trade' in *Foreign Affairs*, New York, Summer, 1979.
9. See Barron, p. 166 and p. 391.
10. *Deutsch-deutsche Pressefreiheit*, p. 34.
11. Roger Bernheim, *Die sozialistischen Errungenschaften der Sowjetunion* (Zurich, 1972), pp. 25–8. The author was Moscow correspondent from 1967–70.
12. For the full text see particularly CSCE/BM/39,41,42,43, 11 November 1977.
13. For Western proposals see CSCE/BM 22, 7 November; BM 34 and 35, 8 November 1977.
14. CSCE/bm/8, 31 October 1977. See also speech of Swiss representative delivered on the same day.
15. For the text of the Soviet, NATO and N+Ndrafts (the N+N was circulated only as an informal document) see also *Das Belgrader KSZE Folgetreffen*, pp. 146–74.
16. In an interview with *Le Monde*, 6 July 1979.
17. See *Report* and *Appraisal*.
18. See also the seven semi-annual implementation reports issued by the US Commission on Security and Co-operation in Europe.
19. I accompanied the Chancellor and was present at the press conference.
20. M. Mihailov, 'Po povodu obmenov i kontaktov', in *Mezhdunarodnaya Zhizn*, 4/1973.
21. See *Frankfurter Allgemeine*, 29 October 1977.
22. *New York Times*, 3 February 1979.
23. AFP from Moscow, 3 December 1979.
24. See for example Bernheim, pp. 33–34.
25. See Report on East-West Journalists Conference, 18–21 October 1976, Berlin, 76/5, Ed. by Michael Haltzel, p. 37, see also pp. 31–43.
26. *Hearings*, p. 63.
27. Ibid.
28. Austrian representative's speech in the Basket Three commission in Belgrade on 25 October 1977.
29. Source: Austrian Foreign Ministry.
30. Source: *Financial Times* and circulation departments of *Le Monde* and *Frankfurter Allgemeine Zeitung*.
31. *International Herald Tribune*, 25–26 March 1978.
32. R.Lynev, 'Nothing but the truth' in the issue of 2 November 1977, quoted after *Osteuropa*, 10/78, pp. A 625–29.
33. According to a survey conducted at the end of the 1960s, engineering-technical and white-collar workers accounted for twenty-three percent of the readership; staff of institutes of

higher education and scientific research institutes 24.6 percent; teachers 10.3 percent; doctors, journalists, humanities nine percent; students eight percent. Circulation in 1973 was 1.55 million. Radio Liberty Research, RL 5/77, 4 January 1977.

34. See *Službeni List*, Belgrade No. 2, 3, 5, 9, 12, 14, 15, 16, 21, 24, 25, 29, 38 1979.
35. See for details, half-annual reports of the US Congress CSCE Commission. Also Richard Portes, 'East Europe's Debt' in *Foreign Affairs*, Summer, 1979.
36. Two years earlier the President of the Polish Foreign Trade Bank told a visitor that he could not give exact figures because data 'on indebtedness are not published, nor are figures on reserves,' *Euromoney*, January 1977. For the 'breakthrough' see *Financial Times*, 16 March 1979.
37. Barry Rubin, *International News and the American media*, The Washington Papers, No. 49 (Beverly Hills and London, 1977).
38. *The New York Times*, 19 July 1978.
39. See Commission reports, and also Kelly, p. 74.
40. The article appeared in the weekly of the Turkmen Writers' Union and Ministry of Culture; it was preceded by several attacks on US and German correspondents in local dailies. Quoted after Radio Liberty Research, RL 263/79, 30 August 1979.
41. *US News and World Report*, 11 and 25 September 1978 and 7 May 1979.
42. *Financial Times*, 27 July, 1 and 4 August 1979; *New York Times*, 27 July 1979.
43. *Süddeutsche Zeitung*, 9 October 1978; Novosti (APN), 25 October 1978; *Arbeiter Zeitung*, Vienna, 20 October 1978.
44. See *Der Spiegel*, 21 May 1979.
45. *Le Monde*, 5 August 1979; TASS 19 October 1978.
46. Details in RL 242/79.
47. Commission Report, July 1979; AP 16 June 1979.
48. RL 242/79.
49. *The New York Times*, 27 July 1979.
50. Report July 1979.
51. For details see *Deutsch-deutsche Pressefreiheit*; *Frankfurter Allgemeine*, 18 May 1979.
52. *Der Spiegel*, 21 May 1979; *Frankfurter Allgemeine*, 18 May 1979.
53. *Frankfurter Allgemeine*, 2 July 1979.
54. Articles 15 and 16 of the Law No. 23/1971 on the 'Protection of State Secrets', *Buletinul Oficial* No. 157, Bucharest, 17 December 1971.
55. *The New York Times*, 17 April 1977.
56. Reuter and DPA, 9 December 1977.

57. For Trevisan see Reuter, 9 May 1978; for Dutch incident see RFE Special from the Hague, 27 and 29 March 1979.

58. Source: RFE Research Department. For an overall balance sheet of working conditions of foreign journalists, still useful for the background, though outdated, see Joachim Krause in *Aus Politik und Zeitgeschichte*, Bonn, 8 October 1977. See also debate about 'Reporting on Eastern Europe' in *Europäische Rundschau*, 2/73 (Péter Rényi), 1/74 (Christian Schmidt-Häuer) and 2/74 (François Fejtö and Nikolai Poljanov).

Index